Championship Racquetball

Fran Davis

Jason Mannino

Human Kinetics

Library of Congress Cataloging-in-Publication Data

Davis, Fran, 1954-
  Championship racquetball / Fran Davis, Jason Mannino.
    p. cm.
  Includes index.
  ISBN-13: 978-0-7360-8979-1 (soft cover)
  ISBN-10: 0-7360-8979-9 (soft cover)
  1. Racquetball. I. Mannino, Jason, 1975- II. Title.
  GV1003.34.D38 2011
  796.343--dc22

                          2010041638

ISBN-10: 0-7360-8979-9 (print)
ISBN-13: 978-0-7360-8979-1 (print)

Acquisitions Editor: Laurel Plotzke Garcia; **Developmental Editor:** Anne Hall; **Assistant Editor:** Elizabeth Evans; **Copyeditor:** Patricia L. MacDonald; **Indexer:** Katy Balcer; **Graphic Designer:** Nancy Rasmus; **Graphic Artist:** Tara Welsch; **Cover Designer:** Keith Blomberg; **Photographer (cover, interior):** Mike Boatman; **Photo Production Manager:** Jason Allen; **Art Manager:** Kelly Hendren; **Associate Art Manager:** Alan L. Wilborn; **Illustrations:** © Human Kinetics; **Printer:** Sheridan Books

Other credits: We thank The Washington Athletic Club (W.A.C) in Seattle, Washington, for assistance in providing the location for the photo shoot for this book.

Human Kinetics books are available at special discounts for bulk purchase. Special editions or book excerpts can also be created to specification. For details, contact the Special Sales Manager at Human Kinetics.

Printed in the United States of America   10 9 8 7 6 5 4 3 2 1

The paper in this book is certified under a sustainable forestry program.

Human Kinetics
Web site: www.HumanKinetics.com

United States: Human Kinetics
P.O. Box 5076
Champaign, IL 61825-5076
800-747-4457
e-mail: humank@hkusa.com

Canada: Human Kinetics
475 Devonshire Road Unit 100
Windsor, ON N8Y 2L5
800-465-7301 (in Canada only)
e-mail: info@hkcanada.com

Europe: Human Kinetics
107 Bradford Road
Stanningley
Leeds LS28 6AT, United Kingdom
+44 (0) 113 255 5665
e-mail: hk@hkeurope.com

Australia: Human Kinetics
57A Price Avenue
Lower Mitcham, South Australia 5062
08 8372 0999
e-mail: info@hkaustralia.com

New Zealand: Human Kinetics
P.O. Box 80
Torrens Park, South Australia 5062
0800 222 062
e-mail: info@hknewzealand.com

E5028

Championship
Racquetball

Contents

Preface   vi
Acknowledgments   ix
Key to Diagrams   x

Part I   The Skills

Chapter 1   **Attacking Forehand**   **3**

Chapter 2   **Penetrating Backhand**   **31**

Chapter 3   **Dominating Serves and Returns**   **57**

Chapter 4   **Winning Offensive and Defensive Shots**   **101**

Part II   The Tactics

Chapter 5   **Maximizing Court Position**   **137**

Chapter 6   **Improving Shot Selection**   **159**

Chapter 7   **Developing Game Plans and Match Strategy**   **183**

Part III   The Competition

Chapter 8   **Practicing Perfectly**   **205**

Chapter 9   **Maintaining Mental Toughness**   **215**

Chapter 10   **Conditioning and Flexibility**   **237**

Chapter 11   **Playing Doubles**   **263**

Appendix A   Training Logs   275
Appendix B   Tournament Logs   277
Index   279
About the Authors   285

Preface

If you were to survey racquetball books written in the past 10 years, you might find that their emphasis has been on the needs of the beginner. These books often begin with a discussion of how to hold the racquet correctly followed by a description of the forehand and the backhand. In other words, the novice is introduced to the fundamentals of the game.

This book, however, is written for intermediate and advanced players who want a systematic method for improving their game, achieving their goals, and gaining confidence. This book is ultimately about playing and winning like a champion. Intermediate and advanced players are committed to constant and steady improvement in their game. In fact, it would be fair to say that intermediate and advanced players are competitive and more likely than beginners to test their skills in tournaments and leagues against other players.

Worldwide, there are various types of intermediate and advanced racquetball players. The sport attracts both male and female participants, as well as young and mature players. We find large numbers of players who come from all over the world in colleges, universities, military service, and health and fitness racquetball clubs.

Racquetball players are motivated to play for different reasons. Some play for recreation and fitness, while others play for competition. Whatever the reason, you will find both groups equally passionate about the game. No one enjoys playing a game in which he or she loses every time. What most people want is to replace their fear of failure with genuine confidence, and this book gives you the tools to do just that. We all enjoy getting better at the game. By using the techniques, strategies, mental toughness tips, peak performance tools and much, much more from this book, you will be able to win more and lose less—a goal of all racquetball players.

This book focuses on the needs of intermediate and advanced players of the 21st century. Players' needs at this level are very different today than they were five years ago. The game has evolved. Larger sizes and innovative materials make today's racquets stronger and more powerful than ever. Since modern racquets hit the ball harder than older ones, the ball moves a lot faster, which in turn cuts down player reaction time. Stringing patterns have increased tension, thus accelerating the speed of the ball when contact is made. Players have also become stronger as the game has evolved.

This is not a book for beginners. Readers of this book already know the basics and are interested in learning how to win and to refine their core game with reliable stroke mechanics, smarter shot selection, better court strategy, more offensive serves, higher percentage return of serves, and mental toughness in order to play at the highest levels of the game.

Some intermediate players seem to have the following problems in common:

- I am too defensive because when I go offensive, I am scared I will miss.
- I can hit the ball hard, but I cannot always control it.

- I don't want to work hard on my game, but I want the results that will make me win.
- My shot selection is poor, and I hit right back at my opponent all the time.
- I am too offensive and shoot everything, even when I am off balance and out of position because I think I can kill the ball.

Some advanced players have these problems:

- I do not know how to effectively return drive serves.
- I do not know how to stop my opponent from attacking my lob serves.
- I do not know how to develop effective neutralizing strategies.
- I do not know how to analyze, determine, and capitalize on my opponent's weaknesses.
- I do not know how to slow my opponent down when he or she is serving.
- I do not know how to avoid unforced errors.
- I do not know how to improve my footwork.
- I do not know how to improve my stroke mechanics.
- I do not know how to prepare for peak performance.
- I do not know how to develop mental toughness.

In today's game, mastery of these skills is a must. The level of one's playing ability can be measured as much by what one cannot do on the court as well as by what one can do. It can also be measured by figuring out an opponent's weaknesses and how to exploit them.

Championship Racquetball provides cutting-edge information and state-of-the-art instruction on the game of racquetball. This book contains a fully developed methodology along with court diagrams, drills, court strategy, shot selection, game tactics, mental toughness, and preparation for peak play by being well conditioned and goal oriented.

The information discussed in this book will help you maximize the development of your game from the ground up. It discusses and demonstrates techniques that are used by the best racquetball players in the world, as well as teaches you how to combine playing racquetball from the neck down (the physical part of the game) with the mental, emotional, and spiritual part of the game (from the neck up), with the following:

- It will teach advanced stroke mechanics using game shots and drills.
- It details court position and shot selection.
- It discusses serve, return of serve, and relocation on the court.
- It maps out advanced game strategy.
- It explains mental toughness in-depth.
- It shows you how to reach your peak performance level.
- It demonstrates conditioning and flexibility exercises so you are able to play at your best.

Championship Racquetball is divided into three sections: The Skills, The Tactics, and The Competition. The skills section is jam packed with the skills and drills that will take you to the next level and make you a champion. You will be given techniques to develop an attacking forehand and a penetrating backhand. If you practice the drills, you undoubtedly will become a more consistent player from both sides of the court, and you will hit the ball harder than ever before. Your opponent will be amazed because of your increased accuracy and added power.

You will be taught a variety of serves that will keep your opponent off balance and guessing. This variety will make you deceptive and less predictable, which are key components needed to become a champion.

In order to move up to an intermediate or advanced level, you will be taught a whole new arsenal of shots, both offensive and defensive, that will keep your opponent off guard. Keeping your opponent off guard gives him or her less time to set up, which in turn will create more unforced errors and give you more opportunities to score.

The return of serve is a critical part of the game for intermediate and advanced players, because you must get your opponent out of the middle of the court. By pulling your opponent out of the middle, you can then move up and control center court. You will learn the precise footwork and shots to hit off of the return of serve so you will find yourself in good center court position and, ultimately, in total control of the match.

The tactics section discusses game plans and strategies (the thinking part of the game) that are crucial to winning consistently. Being in the right place at the right time (court position) and taking the right shot at the right time (shot selection) is an integral part of the game and cannot be taken lightly at the intermediate or advanced level of play. You must be flexible in your approach to the racquetball game. You will play against all types of players. Therefore, you must develop a game plan that incorporates both your strengths and weaknesses and your opponents' strengths and weaknesses that will allow you to be successful against any style of racquetball player. You must have the ability to hit both offensive and defensive shots whether you are serving or are in the middle of a rally with your opponent. But what is most important to develop is a game style that is all your own.

The final section, The Competition, will glue your game together and assist you in getting ready to perform at your best. If you want to become an intermediate or advanced player and champion, you must learn how to combine your mental and physical strategies. It is the healthy combination of the body and mind during a match that produces a champion. In this book you will learn this very concept.

In order to perform at your best, you need to have a plan of action. Once a plan is set, you will then need to set goals to carry out that plan, and we will teach you how. Once you know where you are going, we will help you develop a training schedule, keep a tournament or league log, and get you in condition to compete. We will make sure you have every opportunity to reach those goals by making you as consistent as possible through a wide range of single and partner drills, mental toughness strategies, and conditioning and flexibility exercises. The professional game will be highlighted so you can then compare your levels of commitment, desire, determination, confidence, and your "never say die" attitude to the professional player's.

Lastly, the doubles chapter will shed some light on just how the doubles game compares to the singles game.

Although there are many ways to study racquetball, this book will provide a fairly broad spectrum of choices. It is divided into 11 chapters and can be used in a variety of ways. If a player is totally unfamiliar with the topics discussed in the book and has never had any formal instruction, this book should be read from cover to cover. If a player is familiar with some or part of the contents, the book is like a menu. The reader can select a new topic or revisit one. If a player is taking private lessons, that person can select a topic that coincides with a specific lesson. The organization of this book also introduces the intermediate and advanced player to ways of acquiring precise mental habits when playing the game. Racquetball players will improve their games by learning from a considerable store of exercises to enhance practices. The knowledge and skills in this book should be supplemented generously with the richest of all sources: your experience on the court.

Acknowledgements

We dedicate this book to our beloved friend and mentor, Dr. Learned "Latell" Clark. He not only inspired us to write this book, but he also was an integral part of our journey from the beginning. Latell dedicated his life to racquetball, and anyone that knew him loved him for his kind heart, smile, and infectious laughter. Unfortunately in August 2009, he passed away before seeing the finished product. We love you, Latell.

We would like to thank those in our lives who have helped make this dream a reality.

To Momelou, Russ, Sarah, Richelle, Jack, Christina, Jason, and Jared; without your unconditional love and support, we wouldn't and couldn't have done it. So thank you.

To Diana McNab, owner of Diana McNab LLC and MEd faculty at the University of Denver, our sports psychologist expert, thank you for introducing us to the mind-body connection, a key component needed to become a champion.

To Dan Obremski, owner of Fast Fit in Training Systems and our fitness expert, thank you for sharing with us the fitness techniques used to develop our championship game.

To Doug Ganim, national promotions manager; Ben Simons, senior business manager; and all of HEAD/Penn Racquet Sports, thank you for supporting me and believing in me over the last 27 years in my quest to being the best coach and teacher I could be.

To Mike Boatman, photographer, for his tireless work supplying all the photos for the book.

To Jerry Evarts and Tammarrian Rogers, thank you for your expert eyes and countless hours proofing the book.

A heart-felt thank you goes out to all our campers, clients, and friends who kept on us for years to write a book and share our expertise and experience with the racquetball community. A special thank you goes to Jim Pruitt, Thad Shows, Lamar Hughes, John Delaney, Jon Furbee, George Brewer, Marilyn (Mouse) Scharffenberger, Sparclean Enterprises, Inc., the International Racquetball Tour (www.irt-tour.com), Eric Muller, Patrick Martin, Dr. Phil Singer, and the IRT Network (www.irtnetwork.com).

To the Human Kinetics team, Jason and I appreciate all you have done to get this project to the finish line.

Special thanks to my co-author, Fran, who has been part of the family for many years and who I consider the "Yoda" of racquetball. Without the countless hours she has dedicated to the sport, this book would never have become a reality.

Thanks to my co-author, Jason, who I have known since he was a junior player and who I have been working with for the last 10 years as a coach, partner in camps, co-author in our video "Building Your Racquetball Dream House," and who has become part of my chosen family.

Key to Diagrams

S = Server
R = Receiver
OP = Offensive player
DP = Defensive player
X_1 = Hit 1st wall
X_2 = Hit 2nd wall
X_3 = Hit 3rd wall
Solid line = Ball movement
Dotted line = Player movement
B_1 = Ball bounce 1st time
B_2 = Ball bounce 2nd time
CC = Crosscourt
DTL = Down the line
P_1 = Partner 1
P_2 = Partner 2
OP_1 = Offensive player (Partner 1)
OP_2 = Offensive player (Partner 2)
DP_1 = Defensive player (Partner 1)
DP_2 = Defensive player (Partner 2)

Part I

The Skills

The skills are part of the key components needed to develop your Championship Racquetball game and should not be overlooked or taken for granted. In our coaching, we use the metaphor of the "racquetball sports triangle." For a triangle to be a triangle, it takes all three sides of the triangle to work together and stay connected. The same is true for your championship racquetball game. The base of the triangle reflects the skills, giving your game stability, consistency, and the weapons needed to make the shots required to win the point, the game, and the match. Later on in the book, in part III, we will talk about the two sides of the triangle, mental toughness and conditioning, making the "racquetball sports triangle" complete.

In this section of the book we are not only giving you the core principles we use in our video, "Building Your Racquetball Dream House," we are also showing you what it takes to build your competitive intermediate and advanced championship game. In the following chapters you will learn: how to develop the attacking forehand, the forehand stroke of a champion, how to develop the penetrating backhand, so you are strong from both sides of the court, how to develop dominating serves and returns, setting the tone of the match, and how to develop winning offensive and defensive shots, creating variety so you are unpredictable. Learning how to execute these exact skills correctly and knowing how to drill these skills will create consistency and help to move you from one level to the next, winning every step of the way. When your skills are honed and sharpened, you will be ready for part II, which presents the thinking part of the game.

Chapter 1
Attacking Forehand

In today's game, with the ball traveling in excess of 150 mph (241 km/h), you need to have a forehand that is not only consistent and solid but also strong, powerful, and aggressive—this is called an attacking forehand. The more power you generate, the harder you hit the ball, and the less time your opponent has to react. With less reaction time, your opponent will not be able to set up properly and do the things he wants to do with the ball, thus eliciting weak shots and poor returns. With your new attacking forehand, you can take advantage of your opponent's mistakes and capitalize on his weaknesses. As your opponent sets you up time after time, you will have the opportunity to shoot the ball with confidence and place lots of pressure on the other player.

With the mind-set of an attacking forehand, you will be able to develop a very aggressive game. You will be able to cut the ball off, hit overheads and sidearm passes, hit drive serves with maximum power, and execute very difficult Z serves, just to name a few.

Whether you are serving, receiving the serve, or playing a rally, the goal is to dismantle your opponent's game by attacking at every opportunity and exerting maximum pressure. The mantra of an intermediate player is to first attack the basics before attacking an opponent, but for the advanced player who has mastered the basics, the mantra is attack! attack! attack! The tool to do this is the attacking forehand.

There are many differences between intermediate and advanced players when hitting the forehand. Pointing out these differences requires breaking down each part of the stroke. We have broken the attacking forehand into five different components: (1) grip, (2) stance, (3) step and swing, (4) contact point, and (5) follow-through. Each of the tools of the attacking forehand is equally important and is best described as the cogs of a clock. Each component of a clock acts independently but in unison for the clock to keep accurate time. The same is true for your

All techniques discussed in this book apply to right-handed players. Left-handed players simply reverse positions.

attacking forehand—each of the areas described works independently but in unison for you to have an attacking forehand that is aggressive, consistent, and strong.

When you have accomplished this, you will have developed a weapon that can be used in your game. As a result, you will be able to place pressure on your opponent. You will be able to produce the desired results you are looking for, just like the professionals are able to do. In this chapter, we give you a full breakdown of each component of the attacking forehand.

Grip

The purpose of the grip is to control the racquet and to avoid rotation of the racquet handle in your hand when hitting the ball. The grip should be relaxed. It is a critical part of the stroke because if you hold the racquet incorrectly, your stroke will be wrong from the very beginning, and you will be inconsistent in the execution of any shot.

The proper grip on the racquet is crucial, and the following tips are elemental for all levels of play:

1. You should "shake hands" with the racquet, and the grip should be relaxed.
2. The V of the hand should be near the top of the racquet handle, with the thumb around the handle to avoid an improper grip. An improper grip could lead to problems in the future that would affect your stroke mechanics.
3. The pointer finger should be held in a trigger-grip position for more control of the racquet and better execution of shot selection during game play.
4. Your hand should slide down as far as possible on the handle without exceeding the butt of the racquet; this will give you reliable power that is enhanced by the wrist snap.
5. Never use a hammer grip, which is holding the racquet at the end of the handle with a fisted grip as if you were hammering a nail into a wall. Although this will give you power, it does not give you constant control of the shot.

Proper stroke mechanics start with the grip. All players, regardless of level, need to establish the proper handshake grip in order to be consistent. A proper grip allows the player to naturally contact the ball flat and level, preventing breakdowns in the rest of the swing to compensate for poor grip. An incorrect grip will lead to multiple problems including, but not limited to, hitting with topspin, slicing the ball, dipping the shoulder, and contacting the ball too close to the body. A beginner typically holds the racquet too high on the handle and is ready to change to a lower intermediate grip when he starts to have control of the ball. You will know when to change your grip because you will not be skipping as many balls and you will not be hitting the ball too high on the front wall, generally keeping the ball between 6 and 18 inches (15 and 46 cm) high. A higher grip costs a player significant power and control, which are needed to move through the levels.

Intermediate Grip

The intermediate grip requires the player to lower her hand so that it is close to the butt of the racquet, without any part of the hand or fingers exceeding the butt of the handle (figure 1.1). The purpose of holding the grip low on the handle is to generate power. Power is achieved by snapping the wrist at the end of the stroke to achieve respectable power upon contact with the ball.

Once you lower your grip as an intermediate player and the ball starts popping off the strings of your racquet more quickly, you are ready for the advanced grip. At this point, you have built up enough hand, wrist, and forearm strength to enable yourself to hold the racquet at its lowest point without losing control. Your pinkie should be as low as possible on the racquet, without hanging off the handle. This will increase the lever, allowing for maximum extension and maximum wrist snap on your shots. Advanced players need to squeeze every last drop of power out of the swing without losing control. The advanced grip will create this power, resulting in less reaction time for your opponent and even more control for you.

Figure 1.1   Intermediate grip.

Advanced Grip

The advanced grip is even more exaggerated in terms of how low the player should hold the racquet. At this level, the player should have ample hand strength to hold the racquet at the very edge of the butt of the handle (i.e., as low as possible, increasing the ability to snap the wrist quickly) without the hand exceeding the butt (figure 1.2). With this grip, the snap of the wrist must be very fast and the hand must be relaxed to achieve maximum power and control. Some of the pros customize their grips to acquire more wrist snap.

Figure 1.2   Advanced grip.

The grip must be relaxed enough to hold the racquet as loosely as possible, as if you were holding an egg. If you tighten your hand and your wrist, your grip will be too tight. You will lose power and crack the imaginary egg. This principle applies to all players regardless of skill level.

There are different styles of forehand grips, and the grip you choose will have an effect on the amount of power and control you can generate.

- V of the hand on the top of the racquet handle. This is the grip we advocate because you will hit the ball flat and level and at full extension for maximum power and control.

- V of the hand on the top right edge of the racquet handle. This grip will cost you both power and control; you will naturally hit the ball into the floor because the racquet will be tilted down.

- V of the hand on the top left edge of the racquet handle. This grip will cost you both power and control; you will naturally slice the ball, causing it to hit the side wall first even though you want it to hit the front wall.

When the V of your hand is on the top part of the racquet handle or just slightly to the right or left, you will have the flattest racquet upon ball contact, which will lead to the most consistency.

The only benefits to choosing the last two grips are if you play a different sport. In tennis, if you shift your V to the right, you enable topspin, and to the left, you enable backspin. In squash, players are taught to cut the ball by using a grip that is considered poor for racquetball. In racquetball, you need to hit the ball flat to be successful, and this starts with the correct grip.

COMMON MISTAKES: GRIP

ERROR: You are using a hammer grip.

CORRECTION: Shake hands with the racquet handle using a trigger finger.

SOLUTION: By using the proper grip, you will have more power and control in your shot because your wrist will not be stiff, allowing a complete wrist snap.

Stance

The stance provides the foundation for each attacking forehand shot. The stance, or what we call the power base, establishes your power before you hit the ball. You want to stay low—approximately two-thirds of your body height—and you do not want to stand up unless you are hitting a ceiling ball or you are in between a rally. The proper stance makes it possible for you to always be prepared to return the ball with consistency and power.

1. The forehand stance requires that you are square to, or face, the side wall.
2. Your feet should be spread apart, up to shoulder width plus 2 feet (.6 m) for more power.
3. The left leg is forward, the right leg is back, and your feet are lined up evenly.
4. The knees are flexed and relaxed at approximately 130 to 150 degrees.
5. Your upper body is erect.
6. Your shoulders are level, slightly rotated 5 degrees, and are ready to rotate through the shot.
7. Your weight is evenly distributed or as close to 50/50 as possible. This will allow you to establish a sound power base.
8. You are using the proper forehand grip as described earlier.
9. Your elbow is up and in line with or slightly above your shoulder, which is pointed toward the right corner. You do not want the elbow to be too far above the shoulder, as that will cause the racquet to tilt forward, creating a looping swing.
10. Your racquet is up, above your shoulder, and facing the right front corner (referred to as ERP, early racquet preparation).
11. Your hips are pointing to the side wall, but loose and ready to rotate.
12. The nonhitting arm is relaxed for balance, held approximately at your belly button.
13. You should always keep your eyes on the ball.

Core technique focuses on establishing a power base with feet shoulder-width apart and a knee bend of at least 150 degrees. The following intermediate and advanced techniques focus on a wider and lower power base, increased hip rotation, and higher and more rotated racquet preparation for increased generation of power.

Intermediate Stance

The stance for intermediate players has a wider power base than that of beginner players (figure 1.3).

1. Feet are spread shoulder-width apart plus 1 foot (.3 m), so your body will be lower to the ground.
2. Knees are bent slightly more, to approximately 140 degrees, for a springing action into the stroke.
3. Hips are slightly rotated, pointing to the right front corner, to add power to your stroke.
4. The racquet is up higher, with your elbow in line with the level shoulders (ERP).
5. Racquet is at shoulder level with a slight rotation, approximately 10 degrees.
6. Nonhitting arm is relaxed for balance, moved slightly to the right with your upper-body rotation.

Figure 1.3   Intermediate stance.

As you start to feel more stability and are hitting the ball harder with the wider power base, the more exaggerated knee bend, and the hips starting to rotate, you are ready to transition to a more advanced stance, which has an even wider power base, more bend in the knees, and more rotation in the hips to load the shot with tremendous power.

When a player adds an advanced grip, this is a great time to add an advanced stance, as both will work together to create more power. When you change your grip, it will lengthen the lever, and a player will need to adjust ball toss to compensate for the change in extension. The same holds true for widening your stance; the wider the stance, the lower to the ground a player will be, causing the hitting zone to be larger and farther away from the body. The advanced player will have to toss the ball a little farther away from the body to achieve maximum power at full extension. We advise changing grip and stance together.

Advanced Stance

Like intermediate players, advanced players must widen their power base. The advanced stance should be the widest possible (figure 1.4).

Figure 1.4   Advanced stance.

1. Feet are spread even wider than the intermediate stance—shoulder-width apart plus 2 feet (.6 m)—so your body will be even lower to the ground for maximum power.

2. Knees are bent slightly more, to approximately 130 degrees, for more springing action to enhance movement.

3. Hips are completely rotated, 6 inches to 1 foot (15 to 30 cm) beyond the right corner to obtain maximum power—you coil then uncoil.

4. Your racquet is up higher and your elbow is slightly higher than your shoulder for more power (ERP).

5. Shoulders rotate aggressively, approximately 15 degrees, for maximum power.

6. Nonhitting arm is relaxed for balance, moved another 1 to 2 inches to the right with your upper-body rotation, and serves as a tool to help twist the waist around.

COMMON MISTAKES: STANCE

ERROR: Your feet are too close together, less than shoulder-width apart.

CORRECTION: Feet need to be between shoulder-width apart and up to 2 feet (.6 m) more.

SOLUTION: Having your feet the proper distance apart will create a more stable power base to allow you to generate more power on your shots and eliminate loss of ball control.

ERROR: Your shoulders are dipped rather than level.

CORRECTION: Keep your shoulders as level as possible to develop the most consistency in your swing.

SOLUTION: Keeping your shoulders level and not dipping them or pointing them in the direction you want to hit the ball leads to a more consistent swing. If you do not keep the shoulders level, it could create a pendulum swing, which is similar to a golf swing (high to low then high again), and your ball will go all over the place rather than where you want it to go.

ERROR: Racquet is down not up when moving to the ball or when getting ready to hit the ball.

CORRECTION: As soon as the ball hits the front wall and you know it is a shot to your forehand, get your racquet up immediately.

SOLUTION: By developing good ERP, you will have a more consistent swing because you will have more time to set up, swing, and hit the ball where you want it to go, just like a batter in baseball. If you wait for the ball to approach you, you have to get the racquet up and then swing, which is two motions instead of one, and your shots will be inconsistent.

ERROR: Knees are not bent, and you are standing relatively straight.

CORRECTION: Knees should be bent between approximately 130 and 150 degrees.

SOLUTION: Bending your knees gives you a lower center of gravity, which creates a more solid base to generate power from because of weight distribution and full extension to maximum point of contact. A knee bend also lets you get down on the ball and hit it lower, making it more difficult for your opponent to reach.

Step and Swing

The step begins the stroke. When stepping into the ball, you stride in a straight line toward the front wall, and you must remember to drive off your back hip and pivot your back foot, which unlocks your hips. When you use the proper technique, the power generated from your lower body will be transferred into your upper body and eventually into the racquet and then the ball.

1. Your weight distribution varies depending on your level of play, but it starts at 50/50 as you step forward toward the front wall with your lead foot (front leg).
2. Your feet are lined up and even.
3. The racquet remains up in ERP.
4. Your weight shifts slightly back on the ball of your back foot so you can pivot and drive off your back foot, allowing your hips to generate more power, giving your opponent less time to react.
5. Rotate your shoulders about 5 degrees.
6. Your hips start to open toward the front wall as you turn at the waist.
7. Keep your eyes on the ball.

As you swing, remember the following:

1. Your shoulder leads.
2. The head of the racquet and the elbow start to come down simultaneously.
3. The butt of the handle is perpendicular to the front wall.
4. The face of the racquet is parallel to the side wall.
5. The wrist and racquet begin to come through, and the wrist snaps and is completely relaxed coming through in approximately one second.
6. The nonhitting arm comes through as you turn your shoulders and waist.
7. Keep your eyes on the ball.

The core techniques establish the proper step with the correct weight distribution, utilizing the hips and relaxation of the wrist. In the intermediate and advanced techniques, we discuss how important it is to take a longer step and change the weight distribution so you can get your hips through the shot more quickly and bring the racquet around with more head speed to generate more power, essential for high levels of play.

Intermediate Step and Swing

In the intermediate technique, it is important to take a longer step and change the weight distribution so you can get your hips through the shot more quickly and bring the racquet around with more head speed to generate more power, essential for high levels of play (figure 1.5).

1. Take a longer step, approximately 3 feet (.9 m), which puts you closer to the ground so that you can hit the ball lower with a level swing.

2. Weight shifts slightly back, approximately 5 percent, as you step forward so you can drive off the back foot as you pivot, but weight distribution ends up approximately 55/45 toward the front.

3. Hips fully open and come through quickly for more power.

4. Wrist is relaxed now and allows for greater head speed, one-fourth second faster, which means a faster swing for more power.

5. Nonhitting arm comes all the way through, balanced and allowing for a full follow-through.

Figure 1.5   Intermediate step and swing.

Advanced Step and Swing

Like the intermediate technique, it is even more important for advanced players to take quicker, longer steps and make your movements more forceful (figure 1.6).

1. Take quicker and longer steps, approximately 3.5 feet (1.1 m), to hit balls farther away from the body and at the same time generate more power and hit the ball flat and level.

2. Weight shifts slightly back, approximately 10 percent, as you step forward so you can drive off the back foot as you pivot, but it ends up approximately 60/40 toward the front.

3. Hip rotation is violent. This means getting your hips through your shot as quickly as humanly possible without being off balance.

Figure 1.6   Advanced step and swing.

4. Faster swing speed, approximately half a second faster, for even more power and whip.

5. Nonhitting arm whips around to get maximum rotation.

More About Power

Power gives your opponent less time to react. People always ask the question "Where does power come from?" Well, the answer is not quite as simple as it seems because power comes from many different places. The racquetball stroke is similar to an automatic clock in that there are many different components that work independently and together in order to create the proper timing for the most efficient stroke.

One of the most important areas where power is created is the lower body. The step, pivot, and hip rotation are the core of lower-body power creation and release. Before you step, your weight begins even at approximately 50/50, and then you transfer your weight an additional 5 to 10 percent, depending on your level of play, toward your front leg, using the groin and buttocks as well as the major muscles in your legs. When you pivot, you use your groin, quadriceps, hamstrings, and calf to transfer weight both forward and backward simultaneously between both legs to create energy at point of contact. As this is happening, your hips twist and turn to add to this explosion of energy, creating maximum power. The higher the level of player, the more violent each energy transfer is. The pro players may step, pivot, and turn in unison so quickly that you can hardly see it happen. A novice player may not step or pivot in order to hit the ball.

The biggest problem players have is transferring most of their weight an additional 30 to 40 percent forward, ending up with an 80/20 or 90/10 split, where a majority of the weight is on the front leg and very little weight is on the back leg, putting them off balance and unable to drive off the back leg and hips. The correct weight distribution is critical in order to hit the ball with maximum power and balance. The way to accomplish this is with proper weight distribution at the point of contact, as we discuss in the breakdown of the step and swing. If your weight is correctly distributed, the energy transfer will give you maximum power, the key to an effective attacking forehand.

COMMON MISTAKES: STEP AND SWING

ERROR: You step at a 45-degree angle or toward the side wall rather than straight ahead.

CORRECTION: Step in a straight line toward the front wall.

SOLUTION: Stepping toward the front wall and not at an angle toward the corner or side wall allows for complete and unrestricted use of the hips. If you step incorrectly, your hips lock and you will lose power because you cannot follow through all the way. Locking the hips can also cause hip pain from the abrupt stop.

ERROR: Your step is not long enough, and thus your power base is not wide enough.

CORRECTION: Step a minimum of 3 feet (.9 m).

SOLUTION: This longer step gets you lower to the ground so you can hit the ball lower, level, and farther from your body; all these components help generate more power and consistency.

ERROR: Your hips don't open because your back foot does not pivot, and you end up facing the side wall rather than the front wall upon completion of the swing.

CORRECTION: Pivot on the ball of your back foot as you are coming through your shot, opening up your hips. Think of squishing a bug or putting out a cigarette.

SOLUTION: Full use of the legs and hips creates the most power.

ERROR: You do not lead with the elbow but rather come down with your whole arm, which is straight (i.e., like a tennis swing).

CORRECTION: Lead with your elbow as if you were throwing a ball sidearm.

SOLUTION: By leading with your elbow, you have more of a throwing action; a straight arm results in a pushing or guiding motion. Once again, more power is generated with your elbow leading.

ERROR: Your wrist is stiff when swinging (i.e., no wrist snap), which causes loss of power.

CORRECTION: The wrist needs to be relaxed so you can snap through up to half a second faster, leading to greater head speed.

SOLUTION: A wrist snap and greater head speed result in hitting the ball with more power and whip.

ERROR: The nonhitting arm does not come around as you are swinging; it just stays there and does not move.

CORRECTION: Bring your nonhitting arm all the way across your body.

SOLUTION: Getting the nonhitting arm out of the way and across your body as quickly as possible maximizes upper-body rotation for full power.

ERROR: You have too much weight on your front foot (e.g., 80/20 or 90/10 distribution).

CORRECTION: Weight should be relatively even (50/50) as you are getting into position to hit the ball but then shifts anywhere between 55/45 and 60/40 to the front.

SOLUTION: The weight shift gives you enough weight on your back foot so you can drive off it to create power as well as balance when you are done. This is a key component of being able to hit the ball hard yet get to your next shot without struggling to stay on both feet.

ERROR: Racquet is not parallel to the floor, and the face of the racquet is not parallel to the front wall but moves like a pendulum (i.e., like a golf club upon contacting a golf ball).

CORRECTION: The racquet needs to be parallel to the floor and the face of the racquet parallel to the front wall, like a baseball swing. When you do not hit flat and level at full extension, the hitting zone is very small, and the result is lots of skips and floating balls for setups.

SOLUTION: The flatter your swing, the more consistent you will be. If you have more of a pendulum swing, you will have a tendency to skip more balls as well as set your opponent up because the ball floats to the middle of the court more often.

Contact Point

The contact point is defined as where the ball and racquet make contact in relation to your body. The perfect contact point is off of the front foot, or lead foot. This area can also be referred to as your hitting zone. Keep the ball way out in front of you so that the momentum of your body along with the swing creates more power. In this section you will learn that where you make contact with the ball in your hitting zone will determine where the ball goes.

1. Hit off your front, or lead, foot.
2. Your hitting arm should be at full extension from your body for all shots.
3. The racquet head should be parallel to the floor and parallel to the front wall, knee high or lower, depending on the shot. It's at this point that wrist snap occurs.
4. The wrist should be relaxed, not stiff. A relaxed wrist will allow all the components to move easily with as little resistance as possible.
5. Your chest and belly button begin to face toward the front wall.
6. Your weight distribution varies depending on your level of play, but it starts at 50/50.
7. Your nonhitting arm begins to come through.
8. Keep your eyes on the ball.

Everything about the stroke remains exactly the same (your grip, your stance, your step, your swing, your follow-through) except the contact point. By changing only your contact point and nothing else, you are less predictable and more deceptive. This key principle keeps your opponent guessing and off balance, which gives you the edge. Learning the core techniques of hitting the ball off your lead foot, with the ball away from your body, generally knee high or lower, with the racquet flat and level, gives you a solid understanding of contact point.

Intermediate Contact Point

The intermediate techniques introduce the concept of deception and hitting off different positions off the lead foot and a little farther from the body (figure 1.7).

1. Hit off the lead foot, but start to understand the four racquet contact points (see "Hitting off Your Lead Foot" on page 15).
2. Wrist is completely relaxed, not stiff.
3. Hitting arm is fully extended.
4. Chest and belly button face the front wall.
5. Racquet is parallel to the front wall and floor and is hitting flat.
6. Nonhitting arm leads and stays out of the way.
7. Weight distribution is approximately 55/45 to the front.

Figure 1.7 Intermediate contact point.

Advanced Contact Point

Advanced techniques emphasize deception coupled with power and control; the ball should be the farthest distance from your body to help move you to that higher level of play. (figure 1.8)

1. Hit off the lead foot with complete understanding and execution of the four racquet contact points. Hitting from different positions off the lead foot creates deception, increases variety in your shot selection, and makes you less predictable.

2. Hitting arm is at full extension.

3. Elbow is straight upon contact with the ball.

4. Keep the ball no more than 3 feet (.9 m) away from you at point of contact.

5. Nonhitting arm moves more quickly across the body and stays out of the way on the way to the back wall.

6. Weight distribution is approximately 60/40 to the front.

Figure 1.8 Advanced contact point.

COMMON MISTAKES: CONTACT POINT

ERROR: You contact the ball off your back foot.

CORRECTION: Your contact point is ideally somewhere off your lead foot, depending on the shot.

SOLUTION: When hitting the ball off your lead foot, you achieve maximum power and control. If you hit the ball behind you, off your back foot, you will lose power and control. From a control standpoint, the ball will likely hit the side wall or go directly into the floor if it is hit too far back. In regard to power, you will not be able to achieve maximum weight distribution or maximum wrist snap if the ball is not in proper position to be hit at full extension, resulting in a severe lack of power.

ERROR: You contact the ball too close to your body and not flat at full extension.

CORRECTION: Contact the ball at full extension from your body, with the racquet head flat and level.

SOLUTION: By hitting the ball at full extension, with the racquet flat and level, you will add power and consistency to your stroke and ball control to your game. When the ball is too close to your body, you often get jammed and lose power and set your opponent up too frequently in midcourt.

Hitting off Your Lead Foot

Let's take a closer look at the different contact points relative to your lead foot. Note: pinch, down the line, crosscourt, and reverse pinch will be discussed in detail in later chapters. But for now, these particular shots depend on point of contact relative to your lead foot.

- Pinch: Contact the ball off the heel of your lead foot to the inner thigh (figure 1.9). The ball is hit to the closest corner, hitting the side wall first, the front wall second and then bouncing two times before hitting the second side wall in front of the service line or short line.

- Down the line: Contact the ball off the arch of your lead foot (figure 1.10). The ball hits between you and the closest side wall, bouncing two times before hitting the back wall and not hitting the side wall at all.

- Crosscourt: Contact the ball off the big toe of your lead foot (figure 1.11). The ball hits between you and the farthest side wall, bouncing two times before hitting the back wall and not hitting the side wall at all.

- Reverse pinch: Contact the ball off the little toe of your lead foot (figure 1.12). The ball hits to the farthest (i.e., opposite) corner, hitting the side wall first, the front wall second, and then bouncing two times before hitting the second side wall in front of the service line.

Figure 1.9 Pinch hit off the heel of lead foot.

Figure 1.10 Down-the-line hit off the arch of the lead foot.

Figure 1.11 Crosscourt hit off the big toe of lead foot.

Figure 1.12 Reverse pinch hit off the little toe of lead foot.

Follow-Through

The follow-through completes the swing. When the swing is completed, the head of the racquet is pointing to the back wall. The mistake most people make is not completing the swing. You never want to stop the swing prematurely. An incomplete swing can be the cause of elbow or shoulder problems, inconsistent shots, and loss of power and control. When you stop prematurely, you slow down your swing through the hitting zone, and therefore you are not going to hit the ball as hard.

As you follow through, remember the following:

1. Relax the wrist.
2. The racquet head is below your shoulder and pointing toward the back wall after the swing is completed.
3. Chest and belly button are facing the front wall.
4. Upper body is completely erect, and your weight should be completely balanced, with the back foot pivoted completely.
5. Hips are completely open to maximize your power.
6. The nonhitting arm is completely around the body and pointing toward the back wall.
7. Keep your eyes on the ball.
8. Weight distribution varies based on level of play.

Core techniques focus on making sure you finish your swing completely and do not stop or slow down prematurely, as that adversely affects power. The intermediate and advanced techniques also focus on getting your racquet completely around but they differ slightly in terms of racquet head speed, hip rotation, and the pivot off the back foot with a 90-degree knee bend to get lower on the ball.

Intermediate Follow-Through

The intermediate techniques focus on getting your racquet completely around but with greater racquet head speed, faster hip rotation, and a pivot off the back foot with a 90-degree knee bend to get lower on the ball (figure 1.13).

1. Racquet comes through and around more quickly, approximately one-fourth second faster, ending up between your shoulder and your waist and pointing toward the back wall.

2. Hips open more quickly, approximately one-fourth second faster.

3. Back foot is completely pivoted and bent at an approximately 90-degree angle.

4. The nonhitting arm is pointed toward the back wall.

5. Weight distribution is approximately 55/45 to the front.

Figure 1.13   Intermediate follow-through.

Advanced Follow-Through

Again, the advanced techniques focus on getting your racquet completely around but with the fastest racquet head speed, forceful hip rotation, and a pivot off the back foot with a 90-degree knee bend to get lower on the ball (figure 1.14).

1. Racquet comes through as low (waist high) and as quickly as possible, approximately half a second faster, so your ball is hit low and hard, giving your opponent a tough shot to return.

2. Nonhitting arm also comes completely around as quickly as possible to help balance out the swing.

3. Racquet points a little past the back wall at the end of the swing (an exaggerated follow-through).

4. Back foot is completely pivoted and back leg bends at 90 degrees.

5. Weight distribution is approximately 60/40 to the front.

Figure 1.14   Advanced follow-through.

COMMON MISTAKES: FOLLOW-THROUGH

ERROR: There is no follow-through because you stop your arm prematurely before the racquet is pointing to the back wall.

CORRECTION: The racquet and your nonhitting arm need to be pointing to the back wall when finished, and your chest and belly button need to be facing the front wall.

SOLUTION: By having a complete follow-through, you transfer the maximum power you generated from your legs and hips through your upper body, into the racquet, and then into the ball, resulting in the most powerful shot you could possibly hit. If you stop your swing prematurely, you lose power because you are starting to slow your swing down too soon before contact is made, thus resulting in a slower ball. Also this lack of follow-through and an abrupt stop are what can cause elbow and shoulder problems.

Attacking Forehand Drilling

Our goal in this chapter is to teach you to be fundamentally sound on your forehand side while developing an attacking forehand with all the elements of the intermediate and advanced techniques. Your attacking forehand means nothing unless you are consistent at performing this basic stroke in a game, putting your opponent on the defense and helping you win points. To achieve these things and put pressure on your opponent, we are going to teach you how to drill properly and develop the proper muscle memory needed to hit this stroke time after time with confidence.

Here is the five-step approach to drilling that the professionals use religiously. It allows them to develop and sharpen their timing, their consistency, and their accuracy—a must at the highest levels of racquetball.

1. Drop and hit (intermediate and advanced)
2. Toss, turn, and hit (intermediate and advanced)
3. Toss, turn, shuffle, and hit (intermediate and advanced)
4. Set up and hit (intermediate and advanced)
5. Set up, run, and hit (advanced)

There are many different spots on the court that players can drill from. We have developed nine positions that reflect where most of the game is played (figure 1.15). You will most likely need to hit from these various spots on the court. If you practice from only one position, you will not be consistent from everywhere on the court. Practicing from different areas makes you a more versatile player.

These nine positions are a guide, and once you master them you can create your own all over the court. Until then, practice from these nine positions, which will help you understand the different heights, speeds, and angles in order to hit shots from different depths of the court.

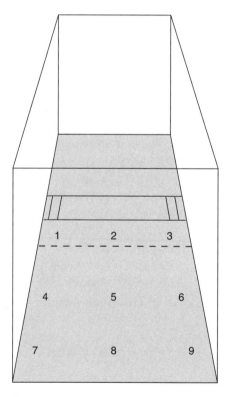

Figure 1.15 Nine practice positions for using the five-step approach.

Position 1: between the short line and dotted receiving line and 3 feet (.9 m) from the side wall

Position 2: between the dotted receiving line and 32 feet (9.8 m) back and 3 feet from the side wall

Position 3: between 32 feet back and the back wall and 3 feet from the side wall

Position 4: between the short line and the dotted receiving line and in the middle of the court

Position 5: between the dotted receiving line and 32 feet back in the middle of the court

Position 6: between 32 feet back and the back wall and in the middle of the court

Position 7: between the short line and dotted receiving line and 3 feet from the side wall

Position 8: between the dotted receiving line and 32 feet back and 3 feet from the side wall

Position 9: between 32 feet back and the back wall and 3 feet from the side wall

Figure 1.16 clearly shows you the zones on the court where you want to practice from using the five-step approach to drilling, regardless of whether you are an intermediate or an advanced player.

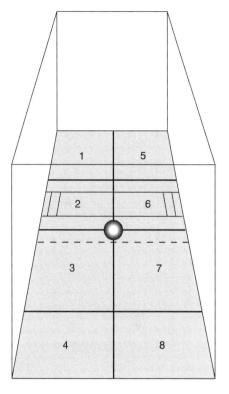

Figure 1.16 Zone diagram for using the five-step approach.

Nine Drill Positions Diagram

1. Drop and hit
2. Toss, turn, and hit
3. Toss, turn, shuffle, and hit

   Intermediate: Do 3, 6, 9, 2, 5, and 8 in that order, always going from closest to the front wall and then moving back, farther from the front wall.

   Advanced: Now add positions 1, 4, and 7

Zone Diagram

4. Set up and hit

   Intermediate: The ball should be set up so it lands in a particular zone, starting with zone 5, zone 6, zone 7, and finally zone 8 in that order, always going from closest to the front wall and then moving back farther from the front wall.

   You want to make sure you set the ball up from zone 6 to land in zone 5, from zone 7 to land in zone 6, and so on, always moving forward into the ball.

   Advanced: Add zone 1, zone 2, zone 3, and finally zone 4.

5. Set up, run, and hit

   Advanced: The ball should be set up so it lands in a particular zone.

   Since you are advanced, you can do whatever zone you are having trouble with and perfect that zone, then move on to the next.

Make sure when you are practicing that you give yourself a variety of setups to zones in front of you, to the side of you, and behind you.

Here are two examples:

1. Stand in zone 2 and set up the ball so it lands in zone 7.
2. Stand in zone 3 and set up the ball so it lands in zone 6.

Now let's get into each of the five steps of drilling in detail.

Drop and Hit

Why do it?

This drill is used primarily to develop stroke consistency, build your confidence, and learn the different facets of the technique.

How to do it?

1. Stand square to the side wall, with the knees bent (1.17a).
2. Racquet is up (ERP).
3. Feet are shoulder-width apart. (Tip: Put two pieces of tape on the floor where your feet correspond with the width of your shoulders.)
4. Drop the ball at full extension off of where your lead foot should end up. (Tip: Place a piece of tape on the floor where you want to drop and make contact with the ball.)
5. Step with the lead foot toward the front wall (1.17b). (Tip: Put a piece of tape on the floor where your foot should step to.)
6. Let the ball drop below your knees and then swing and hit.
7. Keep your eyes on the ball.

Figure 1.17 *(a)* Drop and *(b)* hit drill.

Who does it?

Alone: Do this drill alone. This is the number one drill for developing consistency.

When you are a beginner, using the tape takes the guessing out of where to step and where to drop the ball. Once you move up to the intermediate or advanced level, you will probably not need the tape, but remember this technique as a booster shot regardless of your playing level. You should never abandon the basics.

Toss, Turn, and Hit

Why do it?

This drill is used to transition from the down and ready position (see page 138 in chapter 5) to squaring off to the side wall to hit the ball.

How to do it?

1. Stand square to the front wall in the down and ready position, with feet more than shoulder-width apart, knees bent, waist slightly bent, shoulders level, and weight on the front part of the foot, ready to push off (1.18a). (Tip: As in the drop and hit drill, use tape to mark where feet and ball should be. Use this technique for all drills, if necessary.)

2. Nonhitting arm is fully extended, with ball in hand under hitting arm, making an X.

3. Toss the ball to the right. Pivot on the heel of your right foot, push off with the left foot, and bring the racquet up as you are crossing over so you end up parallel to the side wall (1.18b).

4. Let the ball drop below your knees and then swing and hit (1.18c).

5. Keep your eyes on the ball.

a   b   c

Figure 1.18 *(a)* Toss, *(b)* turn, and *(c)* hit drill.

(continued)

Toss, Turn, and Hit *(continued)*

Who does it?

Alone: Do this drill alone for a while because you want to become comfortable with going from the down and ready position to the hitting position. This will help develop proficiency, consistency, and confidence.

Partner: Once you get comfortable, remove the tape on the floor, grab a bucket of balls, and do this drill with a partner. The partner stands to your right and drops the ball so it is at full extension from you, and all you have to do is concentrate on turning and hitting. Once you hit your allotted number of balls, switch positions with your partner.

Toss, Turn, Shuffle, and Hit

Why do it?

This drill develops reading the ball because now the ball is farther from your body, and you need to turn and shuffle so the ball ends up off the lead foot.

How to do it?

1. Stand square to the front wall in the down and ready position, with feet more than shoulder-width apart, knees bent, waist slightly bent, shoulders level, and weight on the front part of the foot, ready to push off.
2. Racquet is in the middle of the body, waist high and with a relaxed grip.
3. Nonhitting arm is fully extended, with ball in hand under hitting arm, making an X (1.19*a*).
4. Toss ball farther to the right. Pivot on the heel of your right foot, push off with the left foot, bring the racquet up as you are crossing over so you end up parallel to the side wall, and shuffle into the ball (1.19*b-c*).
5. Let the ball drop below your knees and then swing and hit (1.19*d*).
6. Keep your eyes on the ball.

Who does it?

Alone: Do this drill alone for a while because you want to become comfortable with going from the down and ready position to the hitting position and then shuffling into your shot. This will help develop proficiency, consistency, and confidence.

Partner: Once you get comfortable, grab a bucket of balls and do this drill with a partner. The partner stands to your right and drops the ball so it is at full extension and a step from you, and all you have to do is concentrate on turning, shuffling, and hitting. Once you hit your allotted number of balls, switch positions with your partner.

Figure 1.19 *(a)* Toss, *(b)* turn, *(c)* shuffle, and *(d)* hit.

Set Up and Hit

Why do it?

Since you get lots of setups in a game, you must learn how to read the ball going into the front wall to know what angle and what speed it will come off the front wall so that you can move to that spot, set up, and hit the ball off your lead foot.

How to do it?

1. Stand square to the front wall in the down and ready position, with feet no more than shoulder-width apart, knees bent, waist slightly bent, shoulders level, and weight on the front part of the foot, ready to push off.
2. Racquet is in the middle of the body, waist high with a relaxed grip (1.20a).
3. Hit the ball to the front wall softly, and set yourself up.
4. Look at the height at which the ball hits the front wall and the speed that it comes off your racquet or your partner's racquet if you are drilling with a partner, and determine where the ball is going to bounce the second time.
5. After you read the ball, pivot on the heel of your right foot and push off with the left foot.
6. Use ERP as you are crossing over so you end up parallel to the side wall, and shuffle into the ball.
7. Let the ball drop below the knees and then swing and hit (1.20b).
8. Keep your eyes on the ball.

Figure 1.20 *(a)* Set up and *(b)* hit.

Who does it?

Alone: Do this drill alone at first because you want to become comfortable with going from the down and ready position to learning how to read the ball to then setting up to hit the shot. As you are setting the ball up, make sure you are well behind the ball so you are moving into the ball, not back. This will help develop proficiency, consistency, and confidence.

Partner: Once you get comfortable, grab a bucket of balls and do this drill with a partner. The partner sets you up with the same shot over and over again to a zone in front of you, so all you have to do is concentrate on reading the ball, turning, shuffling into the ball, and then hitting the ball. Once you hit your allotted number of balls, switch positions with your partner.

Drilling in itself will enable a player to read the ball better. As you set balls up for yourself, you will be hitting balls at different heights, speeds, and angles, so concentrate on where the ball is going to bounce based on how hard it was hit, at what angle, and at what height. Before trying to hit the ball, give yourself setups and then run and put your racquet on the floor so the ball can hit the racquet. Repeat this over and over again until you start reading the ball more easily. This will come with more experience.

Set Up, Run, and Hit

Why do it?

You must learn how to read the ball going into the front wall so you can move to that spot, set up, and hit the ball off your lead foot. Sometimes the ball may not be in front of you; it may be behind you, off to the side, or off at an angle, and you need to know how to adapt to the situation.

How to do it?

1. Stand square to the front wall in the down and ready position, with your feet no more than shoulder-width apart, knees bent, waist slightly bent, shoulders level, and weight on the front part of the foot, ready to push off.
2. Racquet is in the middle of the body, waist high with a relaxed grip (1.21a).
3. Hit the ball to the front wall softly, and set yourself up.
4. Look at the height at which the ball hits the front wall and the speed that it comes off your racquet or your partner's racquet if you are drilling with a partner, and determine where the ball is going to bounce the second time.
5. After you've read the ball and have determined where it will land in front of you, pivot on the heel of your right foot, then push off with the left foot.
6. Bring your racquet up high as you cross over so you end up parallel to the side wall (1.21b).
7. Shuffle into the ball.
8. If the ball is behind you, pivot on the heel of your right foot so that your toes are pointing toward the back wall as your left foot pushes off and comes around to get you into position behind the ball.
9. Let the ball drop below the knees and then swing and hit (1.21c).
10. Keep your eyes on the ball.

(continued)

Set up, Run, and Hit *(continued)*

Figure 1.21 *(a)* Set up, *(b)* run, and *(c)* hit drill.

Who does it?

Alone: Do this drill alone at first because you want to become comfortable with going from the down and ready position to running to the ball and then hitting the setup shot. As you are setting the ball up, make sure you are giving yourself a variety of setups in front of you, to the side of you, and behind you. This will help develop proficiency, consistency, and confidence.

Partner: Once you get comfortable, grab a bucket of balls and do this drill with a partner. The partner sets you up over and over again, giving you a variety of setups in front of you, to the side of you, and behind you. All you have to do is concentrate on reading the ball, turning, shuffling into the ball, and then hitting the ball. Once you hit your allotted number of balls, switch positions with your partner.

In this chapter, we used the five-step approach as a learning tool for the forehand stroke. The pros use this method, not only to sharpen their timing, but also to regain their consistency and accuracy after coming back from an injury. The chapters for the individual strokes address the five-step approach as a learning tool specific to each stroke and will build the foundation you need in order to have the confidence to hit that stroke or shot with consistency, accuracy, and power based on the level you want to play.

In chapter 8, we expand on the topic of drilling and begin to focus on situations involving multiple strokes and many different shots.

Attacking Forehand Checklist: Core, Intermediate, and Advanced

Core	Intermediate	Advanced
Grip • Shake hands with racquet • V of hand on top with thumb around and pointer finger in trigger-grip position	Grip • Pinkie should be down close to the butt of the handle without exceeding the butt of the racquet in order to get maximum wrist snap	Grip • Pinkie should be as far down as it can go on the handle, but do not go beyond the butt of the racquet, in order to generate even more wrist snap while keeping control • Loose grip • Relaxed wrist
Stance • Good power base with feet shoulder-width apart • Square to side wall • Knees relaxed and flexed approximately 150 degrees • Upper body erect • Shoulders level and ready to rotate • ERP: racquet up • Nonhitting arm relaxed for balance • Weight distribution 50/50 • Eyes on ball	Stance • Wider power base with feet wider than shoulder-width apart, another foot (.3 m) so your body will be lower • Knees bent approximately 140 degrees • ERP: elbow is up and in line with shoulder • Hips slightly rotated to right corner • Nonhitting arm starts to move • Weight distribution 55/45	Stance • Wider power base, another foot (.3 m) compared to intermediate, so body is even lower • Knees bent approximately 130 degrees • Shoulders level and aggressively rotated for more upper-body rotation • ERP: racquet even higher above the shoulder for more power • Hips completely rotated; coil and uncoil for maximum power • Nonhitting arm completely around and pointing to back wall • Weight distribution 60/40

(continued)

Attacking Forehand Checklist: Core, Intermediate, and Advanced *(continued)*

Core	Intermediate	Advanced
Step and swing • Step toward front wall • Feet are lined up evenly • Hips begin to open • Shoulder leads • Racquet head and elbow drop • Butt of handle perpendicular to front wall; racquet face parallel to side wall • Wrist relaxed and snaps through (approximately 1 sec.) • Nonhitting arm begins to come through • Eyes on ball • Weight distribution 50/50	Step and swing • Longer step is needed, approximately 3 ft. (.9 m), to be as low to the ground as possible • Weight shifts slightly back so you can drive off back foot as you pivot • Faster swing speed (1/4 sec.) for more power • Hips fully open faster • Wrist relaxed • Nonhitting arm comes through faster • Weight distribution 55/45	Step and swing • Quicker step is needed to be able to hit balls farther away from you; Jason's step is about 3.5 ft. (1.1 m) long, and he's only 5 ft. 8 in. (173 cm) • Violent hip rotation • Fastest swing speed (1/2 sec. faster) for the most power (more whip) • Nonhitting arm whips around to get maximum rotation • Weight distribution 60/40
Contact point • Off the lead or front foot • Racquet flat and level • Hitting arm extended, knee-high or lower • Chest and belly button begin to face front wall • Nonhitting arm comes through and stays out of the way • Eyes on ball • Weight distribution 50/50	Contact point • Begin to hit off different positions off the lead (front) foot to create deception and variety of shots (visualize the four racquet contact points) • Racquet parallel to front wall and floor • Wrist completely relaxed, not stiff • Chest and belly button face the front wall • Nonhitting arm continues coming through • Weight distribution 55/45	Contact point • Hitting arm at full extension and elbow straight on contact • Ball usually farther than 3 ft. (.9 m) away from you when fully extended to maximize power • Chest and belly button to front wall • Nonhitting arm completely through on the way to the back wall • Weight distribution 60/40
Follow-through • Racquet comes through and around • Racquet ends up below the shoulder and is flat and level • Chest and belly button facing front wall • Upper body is erect • Back foot completely pivots • Weight distribution 50/50 • Hips completely open • Nonhitting arm around and out of the way • Eyes on ball	Follow-through • Racquet comes around 1/4 second faster pointing to back wall when done • Back foot completely pivoted and back leg bent at approximately 90 degrees • Hips completely open • Nonhitting arm pointing to back wall • Weight distribution 55/45	Follow-through • Racquet comes completely around as quickly as possible (approximately 1/2 sec. faster) for more power • Back foot completely pivoted and back leg bent at 90 degrees • Nonhitting arm comes completely around a little past the back wall as quickly as possible for balance • Weight distribution 60/40

Summary

We have given you the proper mechanics for an attacking forehand, one of the weapons you need in order to compete at the intermediate and advanced levels and be a force to be reckoned with. To achieve this, we want to stress again how important it is to understand the differences between the two levels and spend the necessary time to develop these skills one level at a time. Make sure you develop the skill and level you are currently working on before moving on to the next skill. There is nothing worse than moving through the skills and levels too quickly without having a good foundation at each of the levels, as this will lead to major problems down the road because of a weak foundation.

There are no shortcuts for intermediate and advanced players to develop these skills, a necessity for an attacking forehand. To achieve the power, consistency, and accuracy to win at these levels, you need to drill, drill, drill to develop muscle memory so you can not only perform but also perform well under pressure. We provide plenty of drills, from drop and hit all the way through to run, set up, and hit. Using the proper techniques during drilling will create consistency as you move through each level one skill at a time.

In summary, think about this. By holding the racquet lower with a relaxed grip, taking a longer step between 3 and 3.5 feet (.9 and 1.1 m), and having more hip rotation, you will substantially add power to your attacking forehand. Using ERP, having a flat and level swing, contacting the ball at full extension from your body, and having a complete follow-through will dramatically increase your control. By combining both the power aspect and control aspect of your stroke, you will have the complete attacking forehand that is absolutely necessary to become a champion and develop a winning game.

Chapter 2
Penetrating Backhand

George Brewer & Friends

Now you have an attacking forehand, but we don't want you to stop there. We want to teach you how to hit a penetrating backhand so you have confidence from both sides of the court by placing constant pressure on your opponent. The term *penetrating backhand* means to have a backhand that will unravel your opponent's defense. The penetrating backhand will also dismantle your opponent's game plan, making it harder for him to return the ball effectively. The sheer power of a penetrating backhand will not allow your opponent enough time to set up with a good offensive return.

Too often players become what we call lopsided players, which means they have a strong forehand and a weak backhand. When this occurs, these players will usually run around the backhand to hit a forehand because their backhands are not strong enough to make a good offensive shot. This lack of confidence in the backhand places them in a spot where they are out of position. The only time you want to run around your backhand to hit your forehand is for strategic reasons, not because you cannot hit a backhand. Therefore, when you use your forehand on the backhand side, the purpose of this strategy is to trap your opponent along the left side wall and pin him there, which will not allow him to get back into good center-court position (more details on this in chapter 5).

One of the things that separate levels of play is the backhand and a player's ability to shoot the ball offensively with power, consistency, and accuracy. This chapter will help prepare you for just that by developing a pressure-packed backhand. You want to be able to penetrate your opponent's weaknesses with your backhand. Our ultimate goal in this chapter is to get you ready so your attacking forehand and penetrating backhand are equally strong, and your opponent will not know which side of the court to hit to because you will be able to hit good offensive and defensive shots from both sides.

You want to get to this point so that your shots will start to frustrate your opponent. Your opponent will place undue pressure on herself, and she will try to hit more difficult shots and hit them lower and lower (e.g., overhead kills or a kill from 39 feet [11.9 m] back) because no matter what she does she thinks you can't handle it. The more your opponent does this, the more mistakes she will make, which is exactly what you want her to do.

As we did for the attacking forehand, we want to give you the tools for your penetrating backhand so you can start to develop a backhand that your opponents will fear. We have broken your penetrating backhand into five different areas. All the components of your backhand work together, much the same as the forehand to create a penetrating backhand that is aggressive, consistent, very sound, and very strong. When you have mastered your penetrating backhand, you will have another weapon that you can use to create your winning game and produce the desired results you need to become a champion. You will be more of a threat to your opponents, putting more pressure on them and forcing them into making mistakes.

In this chapter, we give you a full breakdown of each component of the penetrating backhand. Following are the tools for a good backhand:

1. Grip
2. Stance
3. Step and swing
4. Contact point
5. Follow-through

There are many differences between intermediate and advanced players when hitting the backhand. Pointing out these differences requires that we break down each part of the stroke.

Grip

The purpose of the forehand grip and the backhand grip is exactly the same: to control the racquet, to avoid rotation of the racquet handle in your hand when hitting the ball, and to make sure the grip is relaxed. Since the grip is a critical part of the stroke, make sure you change your grip from a forehand grip to a backhand grip so the racquet face is flat upon contact with the ball. If you do not change and you hold a forehand grip to hit a backhand, the face of the racquet will be pointing up or be open, and therefore you will be leaving the ball up and constantly setting up your opponent.

The proper grip on the racquet is crucial. The following tips are elemental for all levels of play:

1. You should "shake hands" with the racquet and then turn your hand approximately one-eighth of an inch (.3 cm) toward the back wall, making sure the grip is relaxed.

2. The V of the hand should be at the top left edge of the racquet handle, with the thumb around the handle to avoid an improper grip. If you have an incorrect grip, it will lead to problems in the future that will affect your stroke mechanics.

3. The pointer finger should be held in a trigger-grip position for more control of the racquet and more consistent execution of shot selection during game play.

4. Your hand should slide down as far as possible on the handle without exceeding the butt of the racquet; this will give you reliable power that is enhanced by the wrist snap.

5. Never use a hammer grip, which is holding the racquet at the end of the handle with a fisted grip as if you were hammering a nail into a wall. Although this may give you power, it does not give you constant control of the shot.

All players, regardless of level, need to change their grips when hitting a backhand in order to have a consistent shot. This change of grip allows the player to contact the ball flat and level, preventing breakdowns in the rest of the swing to compensate for a poor grip. An incorrect backhand grip will lead to several problems such as hitting the ball too high, dipping the shoulder, and even soreness and pain in the wrist or elbow. A beginner typically has trouble changing his grip but is ready to change to an intermediate grip when he is able to hit the ball firmly with pace while moderately controlling where it's going, generally keeping the ball between 6 and 18 inches (15 and 46 cm) high. A player who does not change his grip will lose significant power and control and could develop shoulder problems.

Intermediate Grip

This grip requires the player to lower her hand on the racquet. The hand must be close to the butt of the racquet, without any part of the hand or fingers exceeding the butt of the handle (figure 2.1). The purpose of holding the grip low on the handle is to generate power. Power is achieved by snapping the wrist at the contact point to get respectable power.

As an intermediate player, once the ball is coming off the strings of your racquet more quickly and you are hitting the ball relatively harder, you are ready for the advanced grip. At this point, you have developed enough hand, wrist, and forearm strength to hold the racquet at its lowest point without losing control. As in the forehand grip, your pinkie should be as low as possible on the racquet without hanging off the handle. This will increase the lever, allowing for maximum extension and maximum wrist snap on your shots.

Advanced Grip

Advanced players need to squeeze every last drop of power out of the swing without losing control. The advanced grip will create this power, resulting in less reaction time for your opponent and even more control for you.

Figure 2.1   Intermediate backhand grip.

This grip is even more exaggerated in terms of how low the player should hold the racquet (figure 2.2). At this level, the player should have ample hand strength to hold the racquet at the very edge of the butt of the handle (i.e., as low as possible, increasing the ability to snap the wrist quickly) without the hand exceeding the butt. With this grip, the snap of the wrist must be very fast and the hand must be relaxed to achieve maximum power and control. Some of the pros customize their grips to acquire more wrist snap.

Figure 2.2   Advanced backhand grip.

However, the grip must be relaxed enough to hold the racquet as loosely as possible, as if you were holding a raw egg. If you tighten your hand and your wrist, your grip will be too tight. You will lose power and crack the imaginary raw egg. This principle applies to all players regardless of level.

As we did for the forehand, we want to bring to your attention the correct and incorrect backhand grips. The grip you choose will have an effect on the amount of power and control you can generate.

- V of the hand on the top left edge of the racquet handle. This is the grip we advocate because when you are swinging, your natural body mechanics and the way your hand attaches to your wrist will allow you to hit the ball flat and level and at full extension for maximum power and control.

- V of the hand on the extreme left part of the racquet handle. This grip will cost you both power and control. You will naturally hit the ball into the floor because the racquet face will be pointing down, resulting in a lot of skips. In addition, with this exaggerated grip your wrist will lock, not allowing a full wrist snap.

- V of the hand on the top of the racquet handle. This is the grip we advocate for the forehand. Using this grip for the backhand will cost you both power and control because you will naturally slice the ball, causing you to hit the ball high and off the back wall or into the side wall, and your wrist will not fully snap through your shot.

The only grip we advocate and support for the backhand is the first one, V of the hand on the top left edge of the racquet handle (slightly to the left or right is okay) because it will allow you to hit the ball flat, level, and at full extension for maximum power and control. There are no benefits to choosing the last two, but some lower-level pros use these incorrect grips, so we mention them in order to point out incorrect form, drawing your attention to the value of a correct grip.

COMMON MISTAKES: GRIP

ERROR: You are using a hammer grip.

CORRECTION: Shake hands with the racquet using a trigger grip, and then turn your hand approximately one-eighth to one-quarter of an inch (.3 to .6 cm) toward the back wall. The V of the hand should be at the top left edge of the racquet handle, with the thumb around.

SOLUTION: By using the proper backhand grip, most of your hand will be on the handle, giving you more power and control of your shot, and because your wrist will not be stiff, you will have a complete wrist snap.

ERROR: You do not change your grip from forehand to backhand (i.e., you use the same grip).

CORRECTION: Change your grip from forehand to backhand to obtain a flat racquet face upon contact with the ball.

SOLUTION: Changing your grip from forehand to backhand gives you the power and control you need because you are able to hit flatter, which helps keep you from slicing the ball, hitting it high, floating the ball, or hitting it into the side wall by accident.

Stance

The stance provides the foundation for each penetrating backhand shot, as it does for the attacking forehand. The stance, or what we call the power base, establishes your power before you hit the ball. Similar to your attacking forehand, you want to stay low—approximately two-thirds of your body height—and you do not want to stand up unless you are hitting a ceiling ball or you are in between a rally. The only difference is that for your penetrating backhand, you start with your stance at a slight angle rather than square to the side wall. Your front foot should be approximately 3 to 4 inches (8 to 10 cm) closer to the side wall than your back foot. This offset foot position sets the stage for a step toward the corner.

The proper stance makes it possible for you to always be prepared to return the ball with consistency and power. These tips are crucial at all levels of play and will establish a sound power base.

1. The backhand stance requires that you face the side wall.
2. Your feet should be spread apart, a little wider than shoulder width.
3. Your feet are at a slight angle rather than square to the side wall. Your front foot should be approximately 3 to 4 inches (8 to 10 cm) closer to the side wall than your back foot. This offset foot position prepares you for a step toward the corner.
4. The knees are flexed and relaxed at approximately 150 degrees.
5. Your weight is evenly distributed or as close to 50/50 as possible. This allows you to establish a sound power base.
6. You are using the proper backhand grip as described earlier.
7. Your racquet is up and your elbow is in line with your belly button.
8. The racquet face is pointing to the left back corner.
9. Your upper body is erect.
10. Your shoulders are level and rotated so the right shoulder is pointing to the left side wall.
11. Your hips are loose and ready to rotate.
12. Your nonhitting arm is relaxed for balance.
13. Keep your eyes on the ball.

Intermediate Stance

The following intermediate techniques focus on a wide and low power base, increased hip and shoulder rotation, and high and more rotated racquet preparation for increased power (figure 2.3).

1. Feet are spread shoulder-width apart plus 1 foot (.3 m), so your body will be lower to the ground.
2. Knees are bent slightly more, to approximately 140 degrees, for a springing action into the stroke.
3. Hips are rotated, almost facing the back left corner, to add power to your stroke.
4. The racquet is up higher, with your elbow above your belly button (ERP).

Figure 2.3 Intermediate backhand stance.

5. Racquet is at shoulder level, with shoulders slightly rotated, approximately 10 degrees beyond the left back corner.

6. Nonhitting arm is relaxed for balance, moved slightly to the left with your upper-body rotation.

Advanced Stance

To become a solid advanced player, you need to widen your power base because this puts you lower to the ground, making your hitting zone larger and farther away from your body. This enables you to contact the ball at full extension while allowing your legs and hips to strengthen your base and create full weight transfer (60/40) toward the front, leading to maximum power (figure 2.4).

1. Feet are spread shoulder-width apart plus 2 feet (.6 m), so your body will be even lower to the ground for maximum power.

2. Knees are bent slightly more, to approximately 130 degrees, for even more springing action to enhance movement.

3. Hips are completely rotated, facing the back left corner to obtain maximum power—you coil then uncoil.

4. Your racquet is up higher and your elbow is at chest level (ERP) for more power.

5. Shoulders rotate aggressively, with your right shoulder pointing to the left side wall for maximum power.

6. Nonhitting arm is relaxed for balance, moved 1 to 2 inches to the left with your upper-body rotation, and serves as a tool to help twist the waist around.

Figure 2.4 Advanced backhand stance.

COMMON MISTAKES: STANCE

ERROR: Your feet are too close together.

CORRECTION: Your feet should be at least shoulder-width apart and another 1 or 2 feet (.3 or .6 m), depending on your height and level of play.

SOLUTION: By having your feet the proper distance apart, your next step into the shot will be shorter and straight ahead, allowing for less up and down movement and more power going into the shot. If your feet are too close together, then the next step has to be big, resulting in lots of up and down movement and inconsistent shots, creating many setups for your opponent.

ERROR: Your feet are parallel to the side wall, not offset at an angle with the front foot 3 to 4 inches (8 to 10 cm) closer to the side wall than the back foot (i.e., staggered).

CORRECTION: Make sure your feet are staggered so your hips do not open too early and your power is not too far out in front of you, causing too many crosscourt shots.

SOLUTION: By having your feet staggered rather than parallel, your hips will open perfectly, allowing you to go down the line in addition to crosscourt.

ERROR: Your shoulders are not rotated and your right shoulder is pointing to the front wall rather than to the left front corner or left side wall.

CORRECTION: Make sure you rotate your shoulders to between the left front corner and left side wall.

SOLUTION: The correct rotation of your shoulders maximizes your power and develops control so you can choose the shot you want to hit. If your shoulders are not rotated, they will open up too early. As a result, you will make contact way out in front of you and will send all your balls crosscourt.

ERROR: Your shoulders are dipped rather than level.

CORRECTION: Keep your shoulders as level as possible.

SOLUTION: Level shoulders lead to a flat swing, making you more consistent. Dipping your shoulders leads to inconsistency because it creates a pendulum swing, which is similar to a golf swing (high to low then high again), rather than a flat swing.

ERROR: Racquet is down, not up.

CORRECTION: Get your racquet up as soon as the ball is approaching the front wall and you know it's going to your backhand.

SOLUTION: By developing good ERP, you will have a more consistent swing because you will have more time to set up, swing, and hit the ball where you want it to go. If you wait for the ball to approach, you have to get the racquet up and then swing, which is two motions instead of one, and your shots will be inconsistent. If the racquet is already up, all you have to do is swing.

Step and Swing

The step begins the stroke. Unlike for the forehand, you are going to step at a 45-degree angle toward the left front corner (not straight ahead) because now your hitting arm is on the front side of your body rather the back side of your body when setting up. If you stepped straight ahead, your hips would open up too early, and your contact point would be too far forward off of your lead foot. As a result, you would pull all the balls crosscourt, and you would not be able to use the contact point principle (page 13) we used for the forehand and will be using for the backhand. You must remember to drive off your back hip and pivot your back foot, which unlocks your hips. When you use the proper technique, the power generated from your lower body will be transferred into your upper body and eventually into the racquet and then the ball.

1. Your weight remains relatively even as you step at approximately a 45-degree angle toward the left front corner with your lead foot (front leg). Make sure you do not step toward the side wall, as that will lock your hips. Weight distribution varies, however, based on your level of play.

2. Your feet should be staggered, not even, with your right foot closer to the side wall and your left foot slightly back.

3. The racquet remains up in ERP, with your elbow in line with your shoulder.

4. Your weight shifts slightly back on the ball of your back foot so you can pivot and drive off your back foot, allowing your hips to generate more power, giving your opponent less time to react.

5. Rotate your shoulders so your right shoulder is pointing to the left front corner.

6. Your hips start to open as you turn at the waist.

7. Keep your eyes on the ball.

As you swing, remember the following:

1. Your shoulder leads.

2. The head of the racquet and the elbow start to come down simultaneously.

3. The butt of the handle is perpendicular to the front wall.

4. The face of the racquet is parallel to the side wall.

5. The wrist and racquet begin to come through in approximately one second, and the wrist snaps and is completely relaxed.

6. The nonhitting arm comes through as you turn your shoulders and waist.

7. Keep your eyes on the ball.

The core techniques establish the proper step with the correct weight distribution, utilizing hip and shoulder rotation and relaxation of the wrist to allow the racquet to come through quickly. These points are vital for a consistent and powerful backhand.

Intermediate Step and Swing

Practicing intermediate techniques teaches you to take a longer step and change the weight distribution so you can get your hips and shoulders through the shot more quickly and bring the racquet around with more head speed (figure 2.5).

1. Rotate your shoulders even more so your right shoulder is pointing 2 to 3 inches (5 to 8 cm) left of the left front corner for more power.

2. Racquet is up higher, about an inch (2.5 cm), to create more distance between the racquet head and the ball, creating more power.

3. Take a longer step, approximately 3 feet (.9 m), which puts you closer to the ground so that you can hit the ball lower with a level swing.

4. Weight shifts slightly back, approximately 10 percent, as you step at that 45-degree angle toward the left front corner so you can drive off the back foot as you pivot, but weight distribution ends approximately 55/45 toward the front.

Figure 2.5 Intermediate step and swing.

5. Hips fully open and come through quickly for more power.

6. Wrist is relaxed now and allows for greater head speed, one-fourth second faster, which means a faster swing for more power.

7. Nonhitting arm comes all the way through, balanced and allowing for a full follow-through.

Advanced Step and Swing

In the advanced techniques, it is vital to take an even longer step and change the weight distribution so you can get your hips and shoulders through the shot more quickly and bring the racquet around with more head speed. When done correctly, this technique generates more power and consistency, essential for high levels of play (figure 2.6).

1. Rotate your shoulders even more so your right shoulder is pointing to the left side wall for more power, creating a coiling and uncoiling effect.

2. Racquet is up higher, about another inch (2.5 cm), to create even more distance between the racquet head and the ball, creating explosive power.

3. Take quicker and longer steps, approximately 3.5 feet (1.1 m), to hit balls farther away from the body and at the same time to generate more power and hit the ball flat and level.

4. Hip rotation is violent. This means getting your hips through your shot as quickly as humanly possible without being off balance. The faster the hip rotation, with all the other technical parts correct, the more power you will generate.

Figure 2.6 Advanced step and swing.

5. Faster swing speed, approximately half a second faster, for even more power and whip.

6. Nonhitting arm whips through to get maximum rotation.

7. Weight distribution is approximately 60/40 to the front.

The principle of power (page 11) is exactly the same principle we will be using for the penetrating backhand. This section alone is worth its weight in gold. Please do not take it lightly, as it truly is the difference from one level of play to the next. The explosion of energy that creates maximum power from your lower body is the key, not only to obtain consistent, powerful strokes but also to develop a great service game and a relentless return of service game, which we discuss later in this book.

COMMON MISTAKES: STEP AND SWING

ERROR: You step straight ahead rather than at a slight 45-degree angle.

CORRECTION: Step at a slight 45-degree angle so your hips don't open up too early and the ball is pulled crosscourt.

SOLUTION: By stepping at a slight 45-degree angle, your hips will open perfectly, allowing you to go down the line or crosscourt, not just crosscourt. You will have more control of your shot.

ERROR: You step toward the side wall rather than the left front corner.

CORRECTION: Step at a slight 45-degree angle toward the left front corner to allow the hips to open rather than lock.

SOLUTION: By stepping correctly, your hips open as they should, creating the power you need for your shots. If you step toward the side wall, your hips lock and you lose power because you cannot follow through all the way. This poor technique can also create hip problems.

ERROR: Your step is not long enough, and thus your power base is not wide enough.

CORRECTION: Step at least 3.5 feet (1.1 m) based on skill level.

SOLUTION: This longer step gets you lower to the ground so you can hit the ball lower, level, and farther from your body; all these components help generate more power and consistency. If your step is too short, you will lose power because you can't drive with your legs.

ERROR: Your hips don't open and you end up facing the side wall rather than the front wall upon completion of the swing.

CORRECTION: Make sure you pivot your back foot, which unlocks the hips.

SOLUTION: Check to make sure your belly button is facing the front wall when you finish your swing; this is a great indication that you are opening your hips. If your belly button is facing the side wall, that probably means your hips are locked, causing loss of power and possible hip problems.

ERROR: You do not lead with the elbow but rather come down with your whole arm, which is straight (i.e., like a tennis swing).

CORRECTION: Lead with your elbow.

SOLUTION: By leading with your elbow, you assure a flatter swing with power. If you hit with a straight arm, you lose power as you wind up, pushing or guiding the ball rather than ripping through the ball.

ERROR: Your wrist is stiff when swinging (i.e., no wrist snap).

CORRECTION: Make sure your wrist is relaxed through your hitting zone.

SOLUTION: If your wrist is relaxed, the power generated from your legs and hips can move freely through your arm into your wrist and then into the ball, resulting in more power. If your wrist is stiff you undoubtedly lose power.

ERROR: The nonhitting arm does not come around as you are swinging; it just stays there and does not move.

CORRECTION: Bring your nonhitting arm all the way through across your body.

SOLUTION: Bringing your nonhitting arm all the way through and across your body as quickly as possible maximizes upper-body rotation for full power. If you do not get the nonhitting arm through, you lose power because the nonhitting arm helps with a complete follow-through.

ERROR: You have too much weight on your front foot (e.g., 80/20 or 90/10 distribution).

CORRECTION: Weight should be relatively even (50/50) as you are getting into position to hit the ball but then shifts to anywhere between 55/45 and 60/40 to the front.

SOLUTION: The weight shift gives you enough weight on your back foot so you can drive off it to create power as well as be balanced when you are done. This is a key component of being able to hit the ball hard yet get to your next shot without struggling to stay on both feet.

ERROR: Racquet is not parallel to the floor, and the face of the racquet is not parallel to the front wall but moves like a pendulum (i.e., like a golf club upon contacting a golf ball).

CORRECTION: The racquet needs to be parallel to the floor and the face of the racquet parallel to the front wall, like a baseball swing. When you do not hit flat and level at full extension, the hitting zone is very small, and the result is lots of skips and floating balls.

SOLUTION: The flatter your swing, the more consistent you will be. If you have more of a pendulum swing, you will have a tendency to skip more balls as well as set your opponent up because the ball floats to the middle of the court more often.

Contact Point

The contact point for your backhand is no different from that for your forehand; it is where the ball and racquet make contact. The perfect contact point is off of the lead foot. This area can also be referred to as your hitting zone. Keep the ball in front of you so that the momentum of your body along with the swing creates more power. In this section you will learn that where you make contact with the ball in your hitting zone will determine where the ball goes.

1. Hit off your lead foot.
2. Your hitting arm should be at full extension from your body for all shots.
3. The racquet head should be parallel to the floor and parallel to the front wall, knee high or lower depending on the shot. It's at this point that wrist snap occurs.
4. The wrist should be relaxed, not stiff. A relaxed wrist will allow all the components to move easily with as little resistance as possible.
5. Your chest and belly button begin to face toward the front wall.
6. Your weight distribution varies based on your level of play, but it starts with a ratio of 50/50.
7. Your nonhitting arm begins to come through and follows behind your hitting arm.
8. Keep your eyes on the ball.

As with the forehand stroke, everything about the backhand stroke remains exactly the same (your grip, your stance, your step, your swing, your follow-through) except the contact point. By changing only your contact point and nothing else, you are less predictable and more deceptive. This key principle keeps your opponent guessing and off balance, which gives you the edge.

Learning the core techniques of hitting the ball off your lead foot, with your arm extended so you hit the ball away from your body, at knee high or lower, with the racquet flat and level, gives you a solid contact point.

Intermediate Contact Point

The intermediate technique introduces the concept of deception and hitting at different positions off the lead foot, with a slightly different weight distribution (because of the step) and the ball a little farther from the body (figure 2.7).

1. Hit off the lead foot, but start to understand the four racquet contact points (see "Hitting off Your Lead Foot").
2. Wrist is completely relaxed, not stiff.
3. Hitting arm is fully extended.
4. Chest and belly button face the front wall.
5. Racquet is parallel to the front wall and floor and is hitting flat.
6. Nonhitting arm moves more quickly across the body but stays out of the way.
7. Weight distribution is approximately 55/45 to the front.

Figure 2.7 Intermediate contact point.

Advanced Contact Point

Advanced techniques emphasize deception coupled with power and control; the ball should be the farthest distance from your body (approximately 3 feet [.9 m] or slightly farther based on your height), with your arm straight upon contact to help move you to that higher level of play (figure 2.8).

1. Hit off the lead foot with complete understanding and execution of the four racquet contact points. Hitting from different positions off the lead foot creates deception, increases variety in your shot selection, and makes you less predictable.
2. Hitting arm is at full extension.
3. Elbow is straight upon contact with the ball.
4. Keep the ball 3 feet (.9 m) or slightly more away from you at point of contact.
5. Nonhitting arm moves more quickly across the body and stays completely out of the way.
6. Weight distribution is approximately 60/40 to the front.

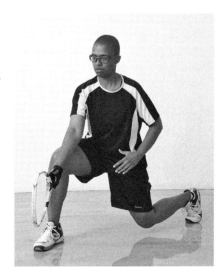

Figure 2.8 Advanced contact point.

Hitting off Your Lead Foot

Let's take a closer look at the different contact points relative to your lead foot. Note: Pinch, down the line, crosscourt, and reverse pinch will be discussed in detail in later chapters. But for now, these particular shots depend on point of contact relative to your lead foot.

• Pinch: Contact the ball off the heel of your lead foot. The ball hits to the closest corner, hitting the side wall first, the front wall second, and then bounces two times before hitting the second side wall in front of the service line (figure 2.9).

• Down the line: Contact the ball off the arch of your lead foot. The ball hits between you and the closest side wall, bouncing two times before hitting the back wall and not hitting the side wall at all (figure 2.10).

• Crosscourt: Contact the ball off the big toe of your lead foot. The ball hits between you and the farthest side wall, bouncing two times before hitting the back wall and not hitting the side wall at all (figure 2.11).

• Reverse pinch: Contact the ball off the little toe of your lead foot. The ball hits to the opposite corner, hitting the side wall first, the front wall second and then bouncing two times before hitting the second side wall in front of the service line (figure 2.12).

Figure 2.9 Pinch hit off the heel of lead foot.

Figure 2.10 Down-the-line hit off the arch of lead foot.

Figure 2.11 Crosscourt hit off the big toe of lead foot.

Figure 2.12 Reverse pinch hit off the little toe of lead foot.

COMMON MISTAKES: CONTACT POINT

ERROR: You contact the ball off your back foot.

CORRECTION: Your contact point is ideally somewhere off your lead foot, depending on the shot.

SOLUTION: When hitting the ball off your lead foot, you achieve maximum power and control. If you hit the ball behind you, off your back foot, you will lose power and control. From a control standpoint, the ball will likely hit the side wall or go directly into the floor if it is hit too far back. In regard to power, you will not be able to achieve maximum weight distribution or maximum wrist snap if the ball is not in proper position to be hit at full extension, resulting in a severe lack of power.

ERROR: You contact the ball too close to your body and not flat at full extension.

CORRECTION: Contact the ball at full extension from your body, with the racquet head flat and level.

SOLUTION: By hitting the ball at full extension, with the racquet flat and level, you will add power and consistency to your stroke and lots of ball control to your game. When the ball is too close to your body, you often get jammed and lose power and control, setting your opponent up too frequently in midcourt.

Follow-Through

The follow-through completes the swing, and the backhand follow-through is no different from the follow-through for a forehand. When the swing is completed, the head of the racquet is pointing to the back wall. The mistake most people make is not completing the swing. An incomplete swing can be the cause of elbow or shoulder problems, inconsistent shots, and loss of power and control. When you stop prematurely, you slow down your swing through the hitting zone, and therefore you are not going to hit the ball as hard.

As you follow through, remember the following:

1. Relax the wrist.
2. The racquet head is below your shoulder and pointing toward the back wall after the swing is completed.
3. Chest and belly button are facing the front wall.
4. Upper body is completely erect, and your weight should be completely balanced, with the back foot pivoted completely.
5. Hips are completely open to maximize your power.
6. The hitting arm is completely around the body and pointing toward the back wall.
7. Keep your eyes on the ball.
8. Weight distribution is 50-50.

The core techniques focus on making sure you finish your swing completely. There is nothing worse than having the proper grip, the correct stance, the right step and swing, and a good contact point only to slow down or stop your swing prematurely. That abrupt stop will adversely affect power as well as put undue stress on your elbow and shoulder, leading to soreness or injury.

Intermediate Follow-Through

The intermediate techniques focus on getting your racquet completely around by slightly changing your weight distribution and using greater racquet head speed, faster hip rotation, and quicker pivoting of the back foot, with a 90-degree knee bend to get lower on the ball (figure 2.13).

1. Racquet comes through and around more quickly, approximately one-fourth second faster, ending up between your shoulder and your waist and pointing toward the back wall.

2. Hips open more quickly, approximately one-fourth second faster.

3. Back foot is completely pivoted and bent at a 90-degree angle.

4. The nonhitting arm comes through across your body.

5. Weight distribution is approximately 55/45 to the front.

Figure 2.13 Intermediate follow-through.

Intermediate players often have extreme difficulty with their follow-through, which affects the entire swing. If you don't follow through, then you'll most likely slow your racquet down in the hitting area before you contact the ball. That deceleration will also keep your hips from properly rotating and your foot from pivoting, leading to your not being able to transfer energy properly to achieve your maximum power.

Advanced Follow-Through

The advanced techniques focus on getting your racquet completely around by slightly changing your weight distribution and using greater racquet head speed, faster hip rotation, and quicker pivoting of the back foot, with a 90-degree knee bend to get lower on the ball (figure 2.14).

1. Racquet comes through low, at waist height, and as quickly as possible, in approximately half a second faster, so your ball is hit low and hard, giving your opponent a tough shot to return.

2. Hips open even more quickly, approximately half a second faster.

3. The hitting arm comes completely through the swing, and the racquet points a little past the back wall at the end of the swing (an exaggerated follow-through).

4. Nonhitting arm also comes completely through as quickly as possible, one second faster, to help balance out the swing.

Figure 2.14 Advanced follow-through.

5. Weight distribution is approximately 60/40 to the front.

One of the ways you can figure out if you're attaining your maximum power stroke is by checking your follow-through. Most pro players, especially the power players, have an extremely violent and complete follow-through. When Sudsy Monchik was on the court, you would often see him hit a backhand from very deep in the court, and his follow-through was so violent that he not only hit the back wall with the racquet but sometimes cracked the racquet in half from the force of impact.

COMMON MISTAKES: FOLLOW-THROUGH

ERROR: There is no follow-through because you stop your arm prematurely before the racquet is pointing to the back wall.

CORRECTION: The racquet and your hitting arm need to be pointing to the back wall when finished, and your chest and belly button need to be facing the front wall.

SOLUTION: By having a complete follow-through, you transfer the maximum power you generated from your legs and hips through your upper body, into the racquet, and then into the ball, resulting in the most powerful shot you could possibly hit. If you stop your swing prematurely, you lose power because you are starting to slow your swing down too soon before contact is made, thus resulting in a slower ball. Also this lack of follow-through and an abrupt stop are what can cause elbow and shoulder problems.

ERROR: You have a high, exaggerated follow-through where the racquet ends up above your shoulder or, worse yet, above your head.

CORRECTION: The follow-through needs to be below your shoulder.

SOLUTION: By swinging flat and level as if you were clearing off a coffee table, you will ensure a flat follow-through that ends up pointing to the back wall. A high follow-through usually indicates a pendulum swing, which is bringing your racquet from high to low to high like a golf swing. This is inconsistent because you will float the ball a lot and give your opponent too many setups. Also, when players finish with the racquet high, their bodies also tend to be high and standing straight up, which causes the ball to stay up and gives the opponent opportunities to set up and shoot the ball.

Penetrating Backhand Drilling

As we shared with you in the introduction to this chapter, too many players out there are lopsided, which means they generally have one stroke better than the other, and usually it is a better forehand than backhand. For example, if you have an A forehand and a C backhand, you might run around your backhand to hit a forehand, which will not work if you want to move to the intermediate level and then to the advanced level and beyond because it can put you out of position. You need to develop a consistent penetrating backhand that you can hit with both accuracy and power, which will build your confidence on the backhand side, so in match play when you are moving, then setting up, and then planting your feet to execute the shot, you can count on your backhand to be a weapon in your game, which will put pressure on your opponent and create weak returns.

So our goal in this chapter is to teach you to be fundamentally sound on your backhand side while developing a penetrating backhand with all the elements of the intermediate and advanced techniques. Your penetrating backhand means nothing unless you are consistent at performing this basic stroke in a game, putting your opponent on the defense and letting you win points. To achieve these things and put pressure on your opponent, we are going to use the same drills as for your attacking forehand but from different positions so that you can develop the proper muscle memory needed to hit your penetrating backhand time after time with confidence and consistency.

Here is the five-step approach to drilling that the professionals use religiously. It allows them to develop and sharpen their timing, their consistency, and their accuracy—a must at the highest levels of racquetball.

1. Drop and hit (intermediate and advanced)
2. Toss, turn, and hit (intermediate and advanced)
3. Toss, turn, shuffle, and hit (intermediate and advanced)
4. Set up and hit (intermediate and advanced)
5. Set up, run, and hit (advanced)

We will use the same two diagrams we used for the attacking forehand to clearly show you the location on the court where you want to practice from using the five-step approach to drilling, regardless of whether you are an intermediate or an advanced player. The only differences are the positions where you will drill from.

Nine Drill Positions Diagram

See page 18 for the nine drill positions diagram.

1. Drop and hit
2. Toss, turn, and hit
3. Toss, turn, shuffle, and hit

   Intermediate: Do 1, 4, 7, 2, 5, and 8, in that order, always going from closest to the front wall and then moving back, farther from the front wall.

   Advanced: Now add positions 3, 6, and 9.

Zone Diagram

See page 19 for the zone diagram figure.

4. Set up and hit

   Intermediate: The ball should be set up so it lands in a particular zone, starting with zone 1, zone 2, zone 3, and finally zone 4, in that order, always going from closest to the front wall and then moving back farther from the front wall.

   You want to make sure you set the ball up from zone 2 to land in zone 1, from zone 3 to land in zone 2, and so on, always moving forward into the ball.

   Advanced: Add zone 5, zone 6, zone 7, and finally zone 8.

5. Set up, run, and hit

   Advanced: The ball should be set up so it lands in a particular zone. Since you are advanced, you can do whatever zone you are having trouble with and perfect that zone, then move on to the next.

   Now add zone 5, zone 6, zone 7, and finally zone 8.

Make sure when you are practicing that you give yourself a variety of setups to zones in front of you, to the side of you, and behind you.

Here are two examples:

1. Stand in zone 7 and set up the ball so it lands in zone 2.
2. Stand in zone 3 and set up the ball so it lands in zone 7.

Now let's get into each of the five steps of drilling in detail.

Drop and Hit

Why do it?

This drill is used primarily to develop stroke consistency, build your confidence, and learn the different facets of the technique.

How to do it?

1. Face the side wall, with the knees bent.
2. Racquet is up (ERP).
3. Feet are shoulder-width apart and at a slight angle, staggered (2.15a).
4. Drop the ball at full extension off of where your lead foot should end up.
5. Step at a 45-degree angle with the lead foot toward the left front corner (2.15b).
6. Let the ball drop below your knees and then swing and hit.
7. Keep your eyes on the ball.

Figure 2.15 *(a)* Drop and *(b)* hit drill.

Who does it?

Alone: Do this drill alone. This is the number one drill for developing consistency.

If you are a beginner, using the tape, like in the drop and hit drill on page 20, takes the guessing out of where to step and where to drop the ball. Once you move up to the intermediate or advanced level, you will probably not need the tape, but remember this technique as a booster shot regardless of your playing level. You can never abandon the basics.

Toss, Turn, and Hit

Why do it?

This drill is used to transition from the down and ready position (see page 138 in chapter 5) to facing the side wall to hit the ball.

How to do It?

1. Stand square to the front wall in the down and ready position, with feet more than shoulder-width apart, knees bent, waist slightly bent, shoulders level, and weight on the front part of the foot, ready to push off (2.16*a*).
2. Nonhitting arm is fully extended, with ball in hand (2.16*b*).
3. Toss the ball to the left. Pivot on the heel of your left foot, push off with the right foot, and bring the racquet up as you are crossing over so you end up at a slight angle to the side wall.
4. Let the ball drop below your knees and then swing and hit (2.16*c*).
5. Keep your eyes on the ball.

Figure 2.16 *(a)* Toss, *(b)* turn, and *(c)* hit drill.

Who does it?

Alone: Do this drill alone for a while because you want to become comfortable with going from the down and ready position to the hitting position. This will help develop proficiency, consistency, and confidence.

Partner: Once you get comfortable, grab a bucket of balls, and do this drill with a partner. The partner stands to your left and drops the ball so it is at full extension from you, and all you have to do is concentrate on turning and hitting. Once you hit your allotted number of balls, switch positions with your partner.

Toss, Turn, Shuffle, and Hit

Why do it?

This drill develops reading the ball because now the ball is farther from your body, and you need to turn and shuffle so the ball ends up off the lead foot.

How to do it?

1. Stand square to the front wall in the down and ready position, with feet more than shoulder-width apart, knees bent, waist slightly bent, shoulders level, and weight on the front part of the foot, ready to push off (2.17a).
2. Racquet is in the middle of the body, waist high and with a relaxed grip.
3. Nonhitting arm is fully extended, with ball in hand (2.17b).
4. Toss ball farther to the left. Pivot on the heel of your left foot, push off with the right foot, and bring the racquet up as you are crossing over so you end up at a slight angle to the side wall, and shuffle into the ball (2.17c).
5. Let the ball drop below your knees and then swing and hit (2.17d).
6. Keep your eyes on the ball.

Figure 2.17 (a) Toss, (b) turn, (c) shuffle, and (d) hit drill.

Who does it?

Alone: Do this drill alone for a while because you want to become comfortable with going from the down and ready position to the hitting position and then shuffling into your shot. This will help develop proficiency, consistency, and confidence.

Partner: Once you get comfortable, grab a bucket of balls and do this drill with a partner. The partner stands to your left and drops the ball so it is at full extension and a step from you, and all you have to do is concentrate on turning, shuffling, and hitting. Once you hit your allotted number of balls, switch positions with your partner.

Set Up and Hit

Why do it?

Since you get lots of setups in a game, you must learn how to read the ball going into the front wall, knowing what angle and what speed it will come off the front wall so you can move to that spot, set up, and hit the ball off your lead foot.

How to do it?

1. Stand square to the front wall in the down and ready position, with feet no more than shoulder-width apart, knees bent, waist slightly bent, shoulders level, and weight on the front part of the foot, ready to push off.

2. Racquet is in the middle of the body, waist high with a relaxed grip (2.18a).

3. Hit the ball to the front wall softly, and set yourself up to the backhand side (2.18b).

4. Look at the height at which the ball hits the front wall and the speed that it comes off your racquet or your partner's racquet if you are drilling with a partner, and determine where the ball is going to bounce the second time.

a

b

Figure 2.18 *(a)* Set up and *(b)* hit drill. *(continued)*

Set Up and Hit *(continued)*

5. After you read the ball, pivot on the heel of your left foot and push off with the right foot.
6. Use ERP as you are crossing over so you end up at a slight angle to the side wall, and shuffle into the ball.
7. Let the ball drop below the knees and then swing and hit.
8. Keep your eyes on the ball.

Who does it?

Alone: Do this drill alone for a while because you want to become comfortable with going from the down and ready position to learning how to read the ball to then setting up to hit the shot. As you are setting the ball up, make sure you are well behind the ball so you are moving into the ball not back. This will help develop proficiency, consistency, and confidence.

Partner: Once you get comfortable, grab a bucket of balls and do this drill with a partner. The partner sets you up with the same shot over and over again to a zone in front of you, so all you have to do is concentrate on reading the ball, turning, shuffling into the ball, and then hitting the ball. Once you hit your allotted number of balls, switch positions with your partner.

Drilling in itself will enable a player to read the ball better. As you set balls up for yourself, you will be hitting balls at different heights, speeds, and angles, so concentrate on where the ball is going to bounce based on how hard it was hit, at what angle, and at what height. Before trying to hit the ball, give yourself setups and then run and put your racquet on the floor so the ball can hit the racquet. Repeat this over and over again until you start reading the ball more easily. This will come in time with more experience.

Set Up, Run, and Hit

Why do it?

Since you get lots of setups in a game, you must learn how to read the ball going into the front wall, knowing what angle and what speed it will come off the wall so you can move to that spot, set up, and hit the ball off your lead foot. The added element is the ball may not be in front of you; it may be behind you or off to the side or off at an angle, and you need to know how to adapt to the situation at this higher level.

How to do it?

1. Stand square to the front wall in the down and ready position, with your feet no more than shoulder-width apart, knees bent, waist slightly bent, shoulders level, and weight on the front part of the foot, ready to push off (2.19*a*).
2. Racquet is in the middle of the body, waist high with a relaxed grip.
3. Hit the ball to the front wall softly, and set yourself up (2.19*b*).
4. Look at the height at which the ball hits the front wall and the speed that it comes off your racquet or your partner's racquet, if you are drilling with a partner, and determine where the ball is going to bounce the second time.
5. After you've read the ball and have determined where it will land in front of you, pivot on the heel of your left foot, then push off with the right foot.
6. Bring your racquet up high as you cross over so you end up parallel to the side wall.
7. Shuffle into the ball.

Figure 2.19 *(a)* Set up, *(b)* run, and *(c)* hit drill.

8. If the ball is behind you, pivot on the heel of your left foot so that your toes are pointing toward the back wall as your right foot pushes off and comes around to get you into position behind the ball (2.19*c*).

9. Let the ball drop below the knees and then swing and hit.

10. Keep your eyes on the ball.

Who does it?

Alone: Do this drill alone for a while because you want to become comfortable with going from the down and ready position to running to the ball and then hitting the setup shot. As you are setting the ball up, make sure you are giving yourself a variety of setups in front of you, to the side of you, and behind you. This will help develop proficiency, consistency, and confidence.

Partner: Once you get comfortable, grab a bucket of balls and do this drill with a partner. The partner sets you up with the same shot over and over again, giving you a variety of setups in front of you, to the side of you, and behind you. All you have to do is concentrate on reading the ball, turning, shuffling into the ball, and then hitting the ball. Once you hit your allotted number of balls, switch positions with your partner.

Try to keep in mind that drilling in racquetball is no different from how any other sport would be, such as tennis, baseball, basketball, or even soccer. To be proficient at any sport, you need to break the skill down and then build it back up step by step. For example, to be proficient in basketball you have to learn how to

1. dribble the ball,
2. shoot the ball from a stationary position (the free-throw line) and from a moving position (running down the court toward the hoop),
3. pass the ball; and
4. read the ball.

Penetrating Backhand Checklist: Core, Intermediate, and Advanced

Core	Intermediate	Advanced
Grip • Shake hands with racquet • V of hand on top left edge of racquet, with pointer finger in trigger-grip position	Grip • Pinkie should be down close to the butt of the handle without exceeding the butt of the racquet in order to get maximum wrist snap	Grip • Pinkie should be as far down as it can go on the handle, but do not go beyond the butt of the racquet in order to generate even more wrist snap while keeping control • Loose grip • Relaxed wrist
Stance • Good power base with feet shoulder-width apart • Face the side wall • Feet are at a slight angle to side wall • Knees relaxed and flexed approximately 150 degrees • Upper body erect • Hips slightly rotated • Shoulders level and rotated so right shoulder faces left front corner • ERP: racquet up • Nonhitting arm relaxed for balance • Weight distribution 50/50 • Eyes on ball	Stance • Wider power base with feet wider than shoulder-width apart, another foot (.3 m) so your body will be lower • Hips rotated almost facing back left corner • Knees bent approximately 140 degrees • ERP: elbow is up and in line with the belly button • Shoulders rotated so right shoulder is 10 degrees beyond left front corner • Nonhitting arm moves slightly to the left	Stance • Wider power base, another foot (.3 m) compared to intermediate so body is even lower • Knees bent approximately 130 degrees • Shoulders level and aggressively rotated so right shoulder points to left side wall • ERP: racquet even higher above the shoulder and elbow is at chest level for more power • Hips completely rotated and facing back left corner—coil and uncoil for maximum power • Nonhitting arm completely around and pointing to back wall
Step and swing • Step at a slight 45-degree angle toward left front corner • Feet are staggered • Hips begin to open • Shoulder leads • Racquet head and elbow drop • Butt of handle perpendicular to front wall • Racquet face parallel to side wall • Wrist relaxed and snaps through and racquet comes through in approximately 1 sec. • Nonhitting arm begins to come through • Eyes on ball • Weight distribution 50/50	Step and swing • Longer step is needed, approximately 3 ft. (.9 m) or slightly farther to be as low to the ground as possible • Weight shifts slightly back so you can drive off back foot as you pivot • Faster swing speed (1/4 sec. faster) for more power • Hips fully open faster • Wrist relaxed • Nonhitting arm comes through faster • Weight distribution 55/45	Step and swing • Quicker and longer step is needed to be able to hit balls farther away from you; Jason's step is about 3.5 ft. (1.1 m) long, and he's only 5 ft. 8 in. (173 cm) • Violent hip rotation • Fastest swing speed (1/2 sec. faster) for the most power (more whip) • Nonhitting arm whips around to get maximum rotation • Weight distribution 60/40

Core	Intermediate	Advanced
Contact point • Off the lead or front foot • Racquet flat and level • Hitting arm extended, knee high or lower • Chest and belly button begin to face front wall • Weight distribution 50/50 • Nonhitting arm comes through and stays out of the way • Eyes on ball	Contact point • Begin to hit off different positions off the lead foot to create deception and variety of shots (visualize the four racquet contact points) • Racquet parallel to front wall and floor • Wrist completely relaxed, not stiff • Chest and belly button face the front wall • Nonhitting arm continues coming through • Weight distribution 55/45	Contact point • Hitting arm at full extension and elbow straight on contact • Ball usually farther than 3 ft. (.9 m) away from you when fully extended to maximize power • Chest and belly button to front wall • Nonhitting arm completely through on the way to the back wall • Weight distribution 60/40
Follow-through • Racquet comes through and around (approximately 1 sec.) • Racquet ends up below the shoulder and is flat and level • Chest and belly button facing front wall • Upper body is erect • Back foot completely pivots • Weight distribution 50/50 • Hips completely open • Nonhitting arm around and out of the way • Eyes on ball	Follow-through • Racquet comes around (approximately 1/4 sec. faster), pointing to back wall when done • Back foot completely pivoted and back leg bent at 90 degrees • Hips completely open • Nonhitting arm comes through all the way for balance • Weight distribution 55/45	Follow-through • Racquet comes completely around as quickly as possible (approximately 1/2 sec. faster) for more power • Violent hip rotation • Nonhitting arm whips through for maximum rotation • Weight distribution 60/40

Summary

Well, we have now given you another weapon you can add to your game—the penetrating backhand. This shot will allow you to be even more competitive in the intermediate and advanced levels. It will make you more aggressive, putting extreme pressure on your opponents.

Having a competent backhand is important because most players are usually weak on the backhand side of the court; their opponents can take full advantage of this and play to their backhands a majority of the time, trying to get them frustrated and create setup, after setup, after setup. To make sure you are not one of those players who have a weak backhand, you want to learn the proper techniques one level at a time, and you want to practice those drills that will make your backhand powerful, consistent, and a force to be reckoned with. Just as you drilled your attacking forehand, you will need to make that same commitment to your penetrating backhand so you can develop the muscle memory you need to not only perform but also perform well under pressure. The more pressure placed on you, the more important it is for you to be technically sound so you can consistently hit your backhand without even thinking about it—you just react to the situation.

You want your backhand to be as strong as your forehand so that you can make all the shots without having to run around the ball. You want to be strong from both sides of the court. This is the only way to become a champion and create the winning game it takes to move up from intermediate to advanced and beyond.

Dominating Serves and Returns

Chapter 3 is broken into three parts. The first part covers the mechanics and technique of how the serves are properly executed as well as factors that adversely affect serves and separate levels of play (placement, deception, variety, power, and consistency). But you must remember the second part—the serve is only as good as your ability to relocate out of the service zone after you contact the ball and be in center court. Lastly, the third part completes the chapter and covers the mechanics and purpose of the return of serve.

The Serve

With your new attacking forehand and penetrating backhand, you are now ready to add a variety of aggressive serves to your arsenal of weapons. It is the serve that establishes the tone for the match.

We cannot stress enough how important the serve is. It is the number one weapon in the game because the only time you can score a point is when you are serving. Your serve is the one time in the game when you are in total control; you are dropping the ball out of your hand and placing it where you want the first point of contact to occur, at the height of your choice. At other times during the game, the ball is coming off a wall at a different angle, speed, and height and with a natural spin, which are all elements that can adversely affect any shot during the rally.

The purpose of the serve is to force a weak return, not to score a point. The more aggressive and consistent your serves are, the more pressure you are able to place on your opponent, forcing weak returns.

Weak returns can be elicited with a number of tactics such as the type of serve, deception, variety, power, and consistency. By utilizing one or more of these, you will keep your opponent off balance or guessing, usually forcing a weak return—which is exactly what you want to accomplish on the serve.

At this point we want to cover the techniques and the mechanics of two types of serves: the low and hard drive and the soft and high lob. We break down the serve into four very precise components to make it easier for you to develop aggressive, consistent serves no matter which serve you choose to use:

1. Footwork
2. Ball toss
3. Contact point
4. Follow-through

Low and Hard Drive Serve

A low, hard drive serve is used to generate power so your opponent has less time to react. In today's game, there are pros who can hit the ball in excess of 170 mph (274 km/h), but for the intermediate and advanced players we are looking to try and get up to 150 mph—imagine having the ball coming at you at that speed!

To give you something to think about, in baseball the pitcher is 60 feet (18 m) from the batter, and the baseball is thrown an average of 85 to 95 mph (137 to 153 km/h). In racquetball the server is only 20 feet (6 m) from the receiver, and the ball is hit at an average speed of 100 to 150 mph (161 to 209 km/h). The speed of the ball in racquetball is an advantage to the server because the harder the server hits the ball, the less time the opponent has to react, and the result is a weak return. This is why so many players like drive serves, but consistency is the key. Controlled power is what you want, not uncontrolled power. So let's take a look at the four components of low and hard drive serves.

Footwork

Footwork is key to the serve because how you step and utilize your lower body will completely affect the speed at which you hit the ball. The attacking forehand technique you learned in chapter 1 is similar to what you will use when hitting drive serves.

Techniques for Developing the Drive Serve Footwork

Intermediate and advanced players use a two-step motion rather than a one-step motion. The two-step motion generates maximum power because you are stepping into the ball with more momentum, utilizing every inch of the service box, thrusting your legs and hips into the ball, increasing the speed of the serve.

Intermediate

The two-step footwork technique for intermediate players is as follows:

1. You are square to the side wall.
2. Your feet are lined up on the short line.
3. Your left foot is forward on the short line, and your right foot is back.
4. Your feet are shoulder-width apart plus 1 foot (.3 m).
5. Knees are flexed approximately 140 degrees, getting you lower to the ground so you can drive off your back leg and hips for more power (3.1*a*).
6. You take a short step, approximately 6 to 12 inches (15 to 30 cm), with the back foot.
7. You take a bigger step with the front foot toward the front wall, about 3 to 4 feet (.9 to 1.2 m), which allows for more power.
8. The end result is that both feet are lined up or at a slight angle with each other, which is similar to the stance of your attacking forehand stroke (3.1*b*).

Figure 3.1*a-b* Intermediate footwork for the drive serve.

Advanced

The two-step footwork technique for advanced players is as follows:

1. You are square to the side wall.

2. Your feet are shoulder-width apart plus 2 feet (.6 m).

3. Knees are flexed approximately 130 degrees, getting you even lower to the ground so you can drive off your back leg and hips for more power (3.2*a*).

4. You take a short step, approximately 9 to 12 inches (23 to 30 cm), with the back foot.

5. You take a bigger step with the front foot toward the front wall, about 4 to 4.5 feet (1.2 to 1.4 m), which allows for even more power (3.2*b*).

Figure 3.2*a-b* Advanced footwork for the drive serve.

Ball Toss

Where you place the ball off of your lead foot—recall the racquet contact points we discussed for the attacking forehand (page 13) and penetrating backhand (page 41)—will determine the serve you are going to hit. This is covered in more detail in the "Placement" section of this chapter.

Techniques for Developing the Drive Serve Ball Toss

The ball toss is critical for the intermediate and advanced players because at these levels you want to start to add deception to your drive serve, and the ball toss is what affects that the most.

Intermediate

The ball toss technique for intermediate players is as follows (figure 3.3):

1. Knees are flexed approximately 140 degrees, getting you lower to the floor.

2. The timing of the toss will be quicker, and it will be a little farther away.

3. Racquet is moving up quicker, ready to start the swing.

4. Your step with your back foot will be quicker and more precise.

5. Your nonhitting arm is close to fully extended, 1 to 2 inches short of full extension (2.5 to 5 cm), with the ball in your hand.

Figure 3.3 Intermediate drive serve ball toss.

Advanced

The ball toss technique for advanced players is as follows (figure 3.4):

1. Knees are flexed approximately 130 degrees, getting you even lower to the floor.

2. The ball toss will be even farther away from the body, at full extension (see "Contact Point") to maximize power. The toss will have no spin in order to be as consistent as possible.

3. The timing of the toss coincides with the back foot hitting the floor, which will establish a fluid motion.

4. You release the ball quicker.

5. Racquet is moving up even quicker, ready to start the swing.

Figure 3.4 Advanced drive serve ball toss.

Contact Point

The contact point is defined as where the racquet and ball make contact. The racquet is fully extended in relation to your body. Whether a serve will be effective is predetermined by the ball toss, which also affects the contact point.

The perfect contact point for the drive serve is off of your lead foot. By tossing the ball way out in front of you, or off of your lead foot, you will create momentum generated from your body.

Techniques for Developing the Drive Serve Contact Point

For intermediate and advanced players, the contact point is farther from the body at full extension, lower on the body, and at a faster swing speed, generating a more powerful drive serve. With a more powerful drive serve, you will give your opponent less reaction time, forcing more weak returns. (See figures 3.5 and 3.6)

Intermediate

1. Contact the ball off your lead foot.
2. Contact the ball at full extension, no less than 3 feet (.9 m) from the body.
3. Contact the ball at shin to knee high, which is the proper height to make the ball bounce twice at or before the back wall.
4. Swing speed is quicker (one-fourth second faster).

Figure 3.5 Intermediate drive serve contact point.

Advanced

1. Contact the ball at fuller extension, slightly more than 3.5 feet (1.1 m), because your step will be bigger in order to get maximum power and control.
2. Contact the ball at shin to ankle high to develop more consistency and power.
3. Swing speed is even quicker (half a second faster).

Figure 3.6 Advanced drive serve contact point.

Where you drop the ball will affect where you make contact with the ball, which will determine where the ball goes (see "Hitting off the Lead Foot to Determine the Drive Serve").

These contact points are only inches apart. Your opponent, the receiver, is approximately 20 feet (6.1 m) behind you and cannot see where your contact point really is. This makes your serve very deceptive and keeps your opponent guessing, an important element in the service game that we will discuss in more detail later in this chapter. We will also discuss the aforementioned serves, where you will be standing in the service zone, and where you want to toss the ball based on which drive serve you want to hit from which position.

Hitting off the Lead Foot to Determine the Drive Serve

This is the same principle that is applied to the attacking forehand and penetrating backhand.

1. If you drop the ball approximately off the inner thigh to the heel or little toe of your lead foot, you will hit a drive Z serve (figure 3.7). Where you stand in the service zone on the court, position 1 or 3 (figure 3.8), determines whether the drop is off your heel or little toe.

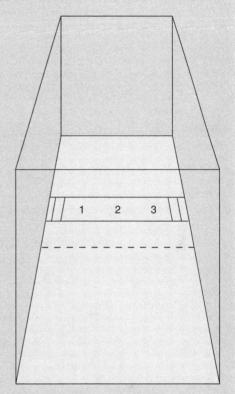

Figure 3.8 Serve position.

Figure 3.7 Drive Z hit off the little toe of the lead foot.

2. If you drop the ball approximately off the arch of your lead foot, you will hit a drive serve down the line (figure 3.9). Where you stand in the service zone on the court, position 1, 2, or 3, determines whether the drop is off the front part or back part of your arch.

Figure 3.9 Drive serve down the line and hit off the arch of the lead foot.

(continued)

3. If you drop the ball approximately off the big toe of your lead foot, you will hit a drive serve cross-court (figure 3.10). Where you stand in the service zone on the court, position 1, 2, or 3, determines whether the drop will be off the front or back of your big toe.

Figure 3.10 Drive serve crosscourt.

4. If you drop the ball in between the big toe and the little toe of your lead foot, you will hit a drive wrap, jam, or nick (figure 3.11a-c). Where you stand in the service zone on the court, position 1, 2, or 3, and which of the three serves you are going to hit, determines whether the drop is closer to your big toe or little toe.

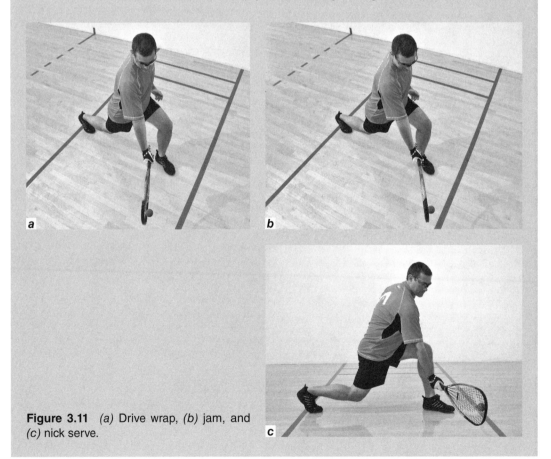

Figure 3.11 *(a)* Drive wrap, *(b)* jam, and *(c)* nick serve.

Follow-Through

The follow-through completes the drive serve, just as it completes the swing for your attacking forehand. When the serve is completed, the head of the racquet is pointing to the back wall and is below your shoulder. Your body and head turn so that your eyes are always on the ball.

The mistake most people make is not completing the swing, which adversely affects the speed of the drive serve. Slowing down your swing or stopping your swing prematurely gives your opponent more time to react to the ball, and often she will have a better return of serve because she has more time to think and move to the ball. An incomplete swing can be the major cause of loss of power and inconsistent serves, but it's also a source of elbow and shoulder problems.

Techniques for Developing the Drive Serve Follow-Through

The key for intermediate and advanced players generating more power on their drive serve is that their racquet moves through their hitting zone more quickly with a complete and full follow-through as they are balanced with the back foot pivoting.

Intermediate

The technique for developing a follow-through for drive serves in intermediate players is as follows (figure 3.12):

1. Racquet will be slightly faster coming around.
2. The racquet will be on its way to the back wall, with your eyes following.
3. Your weight on both feet is balanced, and you are stable and ready to move back into center court position after the serve, with your back foot pivoted.

Figure 3.12   Intermediate drive serve follow-through.

Advanced

The technique for developing a follow-through for drive serves in advanced players is as follows (figure 3.13):

1. Racquet will be even faster coming around and explodes through the swing to generate more power.
2. Weight on the back leg with pivot allows you to push back to center court more quickly.

Figure 3.13   Advanced drive serve follow-through.

Drive Serve Checklist: Core, Intermediate, and Advanced

Core	Intermediate	Advanced
Footwork • One-step technique • Feet shoulder-width apart • Step into ball 2-3 ft. (.6-.9 m) • Knees bent at 150 degrees	Footwork • Two-step technique • Feet shoulder-width apart plus 1 ft. (.3 m) • Step into ball 3-4 ft. (.9-1.2 m) • Back foot moves quicker • Knees bent at 140 degrees	Footwork • Two-step technique • Feet shoulder-width apart plus 2 ft. (.6 m) • Step into ball 4-4.5 ft. (1.2-1.4 m) • Back foot moves even quicker • Knees bent at 130 degrees
Ball toss • Nonhitting arm hanging and attempting to extend • Palm down and holding ball knee high • Racquet starts to come up, ready to swing	Ball toss • Nonhitting arm almost fully extended, another 1-2 ft. (.3-.6 cm) • Ball drop is shin high • Racquet starts to come up quicker, ready to swing	Ball toss • Nonhitting arm fully extended • Ball drop is ankle high • Racquet starts to come up even quicker, ready to swing
Contact point • Off of lead foot • Anywhere in the hitting zone • Waist to knee high and lower • Quick swing speed (approximately 1 sec.)	Contact point • Ball contact at full extension, 3-3.5 ft. (.9-1.1 m) • Ball contact is shin high • Quicker swing speed (approximately 1/4 sec. faster)	Contact point • Ball contact at full extension, slightly more than 3.5 ft. (.9 m) • Ball contact is ankle high • Quicker swing speed (approximately 1/2 sec. faster)
Follow-through • Racquet comes around to side wall to back wall • Racquet below shoulder • Chest and belly button coming around • Eyes on front wall and on ball • Feet in line, with some weight on back foot to push back to center court	Follow-through • Racquet ends up pointing almost all the way to the back wall • Racquet between shoulder and waist • Racquet comes through faster • Weight on back foot and pivots	Follow-through • Racquet ends up pointing to back wall and beyond • Racquet closer to waist high • Racquet comes through even faster and explodes • Weight on back foot and pivots more quickly

High and Soft Lob Serve

High and soft lob serves are used to slow the pace of the game and keep the ball out of your opponent's hitting zone, which is knee high and lower. A soft, high serve puts the ball up at the receiver's chest and shoulder area, which is out of the hitting zone and much tougher to shoot from.

Let's use baseball as an analogy. High and soft lob serves are like off-speed pitches in baseball. Most batters like the fastball right over the plate, where they can tee off on the ball; but changeup pitches usually throw a batter's timing off, forcing pop-ups, grounders, or even strikeouts. This is also true in racquetball. Most racquetball players love to rip and shoot the low, hard drive serves because they are in their hitting zones and do not like the high, soft lob serves, which put the ball out of their hitting zones up by the chest and shoulders. What usually happens is that players get frustrated and try to force balls and shoot them from the chest and shoulders, leading to weak returns and even skipped balls.

Let's take a look at the four components of soft, high lob serves so you can become very consistent and able to use them as an offensive weapon.

Footwork

For lob serves you use a one-step motion because you are not trying to generate power as you are for drive serves. You are just trying to loft the ball over the short line, with off-speed pace and virtually no power.

Techniques for Developing the Lob Serve Footwork

Intermediate and advanced players widen the step to get more leg action, bending their knees in an athletic stance in order to disguise the speed of the serve, while having a consistent motion for all lob serves. These elements assist in adding a little speed. You are making the lob serve a little faster to change the pace of the serve, thus keeping the receiver a little off balance and confused. Apply this new speed to some of the lob serves so your opponent doesn't get used to just one speed, a key component of deception. (See figures 3.14 and 3.15.)

Intermediate

1. You are square to the side wall, starting on the back line of the service area (the short line).
2. Your feet are shoulder-width apart plus 6 inches (15 cm).
3. Knees are softer and a little more flexed (close to 170 degrees for more lofting and spring action off legs).
4. You step into the ball, approximately 6 to 12 inches (15 to 30 cm), to get more push off the legs.
5. Racquet is waist to shoulder high.

Advanced

1. Your feet are shoulder-width apart plus 12 inches (30 cm)
2. Knees are even a little softer and a little more flexed (close to 160 degrees for more lofting and spring action off legs).
3. You step into the ball, about 1 to 3 feet (.3 to .9 m), to get more push off the legs.
4. Racquet is waist to shoulder high.

Figure 3.14 Intermediate high and soft lob serve footwork.

Figure 3.15 Advanced high and soft lob serve footwork.

Ball Toss

Where you place the ball off of your lead foot is no different for a drive serve or a lob serve. The only thing that changes is the height at which you drop or bounce the ball; for lob serves, the ball has to be dropped chest to shoulder high, not knee high or lower as for drive serves. Remember, you will still be using the racquet contact points used for the drive serves (page 61). This will determine the serve you are going to hit, described in more detail in the "Placement" section of this chapter.

Techniques for Developing the Lob Serve Ball Toss

The ball toss is critical for the intermediate and advanced players because at these levels you want to start to add deception into your lob serve, and the ball toss is what affects that the most and is an integral part of deception. (See figure 3.16 and figure 3.17.)

Intermediate

1. Knees are soft and flexed ever so slightly (close to 170 degrees, almost standing straight up).
2. Your nonhitting arm is close to fully extended, another 1 to 2 inches short of full extension. (2.5 to 5 cm), with the ball in your hand, palm down.
3. Bounce the ball higher, quicker, and straight up at the same time as you step and the front foot hits the ground.

Figure 3.16 Intermediate lob serve ball toss.

Advanced

1. Knees are soft and flexed slightly (close to 160 degrees).
2. The ball toss is at full extension to maximize extension. The toss will have no spin in order to be as consistent as possible.
3. The timing of the toss will coincide with your front leg hitting the floor, which will establish a fluid motion.

Figure 3.17 Advanced lob serve ball toss.

Contact Point

The contact point is defined as where the ball and racquet make contact in relation to your body. A consistent service game is based solely on the ball toss. The contact point for lob serves is the same as for drive serves, off your lead foot. What differs is the height at which you contact the ball; for lob serves, the contact point is chest to shoulder high, not knee high or lower as for drive serves. In addition, your wrist is stiff, not loose and relaxed.

By keeping the ball far off your lead foot and chest to shoulder high, with a stiff wrist, you will have a more consistent lob service game and will frustrate many of your opponents by keeping the ball out of their hitting zones. This will force many weak returns, which is the purpose of the serve.

Techniques for Developing the Lob Serve Contact Point

For intermediate and advanced players, the contact point is farther from the body at full extension, higher on the body, and at a slightly faster hip speed, which will help loft the ball over the short line and put the ball deeper into the back corners, thus forcing more weak returns. (See figure 3.18 and figure 3.19.)

Intermediate

1. Hips are engaged but not fast.
2. Contact the ball at close to full extension.
3. Contact the ball closer to chest high, the proper height to make the ball loft over the short line and bounce twice before hitting the back wall.

Figure 3.18 Intermediate lob serve contact point.

Advanced

1. Hips are slightly faster but not too fast because you are not looking to generate power.
2. Contact the ball at full extension in order to get maximum power to loft over the short line.
3. Contact the ball closer to shoulder level and with a stiff wrist for more racquet control.

Where you drop the ball determines where you make contact with the ball. Where you make contact with the ball determines where the ball goes and what serve you are hitting (see "Hitting off the Lead Foot to Determine the Lob Serve"). The same principles apply to both lob serves and drive serves.

Figure 3.19 Advanced lob serve contact point.

Hitting off the Lead Foot to Determine the Lob Serve

This is the same principle that is applied to the attacking forehand and the penetrating backhand.

1. If you drop the ball approximately off the heel to the inner thigh (figure 3.20) or little toe (figure 3.21) of your lead foot, you will hit a lob Z serve. Where you stand in the service zone on the court, position 1 or 3, determines whether the drop is off your heel or little toe.

Figure 3.20   Lob Z serve.   **Figure 3.21**   Backhand lob Z serve.

2. If you drop the ball off approximately the arch of your lead foot, you will hit a lob serve down the line (figure 3.22 and figure 3.23). Where you stand in the service zone on the court, position 1, 2, or 3, determines whether the drop is off the front part or back part of your arch.

Figure 3.22   Lob serve down the line.   **Figure 3.23**   Backhand lob serve down the line.

3. If you drop the ball approximately off the big toe of your lead foot, you will hit a lob serve crosscourt (figure 3.24). Where you stand in the service zone on the court, position 1, 2, or 3, determines whether the drop will be off the front or back of your big toe.

Figure 3.24 Lob serve crosscourt.

4. If you drop the ball in between the big toe and the little toe of your lead foot, you will hit a lob nick or kick (figure 3.25). Where you stand in the service zone on the court, position 1, 2, or 3, and which of the two serves you are going to hit, determines whether the drop is closer to your big toe or little toe.

Figure 3.25 Lob nick or kick serve.

Just as with the drive serves, these contact points for your lob serves are only inches apart. With your opponent, the receiver, being approximately 20 feet (6.1 m) behind you, he cannot see where you're contacting the ball. This makes your serve very deceptive and keeps your opponent guessing, an important element in the service game. Later in this chapter we will discuss this concept in greater detail. We will also discuss the aforementioned serves, where you will be standing in the service zone, and where you want to toss the ball based on which lob serve you want to hit.

Follow-Through

The follow-through completes the lob serve, just as it completes the drive serve. Unfortunately, many players think that just because the lob serve is not a power serve, they do not have to follow through, but this is not true. The follow-through for the lob serve is even more critical because you do not have all the elements that a drive serve has to generate power (e.g., the two-step motion, driving through the ball with an aggressive twisting of the hips, pivoting off the back foot, quicker swing speed, and a faster wrist snap).

The mistake most people make is not completing the swing, which prevents lob serves from getting over the short line and carrying into the back corners on the second bounce. Slowing down your swing or stopping your swing prematurely can cause you to hit short balls, giving your opponent more time to react to the ball and often a better return of serve because she will have more time to think and move to the ball. An incomplete swing can be the major cause for inconsistencies in your lob serves and also can be a source of elbow and shoulder problems.

Techniques for Developing the Lob Serve Follow-Through

The key for intermediate and advanced players to loft the ball over the service line on lob serves is that their racquet and hips moves slightly faster through their hitting zone with a complete and full follow-through as they are balanced with the back foot pivoting. (See figure 3.26 and figure 3.27.)

Intermediate

1. Racquet will be slightly faster coming around.
2. Racquet will be on its way to the back wall, with your eyes following.
3. Hips face front wall.
4. Your weight is on both feet balanced, and you are stable and ready to move back into center court position after the serve, with back-foot pivot.

Advanced

1. Racquet will be faster coming around and will move more quickly through the swing to give you a little more pace on the ball.
2. Racquet faces back wall or beyond.
3. Quicker hip rotation for more lofting of the lob serves.
4. Weight on the back leg with back-foot pivot allows you to push back to center court more quickly.

Figure 3.26 Intermediate lob serve follow-through.

Figure 3.27 Advanced lob serve follow-through.

Lob Serve Checklist: Core, Intermediate, and Advanced

Core	Intermediate	Advanced
Footwork • One short step toward front wall • Feet shoulder-width apart • Step into ball 3-5 in. • Knees bent at 180 degrees	Footwork • One-step technique • Feet shoulder-width apart plus 6 in. (15 cm) • Step into ball 6-12 in. (15-30 cm) • Knees bent at 170 degrees	Footwork • One-step technique • Feet shoulder-width apart plus 12 in. (30 cm) • Step into ball 1-3 ft (.3-.9 m) • Knees bent at 160 degrees
Ball toss • Racquet is waist to chest high, eventually shoulder high • Nonhitting arm hanging and attempting to extend • Palm down and holding ball waist to chest high, ready to drop • Step with left foot and bounce the ball; swing begins	Ball toss • Nonhitting arm 1-2 in. just shy of being fully extended, (2.5-5 cm) • Ball is closer to chest high • Step and bounce the ball at the same time	Ball toss • Nonhitting arm fully extended • Ball is bounced close to shoulder high • Step and bounce fluid and smooth
Contact point • Off of lead foot • Anywhere in hitting zone • Contact ball chest to shoulder high • Wrist likely loose, causing it to snap	Contact point • Ball contact almost at full extension • Ball contact is closer to chest high • Wrist somewhat stiff • Hips move through	Contact point • Ball contact at full extension • Ball contact is closer to shoulder high • Wrist stiff (no wavering) • Hips move slightly faster
Follow-through • Racquet comes around to side wall to back wall • Racquet ideally below shoulder, but often above • Chest and belly button coming around • Eyes on front wall and sometimes on ball • Feet in line, with some weight on back foot to push back to center court	Follow-through • Racquet ends up pointing to back wall • Racquet between shoulder and waist • Hips facing front wall • Weight on back foot and pivot	Follow-through • Racquet ends up pointing to back wall and beyond • Racquet closer to waist high • Hips facing front wall • Weight on back foot and pivot

COMMON MISTAKES: SERVE TECHNIQUE

Footwork (Drive and Lob Serves)

ERROR: You step at a 45-degree angle or greater.

CORRECTION: Step straight ahead toward the front wall, not at a 45-degree angle or greater.

SOLUTION: Stepping toward the front wall allows for maximum power and speed. If you step at a 45-degree angle, your hips are less likely to give you full rotation. At an angle greater than 45 degrees your hips will lock, taking away from the power and speed of the ball.

ERROR: Your feet are too close together.

CORRECTION: Your feet should be 1 to 2 feet (.3 to .6 m) wider than shoulder width.

SOLUTION: With your feet wider than shoulder-width apart, you will be more level going into the serve, allowing for more consistency. If your feet are too close together, then the next step into the ball has to be big, resulting in lots of up and down movement and an inconsistent serve.

ERROR: Your step is too short.

CORRECTION: Your step should be between 3 and 4.5 feet (1.2 and 1.4 m) for drive serves and between 6 inches and 3 feet (15 cm and 1.2 m) for lob serves, based on your level of play.

SOLUTION: Stepping into your serve with a long enough step maximizes your power. With a short step, you can't drive with your legs effectively.

Ball Toss (Drive Serves)

ERROR: You drop the ball too high.

CORRECTION: Drop the ball between shin and ankle high.

SOLUTION: If the ball is dropped correctly, you will be swinging flat and level, giving you more consistent drive serves. If the ball is too high, you will have erratic drive serves, and you will float the ball too deep, giving your opponent a setup off the back wall.

Ball Toss (Lob Serves)

ERROR: You drop the ball too low.

CORRECTION: Drop the ball between your chest and shoulder based on your level of play.

SOLUTION: If the ball is chest to shoulder high, you will have a more consistent lob serve and will be able to loft it over the short line. If the ball is too low, you will have erratic serves and will hit too many short serves because you will be using your wrist rather than keeping it stiff.

Ball Toss (Drive and Lob Serves)

ERROR: You drop the ball too close to your body.

CORRECTION: Ball should be dropped at full extension from the body.

SOLUTION: When the ball is the correct distance from your body, you will have maximum extension for consistent serves with whatever power is needed. If the ball is too close to your body, you will jam yourself a lot, causing loss of power, and you will consistently hit the ball off the side wall, giving your opponent setups off the serve.

ERROR: You drop the ball too far out in front of your lead foot.

CORRECTION: Drop the ball at full extension from the body.

SOLUTION: When the ball is the correct distance from your body, you will have maximum extension for consistent serves with whatever power is needed. If the ball is too far out in front of your lead foot, you will consistently hit your serves crosscourt, making it easy for your opponent to read your serves.

Contact Point (Drive and Lob Serves)

ERROR: You make contact off your back foot instead of your lead foot.

CORRECTION: Make contact off your lead foot.

SOLUTION: By making contact off your lead foot, you will be the most consistent, powerful, and deceptive. If you make contact off your back foot, you will hit the side wall first a lot, resulting in a side-out.

ERROR: Your hitting arm is not at full extension.

CORRECTION: Contact the ball at full extension from the body.

SOLUTION: When the ball is the correct distance from your body, you will have maximum extension for consistent serves with whatever power is needed. If your arm is not fully extended, it leads to less power and an inconsistent swing.

Follow-Through (Drive and Lob Serves)

ERROR: You have little to no follow-through, stopping before the back wall.

CORRECTION: Follow through completely.

SOLUTION: By having a complete follow-through, you will not jeopardize power, consistency, and accuracy. If you do not have a complete follow-through, you will have loss of power on your drive serve, loss of lofting power on your lob serve, and loss of consistency and accuracy on both types of serves. This happens because slowing down your swing through the hitting zone results in a slower ball coming off your racquet or the ball not going where you want it to go.

ERROR: You have no back-foot pivot.

CORRECTION: Make sure you pivot your back foot.

SOLUTION: By having weight on your back foot and pivoting, you completely utilize your hips and maximize your power. If you do not pivot your back foot, your hips lock and you lose power.

ERROR: You watch the front wall when serving rather than watching the ball.

CORRECTION: Watch the ball.

SOLUTION: By watching the ball at all times, you can make a more educated guess as to where it is going to go because you gathered useful, definitive information. If you are not watching the ball, you will not know where it's going or where the correct spot is to relocate to. Furthermore, you will not be able to react quickly enough to the next shot, giving the advantage to your opponent.

Follow-Through (Drive Serves)

ERROR: Your back foot lifts off the ground.

CORRECTION: Keep enough weight on the back foot (see chapter 1 for the exact ratio), and drive off your back foot.

SOLUTION: By keeping your back foot down on the ground, you will have the most power available to you. If your back foot is off the ground, you lose power because you cannot drive off your back hip, and you cannot push back to relocate into good center-court position.

Factors Affecting the Serves

Now that we have covered the techniques and mechanics of the drive and lob serves, which will help you develop your accuracy, we want to cover the five factors that affect the outcome of the serve and also determine your level of play:

1. Placement
2. Deception
3. Variety
4. Power
5. Consistency

These factors have been time tested over a period of many, many years, and rare is the player who has not benefited from their application with regard to the serve.

Placement

The type of serve you are going to hit and where the ball ends up on the court is what we define as placement of the ball. It is based on where you are standing in the service zone, where the ball is dropped, and where the ball is contacted.

Drive Serves

Since you now have a good drive serve, you are ready to move into the intermediate drive serves, the drive Z serve and drive jam. Learning these serves will help you create different angles and add natural spin on the ball. Having more serves in your game gives you variety, another of the five factors that affect the outcome of the serve.

Drive Z Serve

1. Ball hits the front wall between 3 and 5 feet (.9 and 1.5 m) off the floor based on power (figure 3.28).

2. Ball hits the front wall within 4 to 6 feet (1.2 to 1.8 m) of the first side wall (depending on where you are standing in the service zone and how hard you hit it).

3. The ball hits the side wall, moving crosscourt.

4. Ball hits the floor on its first bounce on or near the dotted line within 5 feet (1.5 m) of the second side wall.

5. Ball hits the second side wall about 35 feet (10.7 m) back from the front wall and is not playable off the back wall.

6. Ball is hit between the shin and below the knee.

7. The ball will bounce anywhere between the dotted line and 1 foot from side wall, depending on height and speed of ball.

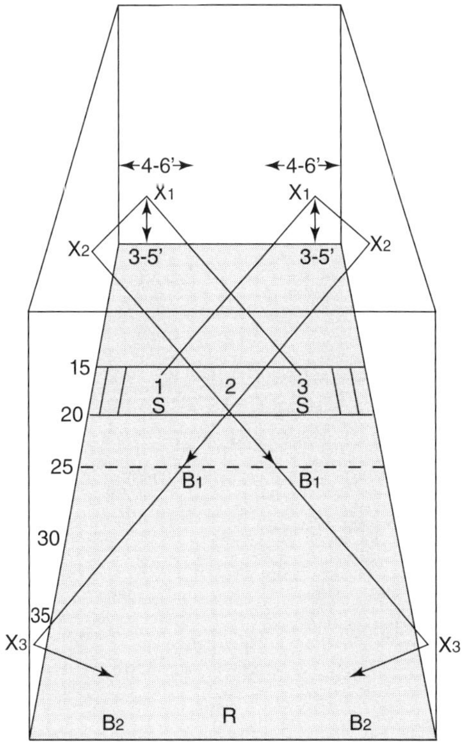

Figure 3.28 Drive Z serve.

Drive Jam Serve

1. Ball hits the front wall between 3 and 4 feet (.9 and 1.2 m) off the floor based on power and about 6 to 9 feet (1.8 to 3 m) from the side wall (depending on where you are standing in the service zone). Hit the ball hard so as not to give your opponent time to react (figure 3.29).

2. Ball hits the side wall on a fly somewhere between the short line and the dotted line about 3 to 4 feet (.9 to 1.2 m) off the floor.

3. Ball comes off the side wall 20 to 25 feet (6.1 to 7.6 m) back from the front wall, bounces, and heads straight for your opponent's belly button, resulting in a jam.

4. Ball is hit between the shin and below knee.

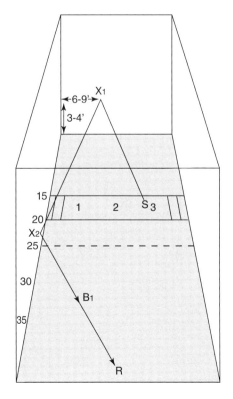

Figure 3.29 Drive jam serve.

Now with more racquet control you are ready to add more advanced drive serves to your game's growing arsenal so you can have more variety, keeping your opponent off guard and forcing more weak returns.

Drive Wrap Serve

1. Ball hits the front wall between 3 and 4 feet (1.2 and 1.8 m) off the floor based on power and about 7 to 10 feet (2.1 to 3 m) from the side wall (depending on where you are standing in the service zone) (figure 3.30). Hit the ball hard so as not to give your opponent time to react.

2. Ball hits the side wall on a fly somewhere between the dotted line, which is 25 feet (7.6 m) from the front wall, and 30 feet (9.1 m), 3 to 4 feet (2.1 to 2.7 m) off the floor.

3. Ball comes off the side wall, bounces, then wraps behind your opponent's body and jams off the back wall, moving away from your opponent. The ball travels at your opponent with pace and angle, which makes it tough to react to.

4. Ball is hit between the shin and the ankle.

Drive Nick Serve

1. Ball hits the front wall between 1 to 3 feet (.3 and .9 m) off the floor based on power and about 6 to 9 feet (1.8 to 2.4 m) from the side wall (depending on where you are standing in the service zone) (figure 3.31). Hit the ball hard so as not to give your opponent time to react.

2. Ball hits the side wall on a fly somewhere between the short line and the dotted line and hits 1 to 3 inches off the floor.

3. Ball comes off the side wall, bounces quite low, and therefore is generally not returnable.

4. Ball is hit between the shin and the ankle

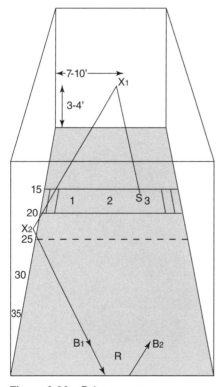

Figure 3.30 Drive wrap serve.

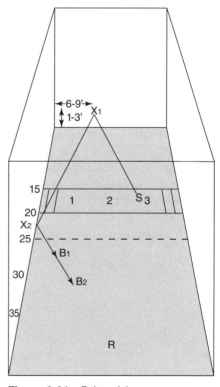

Figure 3.31 Drive nick serve.

Lob Serves

Since you now have a good lob serve, you are ready to move into the intermediate lob serves, the high lob nick and the half lob nick. Learning these serves will add even more variety to your game.

High Lob Nick

1. Ball hits three-quarters to seven-eighths of the way up the front wall and about 6 to 8 feet (1.8 to 2.4 m) from the side wall (depending on where you are standing in the service zone) and hits the side wall on a fly 30 to 35 feet (9.1 to 10.7 m) back from the front wall.

2. Ball bounces deep in the court on its first bounce, between 30 and 35 feet, and then dies before the back wall (figure 3.32).

Half Lob Nick

1. Ball hits one-half to two-thirds of the way up the front wall and about 6 to 8 feet (1.8 to 2.4 m) from the side wall (depending on where you are standing in the service zone) and hits the side wall on a fly 28 to 33 feet (8.5 to 10 m) back from the front wall.

2. Ball ends up deep in the court approximately 30 to 35 feet (9.1 to 10.7 m) back after it bounces and then handcuffs the opponent up by his shoulder (figure 3.33).

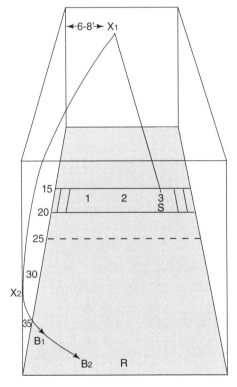

Figure 3.32 High lob nick serve.

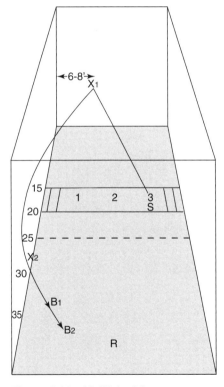

Figure 3.33 Half lob nick serve.

Now with more racquet control, you are ready to add more advanced lob serves to your game, adding to your arsenal of serves, creating lots of variety so your opponent doesn't get used to only one or two serves.

Half Lob Kick

1. Ball hits one-half to two-thirds of the way up the front wall and about 7 to 9 feet (2.1 to 2.7 m) from the side wall (depending on where you are standing in the service zone).

2. Ball bounces within inches of the side wall, approximately 30 to 35 feet (9.1 to 10.7 m) back from the front wall.

3. Ball hits the side wall and then dies and may not be returnable by your opponent (figure 3.34).

Three-Quarter Lob Z

1. Ball hits the front wall 10 to 15 feet up on the front wall (3 to 4.5 m) off the floor based on how hard the ball is hit (figure 3.35).

2. Ball hits the front wall within 6 to 8 feet (1.8 to 2.4 m) of the first side wall (depending on where you are standing in the service zone), then hits the first side wall. Hit a forehand when you're standing at position 3, and hit a backhand when you're standing at position 1.

3. Ball hits the floor on its first bounce on or near the dotted line within 5 feet (1.5 m) of the second side wall.

4. Ball hits the second side wall about 35 feet (10.7 m) back from the front wall and dies.

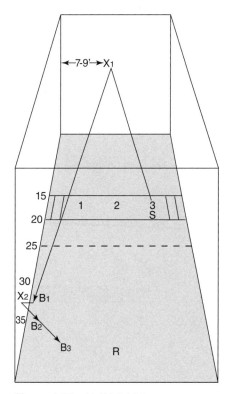

Figure 3.34 Half lob kick serve.

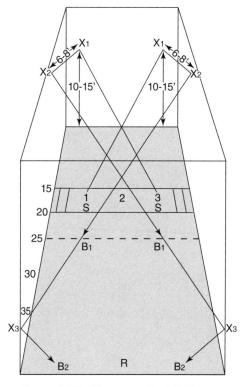

Figure 3.35 Three-quarter lob Z serve.

COMMON MISTAKES: SERVE PLACEMENT

Drive or Lob Z

ERROR: The ball hits the front wall too far from the side wall (i.e., the ball is not tight enough).

CORRECTION: Hit the front wall 4 to 6 feet (1.2 to 1.8 m) for the drive serve and within 6 to 8 feet (1.8 to 2.4 m) for the lob serve off the first side wall (depending on where you are standing in the service zone and how hard you hit the ball).

SOLUTION: Placing the ball the correct distance on the side wall with the correct pace on the ball will get the serve to hit the second side wall deep in the court, forcing a weak return or no return at all. If the ball does not hit the second side wall before the back wall, it will result in a setup off the back wall for your opponent.

ERROR: You hit the Z serve from position 2.

CORRECTION: Hit the Z serve from positions 1 or 3.

SOLUTION: There is not enough angle when you hit the Z serve from position 2, and you have a greater chance of hitting yourself after the ball hits the front wall than the side wall because the ball will come through the middle of the court, which is where you are standing.

Drive Jam

ERROR: The ball hits the side wall too far up, between 15 and 20 feet (4.6 to 6.1 m) instead of between 20 and 25 feet (6.1 and 7.6 m).

CORRECTION: The ball should come off the side wall 20 to 25 feet back from the front wall.

SOLUTION: By hitting the correct height and speed off the front wall, you will give your opponent little time to react because the ball will be moving right at him. If the angle off the side wall is too sharp, it will be a setup for your opponent.

Drive Wrap

ERROR: The ball hits the side wall too far back, between 30 and 35 feet (9.1 and 10.7 m) instead of 25 and 30 feet (7.6 and 9.1 m).

CORRECTION: The ball should come off the side wall 25 to 30 feet back from the front wall.

SOLUTION: By hitting the correct height and speed off the front wall, you will give your opponent little time to react because the ball will wrap behind her and jam off the back wall, moving away from your opponent. If the angle is off slightly, it could lead to a setup off the back wall for your opponent.

High Lob Nick

ERROR: The ball hits too far up, 20 to 25 feet (6.1 to 7.6 m), on the side wall.

CORRECTION: The ball should hit the side wall on a fly 30 to 35 feet (9.1 to 10.7 m) back from the front wall.

SOLUTION: If the ball hits 30 to 35 feet back, it is not likely to come off the back wall, making it tougher for your opponent to return from deep court. If the ball hits too far up on the side wall at 25 to 30 feet (7.6 to 9.1 m), it will drop short and be a setup for your opponent.

Half Lob Nick

ERROR: The ball hits too far back on the side wall.

CORRECTION: The ball should hit the side wall on a fly 28 to 33 feet (8.5 to 10 m) back from the front wall.

SOLUTION: If the ball hits 28 to 33 feet (8.5 to 10 m) back and then bounces, it ends up at your opponent's shoulder, which will make it difficult to return. If the ball hits too far back on the side wall at beyond 35 feet (10.7 m), it will be a setup off the back wall for your opponent.

Half Lob Kick

ERROR: The ball bounces too far from the side wall on its first bounce.

CORRECTION: The ball needs to bounce within 1 to 3 inches of the side wall.

SOLUTION: If the ball hits within inches of the side wall deep in the court, it will be very difficult to return and may even die before the opponent figures it out. If the ball does not hit within inches of the side wall, it will not hit the wall with natural spin and die, and therefore it will be a setup for your opponent.

Deception

The element of surprise, keeping your opponent off balance, is the key to eliciting a weak return from your opponent or no return at all. If the receiver has no idea where the ball is going or which serve is coming, you've got your opponent where you want her. This deception is created by two major elements: your footwork and ball toss. The one-step or two-step motions we taught you earlier should be exactly the same for all the lob serves and all the drive serves no matter which particular serve you are going to hit.

What changes ever so slightly is the ball toss, which ultimately affects your contact point. To the receiver it will appear that the ball toss is in the same spot, off your front foot, but you could drop the ball off your big toe for a drive serve crosscourt, or off your heel for a drive Z, or in between the big toe and little toe for a lob nick—this keeps your opponent guessing.

Variety

The old saying "Variety is the spice of life" is true in racquetball, too. Having a variety of serves makes you a more powerful racquetball player because no matter whom you play and what their weaknesses are, you will have a good pool of serves to choose from.

You want to be just like a pitcher in baseball. To keep the batter off balance and guessing, the pitcher throws different pitches to force a strikeout, a grounder, or a fly ball. The pitcher might be known for his fastball, but if he throws only fastballs, the batter will get used to this pitch and become comfortable with it, making it more likely for him to hit the ball and hit it effectively. The same is true for a serve in racquetball. If the server has only one, two, or three types of serves that she is good at, the receiver will get used to them, will be physically and mentally prepared for those serves, and will be comfortable returning them and returning them well. Therefore, variety is the key. The higher the level of player you are, the more important variety is in your game.

There are four variables you can change in your serve to force weak returns:

1. **Height:** By changing the height at which the ball hits the front wall (low, one-half, three-quarters, high), you can find a height that your opponent is uncomfortable receiving.

2. **Speed:** As we discussed earlier in this chapter, there are low and hard drive serves as well as soft and high lob serves. Not all your opponents will be able to handle or feel comfortable at the different speeds. It is your job to find out which speeds they are uncomfortable receiving.

3. **Angle:** By moving around in the service zone and utilizing all three positions (see figure 3.8), you will create different angles, which can cause problems for some receivers.

4. **Type of serve:** Changing what serve you hit based on your opponent's weaknesses will help create that weak return you are looking for.

The service zone is broken into three positions. Now let's take a look at all the possible serves from the three positions, creating the variety we have been talking about.

Where and What to Hit: Options

POSITION 1				POSITION 2				POSITION 3			
Drive		**Lob**		**Drive**		**Lob**		**Drive**		**Lob**	
Drive	Regular hard R & L	Lob	High R & L	Drive	All	Lob	All	Drive	Regular hard R & L	Lob	Regular high R & L
	Off-speed R & L		Half R & L						Off-speed R & L		Regular half R & L
	Wrap-around R & L		Nick R & L						Wrap-around R & L		High and half nick L
	Jam R & L								Jam regular & overhead R		
									Backhand R & L		
									Backhand off-speed R & L		
Z	Low & hard R & L	Z	High soft L	Z	None	Z	None	Z	Low & hard R	Z	High soft R
	Low & off speed L		Off-speed ¾ L						Overhead R		Off-speed ¾ R
Total Serves	11		8	Total Serves	8		6	Total Serves	14		8

R = right, L = left

Power

The topic of power is twofold. We first address power in terms of creating it to your benefit, as Sudsy Monchik did with his low, hard drive serves, and then we talk about power in terms of defusing it to your benefit, as Jason did with his soft, high lob serves.

Creating Power

The simplest way to look at power is in terms of physics.

$$\text{Power} = \text{force} \times \text{velocity}$$
$$\text{Force} = \text{mass} \times \text{acceleration}$$
$$\text{Power} = \text{mass} \times \text{acceleration} \times \text{velocity}$$

Since you want to create a more powerful serve, you need to increase the acceleration and velocity of your swing (by using a lighter racquet with the attacking forehand mechanics) coupled with putting more mass behind the serve (your body weight and racquet weight). To increase the mass without using a heavy racquet, which would take away from the acceleration and velocity, you want the body and racquet to work together in unison, like the cogs of a clock we talk about for the attacking forehand. Remember, forehand power starts with the lower body during the step (utilizing the legs, the back-foot pivot, and the hips), and then it transfers to the upper body (utilizing the shoulders, the chest, the elbow, and the wrist), and then into the racquet. The power hitters (the drive servers) must have this chain reaction where the whole body is connecting and working together in order to create that power. This is why Sudsy Monchik was the hardest hitter in his day even though he was not the biggest player on tour at 5 feet 9 inches (175 cm)—he had his entire body working in unison to maximize his power.

Defusing Power

When Jason returned to playing racquetball following a two-year absence after breaking his back in a car accident in the early 1990s, he joined the professional tour in 1995. When he arrived on tour he realized two things:

- With his injury, he knew pound for pound he would not be able to fight fire with fire and use the powerful drive serves that Sudsy Monchik, Cliff Swain, and John Ellis were using because his back could not take that kind of rotation and torque.
- The pros also loved to "rock and roll, turn and burn." The lower and harder the ball was hit, the more they liked it, and the better they were.

At this point Jason began to study the pro game, week after week. He realized that instead of learning how to create this kind of power with his body, he could defuse it by keeping the ball out of his opponents' hitting zones and up by their shoulders, which most players hate. This is exactly how he developed his arsenal of soft and high lob serves, a strategy now widely used by men and women pros as well as the top amateurs. Jason was instrumental in changing the game from sheer power to control and power. Just in case you think this wouldn't work for you, Jason's record speaks for itself, and he played against the best in the world. Give it a try—you will be successful.

Consistency

There are many players who can hit the ball hard, many who can be deceptive, many who develop variety, and many who are able to place the ball. However, very few players have mastered all of these aspects in order to gain consistency, which is developed by drilling correctly on a regular basis. You must first find your comfort zone in terms of power. Players tend to over hit their drive serves and try to be too perfect with their lobs.

To avoid overhitting, you must find your effective power swing that allows you to hit the ball hard without sacrificing form. A player can drill until she is blue in the face and not be able to develop consistency because she will drift away from good mechanics to make way for hitting the ball as hard as she can. Although power is important, it loses its luster when the player can't hit the ball over the line without it's coming off the back wall.

Serve Drills

Remember, when you are serving you are in the driver's seat. You are in total control of the situation because you are picking the type of serve you want to hit, which position you will be standing in to serve, and where you will be dropping the ball. At all other times in the match, you are not in control because the ball is coming at you from different directions, with different speeds, at different angles, and at different heights, and then you have to read the ball and make a decision as to where to place your body based on the shot you want to hit. All these variables should make it obvious why you would want to take advantage of your one opportunity for total control.

Since you can score points only when you are serving and the purpose of the serve is to force a weak return (an ace is a bonus), then we want to get you ready to deliver the most consistent and accurate serves possible with the right height, speed, and angle based on the serve you are attempting to hit. The only way to accomplish this is to drill and practice. Now that you have the proper techniques and mechanics of both drive serves and lob serves, let's get started on making you a more consistent server—a player who has lots of variety in the service game, from height, to speed, to angle, to deception, to placement, to power, and most of all, to consistency and accuracy. This variety will give you the weapons you need so there's no need to second-guess yourself about going after anyone and everyone in a match—you will never be doubtful again.

Drop-and-Hit Serve

Have a bucket of 15 or 20 balls.

Drill from all three serve positions.

Practice low and hard drive serves first from all three positions (except drive Zs from position 2; look at the table on page 83 to see what serves you can practice from what position). Do one position at a time, pick one type of serve at a time, and then perform the serve to both sides of the court, if applicable (15 or 20 to the right and then 15 or 20 to the left, depending on your level of play).

Intermediate drive serves: Now practice the drive Z and drive jam, repeating the sequence from the appropriate positions.

Advanced drive serves: Now practice the drive wrap and drive nicks, repeating the sequence from the appropriate positions.

Target Serve

Low and Hard Drive Serves

Use painter's tape to put 2 feet by 2 feet (.3 m by .3 m) boxes on the front wall, as well as the side wall or back floor, where the ball should hit for the following serves:

Intermediate: drive Z and drive jam

Advanced: drive wrap and drive nick

High and Soft Lob Serves

Use painter's tape and put 2 feet by 2 feet (.3 m by .3 m) boxes on the front wall, as well as the side wall or back floor, where the ball should hit for the following serves:

Intermediate: high and half lob nick

Advanced: half lob kick and three-quarter lob Z

Partner Serve Drills

- Serve the entire game using the same serve. A point is scored on every rally.

One person serves and the other person returns serve for the entire game. The person serving can serve only one serve from one position, which gives him a chance to practice that particular serve. You can play an entire game to 15 or to 11 or to whatever number you pick. The first person to the chosen number wins, and then the players switch roles.

- Serve the entire game using a different serve. A point is scored on every rally.

One person serves and the other person returns serve for the entire game. The person serving can now use different serves from the same position, which gives her a chance to practice being more deceptive on her serve. You can play an entire game to 15 or to 11 or to whatever number you pick. The first person to the chosen number wins, and then the players switch roles.

Relocation After the Serve

Your serve is relatively useless unless you relocate out of the service zone afterward so you can get back into good center-court position, which is on or behind the dotted line (see chapter 5). Often players hit a serve, admire it, and remain in the service zone—a major mistake because then they are not ready for the opponent's return of serve. It doesn't matter how good your serve is; unless it is an ace, you must get back into good center-court position as quickly and efficiently as possible. If you don't come back into good center-court position, you are vulnerable to getting passed, preventing you from returning your opponent's return of serve (resulting in a side-out) or causing you to hit a weak return (giving your opponent an offensive opportunity). The last thing you want to do is voluntarily give up the chance to serve because you are not in position. Remember, the only time you can score a point is when you are serving, so getting back after the serve is critical. Let's take a look at a technique you can use to move out of the service zone after you serve.

Footwork and Body Technique for Relocating After the Serve

Regardless of whether you just hit a drive serve or a lob serve, you want to do the following after you finish your service motion:

1. Make sure your feet are lined up parallel.
2. Pivot your back foot, with a substantial amount of weight on the foot (see chapter 1 for the exact ratio), so you are ready to push back to good center-court position.
3. Keep your eyes on the ball.
4. Look over your shoulder to the side of the court the ball is on. That is, if the ball is on the left side of the court, look over your left shoulder; if the ball is on the right side of the court, look over your right shoulder.
5. Push off with your lead (front) foot, and take a big step back toward center court.
6. Point your shoulder into the back corner of the side the ball is on (left side, left back corner; right side, right back corner). This creates a straight line to get you back quickly to center court (as opposed to a semicircle).
7. Shuffle back, with the shoulder still pointing into the back corner of the side the ball is on, to the dotted line or farther back. Where you stand in center court is based on how well you hit your serve and what type of serve you hit. This is discussed in chapter 5.
8. Square up to the front wall in the down and ready position.
   - Legs are about 1 to 1.5 feet (.3 to .5 m) wider than shoulder-width apart.
   - Knees are bent approximately 140 to 150 degrees.
   - Waist is bent slightly, approximately 140 to 150 degrees.
   - Shoulders are level.
   - Racquet is up around waist high, in a relaxed backhand grip because most serves are returned to the backhand side.
   - Weight is slightly forward and inside, just enough to push off and move toward the ball.
   - Eyes are on the ball and looking over the appropriate shoulder.

All the serves follow this footwork and body motion, with the following exceptions. When studying these, pay close attention to points 4 and 5 (looking over your shoulder and pushing back):

Intermediate

Drive Z from position 1 to the left side of the court:

1. Steps 1 to 3 of the sequence are the same (3.36*a*).
2. Look over your right shoulder as the ball crosses the short line.
3. Push off with the lead foot, and take a big step toward center court (3.36*b*).
4. Head turns back so you can look over your left shoulder to follow the ball (3.36*c*).
5. Continue with steps 6 through 8 (3.36*d*).

Figure 3. 36*a-d* Relocation after drive Z serve from position 1.

Drive Z from position 3 to the right side of the court:

1. Steps 1 to 3 of the sequence are the same.
2. Look over your left shoulder as the ball crosses the short line.
3. Push off with the lead foot, and take a big step toward center court.
4. Head turns back so you can look over your right shoulder to follow the ball.
5. Continue with steps 6 through 8.

Advanced

Drive wrap from all three positions to the left side of the court:

1. Steps 1 to 3 of the sequence are the same.
2. Look over your left shoulder as the ball crosses the short line (3.37a).
3. Push off with the lead foot, and take a big step toward center court (3.37b).
4. Head turns back so you can look over your right shoulder to follow the ball (3.37c).
5. Continue with steps 6 through 8 (3.37d).

Figure 3.37a-d   Relocation after serve for drive wrap.

Three-quarter lob Z from position 3 to the right side of the court:

1. Steps 1 to 3 of the sequence are the same.
2. Look over your left shoulder as the ball crosses the short line (3.38a).
3. Push off with the lead foot, and take a big step toward center court (3.38b).
4. Head turns back so you can look over your right shoulder to follow the ball (3.38c).
5. Continue with steps 6 through 8 (3.38d).

Figure 3. 38a-d   Relocation after serve for a three-quarter lob Z serve.

Drills for Relocating After the Serve

Practice the proper footwork and body position for relocating after you serve without a ball first, especially off the Z serves and wrap serves. Once you start to feel comfortable with the proper footwork and body position without a ball, serve and then relocate to good center-court position with a ball.

Now that you have served and relocated out of the service zone into good center-court position, you are ready to play and play hard.

COMMON MISTAKES: RELOCATING AFTER THE SERVE

ERROR: You do not get out of the service zone quickly enough into center-court position, probably because you think your opponent cannot return the serve.

CORRECTION: As soon as the ball crosses the short line, get back quickly so you are ready for the return of serve from the opponent.

SOLUTION: Getting back to center-court position quickly puts you in the best possible position to hit a good shot. Being slow or admiring your serve and not getting back quickly makes you vulnerable to getting passed or jammed.

ERROR: You get out of the service zone quickly enough but do not get back to the dotted line or beyond into center-court position.

CORRECTION: Get back to the dotted line or farther based on if the serve is a drive or lob.

SOLUTION: The dotted line is your goal for a drive serve, farther back if it is a lob serve. If you do not get back to good center-court position, you will not be ready for your opponent's return of serve. Because of your poor court position, you will lose the serve because you cannot return your opponent's shot, or you will hit a poor return.

ERROR: After you hit the serve, you backpedal (which means your back is square to the back wall) rather than lead with the shoulder to the side the ball is on.

CORRECTION: Move back into good center-court position, leading with your shoulder.

SOLUTION: As you come back leading with your shoulder, two good things occur: (1) You get back quicker, and (2) you can keep your eyes on the ball, watching for what return your opponent is most likely going to hit. If you backpedal, it will take you longer to get back, and you cannot watch the ball because you are not looking over your shoulder, and so you have no idea what your opponent is going to hit.

ERROR: When you come out of the service zone after the Z serve at position 3, you move in a semicircle because you are following the ball around.

CORRECTION: Come out of the service zone looking over your right shoulder and then immediately over your left as you shuffle back.

SOLUTION: The most efficient way to get back into center court is a straight line. By relocating to good center-court position using a semicircular motion rather than a straight line, it takes you longer to get back and set, and therefore you are not ready.

Return of Serve

Just as the serve sets the tone of a match, the return of serve sets the tone of a rally. Both are extremely important, and combined they are worth 40 to 50 percent of your game—nothing to take lightly. When you are returning the serve, you are positioned in the back of the court about 2 to 3 feet (.6 to .9 m) from the back wall. You are as far away from the front wall (which is the target) as possible and on defense. The server, who is on offense, is positioned in the middle of the court approximately 20 feet (69.1 m) from the front wall and is hitting the ball out of her hand.

With this in mind, the purpose of the return of serve is to move the server out of center court and put her in the most difficult position to score from—the very back of the court, which is the farthest from the target. Your goal is to regain strategic control of center-court position by placing your opponent in the back court (see chapter 5). The two shots that will accomplish these objectives are the ceiling shots and the passing shots (see chapter 6). These two shots will help you neutralize the server, who is in total control of the match at this point.

It is plain and simple. If you cannot return the serve well, you will not be able to get your opponent out of the middle, nor will you be able to get yourself into good position so you can rally and possibly force a side-out. To accomplish your goals, your return of serve mechanics must be sound. Let's take a closer look at the techniques of the return of serve and drills you can use to make your return more consistent, which will put more pressure on the server.

Return of Serve Mechanics

The return of serve mechanics are crucial because the ball will be coming into the back corners or off the side wall at you at different speeds, angles, and heights, and you must be able to read, react, and execute as quickly and efficiently as possible, especially when the ball is traveling in excess 150 mph (161 km/h). You undoubtedly have less time to think and react, so crossing over and getting square to the side wall is important so you can engage your legs and hips in the stroke to generate power on a passing shot or get the ball to the ceiling. Also, the proper mechanics ensure you are using the most efficient technique to be able to quickly react and adapt to most any situation.

If you do not have proper mechanics for returning the serve, you will most likely do one of three things:

1. Skip the ball, which is a present for your opponent because he did not have to earn the point.
2. Hit a weak return of serve that sets your opponent up for an offensive opportunity.
3. Completely miss the return, which again is a present for your opponent.

The mechanics and techniques of the return of serve are the same for both drive serves and lob serves except for a few minor variations. We break down the return of serve as follows:

1. Down and ready
2. Pivot
3. Crossover step
4. Swing and contact point
5. Follow-through

Down and Ready

1. Legs are spread a little wider than shoulder-width apart (about a foot wider) for return of lob serves (3.39*a*).
2. Legs are spread another 1 to 2 feet (.3 to .6 m) wider for return of drive serves (3.39*b*).
3. Knees are bent at 160 to 170 degrees for return of lob serves.
4. Knees are bent at 130 to 140 degrees for return of drive serves.
5. Bend slightly at the waist for return of lob serves.
6. Bend more at the waist for return of drive serves.
7. Racquet is up about waist high to go forehand or backhand.
8. Grip should be a relaxed backhand because 90 percent of serves go to the backhand side.
9. Eyes are on the ball.
10. Weight should be forward on the front part of your foot, ready to push off and pivot.

Figure 3.39   Down and ready position for return of serve for *(a)* lob serve and *(b)* drive serve.

Pivot

1. Pivot your foot on the heel of the side the ball is going to (figure 3.40). If the ball is going to the left side of the court, pivot off the heel of your left foot. If the ball is going to the right side of the court, pivot off the heel of your right foot. This opens your hips so you can move in that direction.
2. Move toward the ball.
3. Racquet begins to come up (ERP).

Figure 3.40   Pivot position for return of serve.

Crossover Step

1. Push off on the ball of your opposite foot (figure 3.41).
2. Cross over the pivoted foot when returning lob serves, and add a shuffle step if the ball is farther from you.
3. Cross over with a lunge step when returning drive serves that are well hit into the corners.
4. Move toward the dotted line or side wall, depending on the serve, not the back corners.
5. Racquet comes up completely before your opposite foot hits the floor when returning lob serves.
6. Racquet fully extends before your opposite foot hits the floor when returning good drive serves.

Figure 3.41 Crossover step for return of serve.

Swing and Contact Point

1. Hitting arm is fully extended.
2. Racquet head is flat or slightly up on contact based on whether you are shooting the pass or going to the ceiling.
3. Hit off of lead foot, getting under ball.
4. Move quickly and do whatever it takes to get the ball up to the ceiling if the serve is well hit or shoot a pass if it is a setup.
5. Ball contact is approximately waist to chest high when returning lob serves.
6. Ball contact is approximately ankle to knee high when returning drive serves (figure 3.42).

Figure 3.42 Contact point for return of serve.

Follow-Through

1. The racquet head is pointing to the back wall or as far around as it can possibly go based on whether you are off balance or not (figure 3.43).
2. Chest, belly button, and hips are facing the front wall.
3. Eyes are looking up at the ball.

Figure 3.43 Follow-through position for return of serve.

Drills for the Return of Serve

Returning serves is extremely important because it sets the tone of the rally. When you are back receiving serve, you are in the most defensive position possible, farthest from the front wall (37 to 38 feet [11.3 to 11.6 m] back), with absolutely no control over what the server is going to hit or where. You want to be able to return the serve well and neutralize the server's power (i.e., pull the server out of the middle while you move up to regain control of center court). If you are able to do this, most of the time you will place an enormous amount of pressure on the server, and she will not know what to serve. Everything she serves, you will be able to handle.

Many pros become bewildered while playing Jason because it seems he gets to almost every serve and does something with it. Therefore, his opponents do not know what to serve to him, which makes their serves much weaker. They not only are second-guessing themselves but also have let doubt creep into their games, and this creates a mental weakness. Here are some drills so you can be like Jason, known as the best service returner in the game.

Returning Drive Serves

Shoot the Pass

Level: All

1. Get into the down and ready position.
2. Toss the ball so it is a setup (forward and up, about knee to waist high), then do other variations such as the following:
   o Sideways toward the side wall, knee to waist high
   o Off back wall, knee to waist high
   o Into corner, knee to waist high
3. Cross over and shuffle, if necessary.
4. Set up and shoot the pass.
5. Hustle back to center court.

Go Up to the Ceiling

Level: All

1. Get into the down and ready position.
2. Toss the ball so it is out of your reach (forward and way up, about ankle to knee high).
3. Cross over and lunge.
4. Pop ball up to ceiling.
5. Hustle back to center court.

Drive Jam Serve

Level: Intermediate

1. Get into the down and ready position.
2. Drop the ball very close to the body about waist high, assimilating a jam serve right at the belly button.
3. Step back with the leg on the side where the ball is going (if the ball is coming on the left side, step back with the left leg; if the ball is coming on the right side, step back with the right leg), and go up to the ceiling.
4. Hustle back to center court.

Drive Wrap Serve

Level: Advanced

Cannot practice alone, only with a partner, but here's the proper footwork for the return:

1. Get into the down and ready position.
2. Turn and follow the ball, without taking your eyes off it.
3. Shuffle with the ball off the back wall.
4. Good serve: go up to ceiling.
5. Bad serve: shoot the pass.
6. Hustle back to center court.

Returning Lob Serves

Go Up to the Ceiling

Level: All

1. Get into the down and ready position.
2. Bounce the ball about waist to chest high at about 30 feet (9.1 m).
3. Cross over and run up at an angle toward the front corner.
4. Step up and take the ball to the ceiling before it hits the side wall.
5. Hustle back to center court.

Shoot the Pass

Level: All

1. Get into the down and ready position.
2. Toss the ball about knee to waist high at about 30 to 35 feet (9.1 to 10.7 m).
3. Cross over and run up at an angle toward the front corner; do not let the ball bounce.
4. Cut off the ball and shoot the pass before it hits the side wall.
5. Hustle back to center court.

Shoot the Overhead Pass (Forehand Side)

Level: All

1. Get into the down and ready position.
2. Bounce the ball about shoulder to head high at about 30 to 35 feet (9.1 to 10.7 m).
3. Cross over and run at an angle to the front corner.
4. Attack the ball and hit an overhead pass.
5. Hustle back to center court.

Short-Hop or Mid-Hop the Ball

Level: All

1. Get into the down and ready position.
2. Bounce the ball about 30 to 35 feet (9.1 to 10.7 m), knee to waist high.
3. Cross over and run at an angle toward the front left corner.
4. Short-hop or mid-hop the pass before it hits the side wall.
5. Hustle back to center court.

High and Half Lob Nick Serve

Level: Intermediate

Cannot practice alone, only with a partner, but here's the proper footwork for the return:

1. Get into the down and ready position.
2. Cross over and move at an angle toward the ball.
3. Hit the ball after it hits the side wall.
4. Once it bounces, hit it knee to waist high; do not wait for it to bounce shoulder high.
5. Go up to the ceiling.
6. Hustle back to center court.

Half Lob Kick Serve

Level: Advanced

Cannot practice alone, only with a partner, but here's the proper footwork for the return:

1. Get into the down and ready position.
2. Cross over and run at an angle to the ball.
3. Hit the ball before it hits the side wall, about waist high.
4. Go up to the ceiling.
5. Hustle back to center court.

Three-Quarter Lob Z Serve

Level: Advanced

To practice this serve, perform the following drills:

Go Up to the Ceiling

Shoot the Overhead Pass (Forehand Side)

Partner Drills

- Each person serves 15 or 20 of the same serves to the same side of the court. The receiver practices returning those serves, hitting the same return each time based on whether the serve was good or bad. If the serve is a good one, respect it and go to the ceiling. If the serve was poorly hit and you have a setup, shoot the pass and take advantage of the server's mistake.

- Each person serves 15 or 20 of the same serves but to different sides of the court. The receiver practices returning those serves, hitting the same return each time based on whether the serve was good or bad. If the serve is a good one, respect it and go to the ceiling. If the serve was poorly hit and you have a setup, shoot the pass and take advantage of the server's mistake.

- Each person serves 15 or 20 different serves to the same side of the court. The receiver practices returning those serves, hitting the correct return based on whether the serve was good or bad. If the serve is a good one, respect it and go to the ceiling. If the serve was poorly hit and you have a setup, shoot the pass and take advantage of the server's mistake.

- Each person serves 15 or 20 different serves to different sides of the court. The receiver practices returning those serves, hitting the correct return based on whether the serve was good or bad. If the serve is a good one, respect it and go to the ceiling. If the serve was poorly hit and you have a setup, shoot the pass and take advantage of the server's mistake.

COMMON MISTAKES: RETURN OF SERVE

Down and Ready

ERROR: Your feet are too close together.

CORRECTION: Your feet should be spread wider than shoulder-width apart for lob serves and another foot (.3 m) wider for drive serves.

SOLUTION: Having your feet wider than shoulder-width apart means you need to take only one step to the ball, the crossover step, which lets you reach the ball faster. If your feet are too close together, your first step will have to be to widen your stance, then to cross over, making you slower in your return of serve.

Pivot

ERROR: You take a jab step or a side step to the right or left and then pivot instead of just pivoting right to the ball.

CORRECTION: Pivot immediately, no jab step or side step, to the side of the court the ball is going to.

SOLUTION: Not taking an extra step before pivoting gets you to the ball faster. If your feet are too close together and you take a jab step or side step out of habit instead of pivoting right to the ball, it will slow down your return of serve.

Crossover Step

ERROR: Instead of using a crossover step, which gets you square to the side wall, you shuffle sideways and are square to the front wall when you hit the return.

CORRECTION: Take a crossover step, not a shuffle step, sideways.

SOLUTION: Taking a crossover step puts you square to the side wall, just as for your attacking forehand and penetrating backhand, making your return of serve more powerful, consistent, and accurate. If you do not cross over you will lose power, control, and accuracy on all your returns.

Swing and Contact Point

ERROR: The ball is too close to your body.

CORRECTION: The ball should be at full extension from your body.

SOLUTION: By having the ball at full extension from your body, you can generate maximum power and consistent returns. If the ball is too close, you will get jammed and force a weak return.

Follow-Through

ERROR: You do not follow through.

CORRECTION: Completely follow through on every return.

SOLUTION: A complete follow-through ensures maximum power, control, and accuracy. No follow-through leads to loss of power, control, and accuracy on all your returns.

ERROR: You are not watching the ball.

CORRECTION: Watch the ball so you know what your opponent is going to do, which gives you a jump on the ball and will help you get to the serves quicker. If you do not keep your eyes on the ball, you will not know what's happening and cannot react quickly enough to the next shot.

SOLUTION: Watching the ball helps you to know what is going on, and you can make appropriate decisions based on facts.

Summary

We just covered the serve, relocation out of the service zone after the serve, the mechanics of the return of serve, and just how important all these components are in developing your championship racquetball game.

The purpose of the serve is to force a weak return, and the reason you relocate is to get into good court position to take advantage of that weak return of serve you just created. Do not take any of these areas lightly if you want to be in the driver's seat during the match. Having mediocre serves versus good serves versus great, aggressive serves is the difference from one level to the next. Putting yourself in the right position after your serve gives you the best chance to cover a majority of the returns. Since you are looking to move up to an intermediate or advanced level, we recommend spending time practicing your serves and getting back into position.

The server in racquetball is like the pitcher in baseball, who sets the tone of the game right out of the gate. We hear it all the time: If the pitcher is "off" in baseball, then the rest of the player's game suffers. This is how racquetball players think, too. It might not be accurate, but if you think it's true, it is—the self-fulfilling prophecy. Since the serve holds that kind of power over our minds, you need to spend time practicing the serve and giving it the attention it needs.

Practicing the mechanics of the return of serve will help you become technically sound in order to move comfortably into the intermediate or advanced level of play. The receiver in racquetball is like a batter in baseball. If the batter can handle all pitches the pitcher throws to him, the pitcher will get frustrated, lose confidence, and not have a good game. The same is true in racquetball. If the receiver can handle all the serves the server hits, then the server will get flustered, lose confidence, not serve very well, and thus have a bad game. If your opponent is confused about what to serve you because her perception is that you can handle any serve, she will focus on that and not be able to focus on the rest of the match—this will give you a great advantage. This advantage is a match breaker! If implemented correctly, you will take what most people think is a vulnerable position and make yourself the aggressor, which will increase your chances of winning.

Hitting aggressive serves, relocating after the serve to get into good center-court position, and being technically sound on the return of serve so you will be a consistent returner all dictate how the match will play out. These are the critical components you need in order to become the champion you want to be.

Chapter 4

Winning Offensive and Defensive Shots

In this chapter we continue to lay the groundwork for your new racquetball game so you can develop a stronger foundation on your way to becoming a champion. You already have an attacking forehand, a penetrating backhand, and consistent and aggressive serves, so you are well on your way to being the racquetball player you've always wanted to be.

To develop your game and become a solid intermediate or advanced player, you need to learn the different shots of the game. A beginner is more of a one-dimensional player, with very limited shots in his game, because he does not have the racquet control to make a variety of shots and has not developed the ability to select shots in different situations. Often beginners just hit the ball with no plan or understanding of what is going on. As you move up in level and embark on becoming a competitive intermediate or advanced player, you gain racquet control and have a more complex thought process when hitting the ball because you are deliberately selecting your shots. As a higher-level player, you need to acquire more shots so that you have an arsenal to choose from and call on in different situations so you do not become predictable. The more shots you have in your bag of tricks, the more you will keep your opponent on his toes, putting him off balance and making him guess what shot is coming next.

The shots of the game are broken down into the aggressive offensive shots and the aggressive defensive shots. An offensive shot is defined as a shot that can score you a point (if you are serving); end the rally; or force a weak return, giving you an opportunity to score. A defensive shot is defined as a shot that can buy you time to get you back into good center-court position while forcing your opponent out of center court, putting her deep in the court in poor position (see chapter 5).

Let's take a closer look at the different shots of the game and how to hit them so that when you get to chapters 5 and 6, you can call on these shots in different situations to execute the game plan you need in order to win the match.

Aggressive Offensive Shots

Core Techniques

This section reviews the core techniques of the various intermediate and advanced offensive shots. The more shots you can make with consistency, accuracy, and power, the higher the level you will be able to play.

Kill   This shot hits approximately 6 inches (15 cm) or lower on the front wall. It bounces twice before the short line (4.1*a*). Contact point is approximately shin high or lower off of the lead foot.

Pass-Kill   This shot hits approximately 12 inches (30 cm) or lower on the front wall and bounces twice before the dotted line (4.1*b*). Contact point is approximately shin high or higher off of the lead foot.

Pass   The pass hits approximately 18 inches (46 cm) or lower on the front wall and bounces twice before the back wall (4.1*c*). Contact point is approximately knee high or lower, based on how hard you hit the ball, and off of the lead foot.

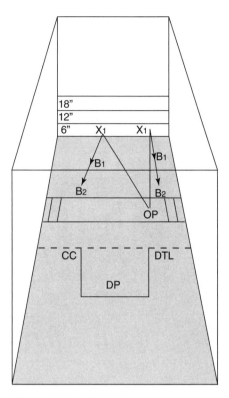

Figure 4.1*a*   Kill shot.

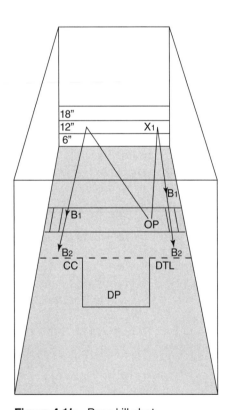

Figure 4.1*b*   Pass-kill shot.

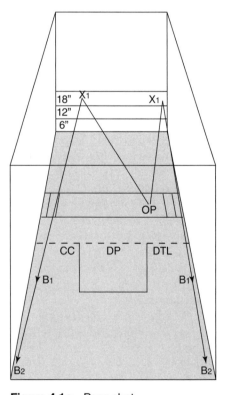

Figure 4.1*c*   Pass shot.

The harder you hit the ball, the lower on the front wall it can hit (maybe 17, 16, or 15 inches). Experiment to find that magic height that makes the ball hit the back wall on two bounces.

The reverse is true the softer you hit the ball, so you would need to hit it closer to the 18-inch (46 cm) mark or maybe even slightly higher. Experiment to find that magic height that makes the ball hit the back wall on two bounces. The pass—not the kill—is the number one offensive shot in the game of racquetball because it has the highest percentage of success. Because the ball hits 18 inches (46 cm) rather than 6 inches (15 cm) on the front wall, there is more room for error. If you miss the pass low, the play can become a pass-kill or a kill, but if you miss the kill low, it becomes a skip—a big no-no. This is why the pass is the number one choice of the pros and wins more rallies.

Pinch This shot hits 6 inches (15 cm) or lower on the side wall, as close to the corner as possible, and closest to where you are standing, then hits the front wall. It then bounces twice before hitting the second side wall and in front of the service line. The ball is hit when you are 2 to 3 feet (.6 to .9 m) from the side wall (4.1*d*). Contact point is approximately ankle high off the heel of your lead foot.

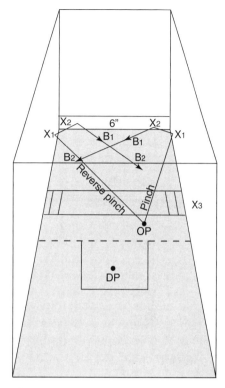

Figure 4.1*d* Pinch and reverse pinch shots.

Reverse Pinch This shot hits 6 inches (15 cm) or lower on the opposite side wall or farthest corner. It then hits the front wall and bounces twice before hitting the second side wall in front of the service line (4.1*d*). Contact point is approximately ankle high off the little toe of your lead foot.

You have two options with the kill, pass-kill, and pass shots. You can hit the ball down the line or crosscourt.

1. Down the line is between you and the closest side wall. Contact point is off the arch of your lead foot.

Core Offensive Shots

	Kill	Pass-kill	Pass	Pinch	Reverse pinch
Contact height on wall	6 in. (15 cm) or lower on front wall	12 in. (30 cm) or lower on front wall	18 in. (46 cm) or lower on front wall	6 in. (15 cm) or lower on side wall (closest corner)	6 in. (15 cm) or lower on side wall (farthest corner)
Bounces (2x)	Before short line	Before receiving line (dotted line)	Before back wall	Before 2nd side wall and service line	Before 2nd side wall and service line
Contact height relative to body	Shin high or lower	Shin high or higher	Knee high or lower	Ankle high	Ankle high

2. Crosscourt is between you and the farthest side wall. Contact point is off the big toe of your lead foot. At no point should the ball hit the side wall. The ball should end up in one of the back corners on its second bounce.

Your choice between shooting down the line or crosscourt will depend on where your opponent is located on the court, which we cover in chapters 5 and 6.

Intermediate Techniques

As an intermediate player, it is important to have a variety of shots in your game so you are less predictable. By adding more shots you become a more versatile and deceptive player, able to keep your opponent off balance and guessing.

Off the Back Wall

Off the back wall is one of the most effective offensive shots in the game today because it is the only shot that is moving in the direction of the target, the front wall. It hits the front wall first, bounces, and comes off the back wall, making it a setup. Too often, players opt to hit a ball coming off the back wall defensively back into the wall, or they hit the ball to the ceiling, or they don't even let a long ceiling shot come off the back wall before jumping in to play another ceiling ball. To take full advantage of the offensive opportunity created when the ball comes off the back wall, you need to gain the confidence to use this shot offensively rather than defensively. To teach you how to take the ball off the back wall, we break the shot into two parts: footwork and judgment.

Footwork   To make an effective shot off the back wall, you need to master the correct footwork.

Initial stance

- Get in the down and ready position (4.2*a*).
- Legs are spread 1 to 1.5 feet (.3 to .5 m) wider than shoulder-width apart.

a

Figure 4.2*a*   Down and ready position for off the back wall.

- Knees are bent to approximately 140 to 150 degrees.
- Waist is bent slightly to 140 to 150 degrees.
- Shoulders are level.
- Racquet is up in the ready position.
- Stand on the balls of your feet, ready to push off.

First Step

- Eyes are on the ball at all times.
- Take a slight step back toward the back wall with the right leg to get behind the ball.
- Racquet starts to come down (4.2*b*).

Second Step

- Take a shuffle step back so the racquet touches the back wall.
- Racquet is completely up (4.2*c*).

Swing

- Shuffle forward to get set for the ball.
- Racquet is starting to come down.
- Eyes remain on the ball.
- Legs are spread, ready to hit the ball with an attacking forehand stroke (4.2*c*).

Contact Point and Follow-Through

- Feet are stopped, set, and spread.
- Use an attacking forehand or a penetrating backhand (4.2*d*).

Figure 4.2*b* First step for off the back wall.

Figure 4.2*c* Second step and start swing for off the back wall.

Figure 4.2*d* Contact point and follow-through for off the back wall.

Judgment   The key to hitting off the back wall, once you have the proper footwork and the proper stroke mechanics, is judging how the ball comes off the wall so you know where it will bounce on its second bounce. Two factors determine this:

1. The height at which your opponent hits the ball on the front wall
2. How hard the ball leaves the racquet

You need to know this information so that when you set up to hit a shot off the back wall, you are 1 to 1 1/2 steps behind where you think the ball will bounce the second time. You shuffle forward with the ball off the back wall, not ahead of the ball. This allows you to get behind the ball to achieve better leverage. This will give you the timing needed to generate the power and consistency you want.

Never wait for the ball where you think it's going to bounce on its second bounce (called "camping out"). Too often you'll guess wrong by waiting for it and not shuffling with it; therefore, you will lose accuracy and power and probably hit off your back rather than lead foot.

A great analogy to help you remember the correct technique is that you want to move back with the ball and out with the ball, like a wave in the ocean.

Wide-Angle Pass

As we said earlier, the pass is the number one offensive shot in the game of racquetball. We want you to master the standard pass shot so you will be ready to add more pass options to your game, making you a more well-rounded player, a must to start climbing the ladder to the next level of play.

The wide-angle pass is the first of three passes we will teach to help you improve your intermediate level of play. Both the down-the-line pass and the crosscourt pass do not hit the side wall at any time before hitting either back corner on the ball's second bounce. The wide-angle pass takes much more racquet control than the standard pass because now you want the ball to hit the side wall. For a wide-angle pass (figure 4.3):

1. The ball hits the front wall and then the side wall on a fly, even or slightly behind your opponent.

2. The wide-angle pass is not usually hit when your opponent is behind the dotted line, but rather when he is on or in front of the dotted line.

3. You want to be 30 feet (9.1 m) and up when attempting to hit this shot because you will not be able to hit the correct angle if you are farther back.

4. Your hitting arm is at full extension from your body.

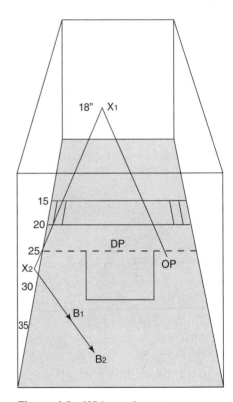

Figure 4.3   Wide-angle pass.

5. Contact point off your lead foot is in between the big toe and the little toe, depending on where you are standing, in order to hit the side wall on a fly.

6. The ball is hit approximately 18 inches (46 cm) and higher depending on how hard you hit the ball.

7. Where the ball hits on the front wall and how close to the side wall it hits are based on where you are hitting the ball from on the court.

8. When the ball hits the side wall after the front wall, it will angle out, and then it will hit the floor and move away from your opponent, causing your opponent to spin to get to the ball.

9. The ball should ideally hit the back wall on two bounces.

The wide-angle pass is an intermediate shot, so racquet control is important. If the shot is not hit correctly and hits too far up on the side wall in front of your opponent, it will wind up coming back to middle court for a setup. If the ball hits the side wall too far back or too far behind your opponent, it will be a setup off the back wall.

The wide-angle pass is a more unforgiving pass shot than the standard pass because when the ball comes off the side wall, it comes off at an angle and with natural spin, making it harder for your opponent to read and track the ball, causing more mistakes than a standard pass that comes straight in and out.

Overhead Pass

The overhead pass is the second pass we will teach to help you master the intermediate level of play. The overhead pass is exactly what the name depicts—it is a pass shot hit from above your head. What makes it so effective is that it is hit with the same motion as the ceiling shot, the number one defensive shot, which we teach you when we cover the defensive shots. Since the motion is exactly the same and the only difference is the contact point, this shot is very deceptive, an added bonus.

For an overhead pass (figure 4.4):

1. The hitting arm is at full extension above your head.

2. Contact point is made approximately at eye level as the ball is coming down, with the racquet face angled slightly down and off the lead foot (it looks like the serve in tennis).

3. The ball hits the front wall at approximately 18 inches (46 cm) and lower and bounces two times before hitting the back wall.

4. The overhead pass can be hit down the line or crosscourt, and when you move up a level, you can even kick it off the side wall. With all three options, the ball winds up deep in one corner or the other.

5. The overhead pass is hit only with the forehand, not the backhand because you will not have the proper angle since your arm is in front of your body.

Figure 4.4 Overhead pass.

The reason you want to add the overhead pass to your shot-making ability is it makes you a more aggressive player, putting more pressure on your opponent. This shot lets you take a shorter ceiling ball that your opponent hits and then hit an offensive shot, the overhead pass, rather than a defensive shot, the ceiling ball. What most players do is take that short ceiling ball back up to the ceiling, which lets your opponent off the hook. By going for an overhead pass, you are taking advantage of your opponent's mistake, which puts you on offense and your opponent on defense.

Sidearm Pass

The sidearm pass is the last pass we will teach to help you master the intermediate level of play. The sidearm pass is another aggressive shot that is an offspring of the standard pass.

The beauty of the sidearm pass is that it is hit exactly the same as a standard pass, but instead of hitting the ball knee high and lower, you are going to hit the ball higher on your body with a slightly different racquet position. Since the motion is exactly the same and the only difference is the contact point, the aggressive posture you develop puts more pressure on your opponent. For the sidearm pass (figure 4.5):

1. The hitting arm is at full extension from your body.

2. Contact point is off your lead foot, and the ball is hit approximately waist to shoulder high. The racquet face is angled slightly down and pointing into the side wall.

3. The ball hits the front wall at approximately 18 inches (46 cm) and lower and bounces two times before hitting the back wall.

4. The sidearm pass, like the overhead pass, can be hit down the line or crosscourt, and when you move up a level, you can even kick it off the side wall. With all three options, the ball winds up deep in one corner or the other, making it more difficult for your opponent to score and putting him on the defense rather than offense, or the ball may not be returnable at all off the back wall.

5. The sidearm pass is hit only with the forehand, not the backhand.

Figure 4.5 Sidearm pass.

Adding the sidearm pass, like the overhead pass, to your shot-making ability makes you a more aggressive player. This shot lets you take a floating ball—a mishit by your opponent—and turn it into an offensive opportunity, the sidearm pass. Most players really don't know what to do with that short floating ball, so they either just hit it or go defensive and hit a ceiling ball. As with the overhead pass, by going for a sidearm pass you are taking advantage of your opponent's mistake.

Advanced Techniques

With the intermediate techniques under your belt, you are clearly gaining more racquet control and developing a better sense of the game. You are now ready for the advanced techniques. Remember, though, the cardinal rule of not working on the next level's shots until you have mastered the previous level's shots. Make sure your shots off the back wall and all three intermediate passes are consistent before moving on.

Chapter 8 gives more details on how to know when you're ready to progress to the next level. When drilling, players should aim for a success rate of 10 out of 15 (or 66 percent) for the intermediate level and 17 out of 20 (or 85 percent) for the advanced level of play. Once an intermediate player reaches 10 out of 15, he is ready to add more shots to his repertoire and tackle the advanced techniques.

Cutting the Ball Off

When you cut the ball off, you hit it out of the air before it bounces, which opens up a whole new possibility for aggressive play. The basic shots we talked about—kill, pass-kill, and pass—as well as the pinch and reverse pinch can all be hit on one bounce, as you learned earlier, and without a bounce. Learning how to cut the ball off increases the number of shots in your arsenal. In essence, you are doubling the number of shots you can make, which makes you less predictable, a very important factor to consider. The other reasons for incorporating this tactic into your game are very simple:

1. It cuts down on your opponent's reaction time.
2. It catches your opponent off balance.
3. It keeps your opponent guessing.
4. It puts an enormous amount of pressure on your opponent.

Remember these key factors when cutting the ball off:

1. Only cut off high lofting balls, which give you time to decide whether to make the play or not.
2. Commit early—he who hesitates is lost.
3. Hit the ball with the same mechanics as for your attacking forehand and penetrating backhand, just don't let the ball bounce. Absolutely nothing else changes; that's what makes the shot so effective and deceptive (figure 4.6).

Figure 4.6 Cutting the ball off.

Splat

The splat shot is nothing more than an advanced pinch shot, but you hit the ball when it is within 1 foot (.3 m) from the side wall (figure 4.7); for the pinch shot, you hit the ball farther out from the side wall.

1. Contact point is approximately ankle high and lower and off the heel of your lead foot (figure 4.8).

2. This shot hits 6 inches (15 cm) or lower on the side wall.

3. The ball hits the side wall deep, about 1 to 2 feet (.3 to .6 m) from your body, unlike the pinch shot, which hits close to the corner.

4. After the ball hits the side wall, it hits the front wall and then bounces two times before hitting the second side wall, like the pinch, which generally makes it unreturnable or results in a weak return—exactly what you want.

This is a great shot to hit, especially if your opponent is leaning to the same side of the court you are hitting the ball from or if your opponent is notoriously behind you. Many young players who are just entering the open and pro levels have a tendency to be "splat happy," but over the years they learn the hard way not to splat everything because all it does is leave the ball up front for their opponents most of the time. There is a time and place to splat. When your opponent gets used to the pass shot, use the splat shot.

Remember, the splat shot is advanced, so until you have the intermediate shots down pat, such as off the back wall, wide-angle pass, overhead pass, and sidearm pass, don't attempt this shot. It's fun, it's exciting, and it's cool, but don't lose matches unnecessarily—be smart about your shot selection.

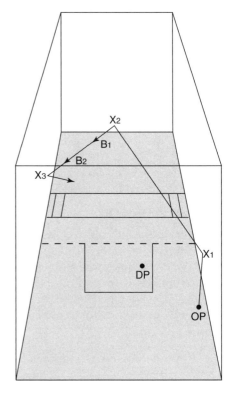

Figure 4.7 Splat shot.

Figure 4.8 Splat shot contact point.

Short Hop and Mid Hop

The short hop and mid hop are the most difficult shots to hit in the game of racquetball because they require impeccable timing. You want to hit the ball immediately after it hits the floor and bounces, roughly knee to ankle high or lower. It almost looks as if you are cutting the ball off rather than short-hopping or mid-hopping it because the ball is hit so low (figure 4.9).

By hitting these very aggressive shots, you will put a tremendous amount of pressure on your opponent because it takes away her reaction time and catches her off guard. Most players are expecting you to wait and play the ball in the back court; instead, you step up and take it early, on or slightly behind the dotted line, which makes the play that much more effective.

1. Contact point is critical because it differs for the short hop and mid hop. When you are hitting a short hop, you want to hit the ball between your ankle and your shin (*a*); when you are hitting a mid hop, you want to hit the ball between your shin and your knee (*b*).

2. The racquet gets down faster to where you contact the ball, so you can be very aggressive with the shot.

3. Generally go for pass or pass-kill returns off the short hop or mid hop, not the kill, because the precise timing of the shot makes the success percentage lower.

These shots are extremely difficult to hit, but when you are down and ready and see an opportunity to short-hop or mid-hop, commit early and go for it. The short hop and mid hop are primarily hit off of passes because these shots are already too low to do anything else. We don't recommend trying them until you have complete racquet control and can hit not only all the intermediate shots but the other advanced shots as well. Our philosophy is crawl, walk, and then run.

Figure 4.9 *(a)* Short hop and *(b)* mid hop.

Aggressive Offensive Shot Drills

For you to be able to use these offensive shots consistently in a game situation, you will need to drill them over and over again. When we cover shot selection in chapter 6 and game plans and match strategy in chapter 7, you will be calling on these offensive shots to help you win matches, and you do not want to waste scoring opportunities because you did not practice and put the time in on the court. It is one thing to know what to do to win a match, but it is an entirely different thing to be able to carry out what you want to do to accomplish that goal.

As we did in the first three chapters, we recommend you have regular drill sessions so you can develop the level of consistency needed in order to win matches at your appropriate skill level on the road to becoming a champion. Remember, we suggest 15 times for intermediate, 20 times for advanced.

Progression of Drills

1. Practice the particular shot (e.g., drop and hit), only one shot at a time, 15 or 20 times, and keep track as discussed in chapter 8. Practice all the shots within your skill level and only add new shots as your start to perfect the shots you are working on.

   Example: Drop and hit a pass, 15 or 20 times.

   Drop and hit a pinch, 15 or 20 times.

2. Practice the particular shot (e.g., set up and hit), only one shot at a time, 15 or 20 times, and keep track. Practice all the shots.

   Example: Set up off the back wall into a pinch, 15 or 20 times.

   Set up off the back wall into a pass down the line, 15 or 20 times.

   Set up off the back wall into a pass crosscourt, 15 or 20 times.

3. Practice the particular shot (e.g., set up and hit) one time each until you have hit 15 or 20 shots. Practice all the shots.

   Example: Set up off the back wall into a pass crosscourt, 1 time.

   Set up off the back wall into a splat, 1 time.

   Set up off the back wall into a pass-kill down the line, 1 time.

You will use the same five-step approach to drilling that you learned in chapters 1 and 2:

1. Drop and hit
2. Toss, turn, and hit
3. Toss, turn, shuffle, and hit
4. Set up and hit
5. Set up, run, and hit

Everything else is the same except for the ball drop, which is different for each of the core, intermediate, and advanced shots. Please refer to pages 18-19 for more details on which of the nine positions and what zones you will be practicing the shots from and for a review of the five-step approach.

Level: All

Kill

- Drop the ball approximately shin high or lower, or 6 inches (15 cm) or lower.
- Down the line will be off the lead foot at the arch.
- Crosscourt will be approximately off the big toe.
- Practice only one shot at a time, 15 or 20 times, and keep track.

Pass-Kill

- Drop the ball approximately shin high or higher, or 12 inches (30 cm) or lower.
- Down the line will be off the lead foot at the arch.
- Crosscourt will be approximately off the big toe.
- Practice only one shot at a time, 15 or 20 times, and keep track.

Pass

- Drop the ball approximately knee high or lower, or 18 inches (46 cm) or lower.
- Down the line will be off the lead foot at the arch.
- Crosscourt will be approximately off the big toe.
- Practice only one shot at a time, 15 or 20 times, and keep track.

Pinch

- Drop the ball approximately ankle high or lower, or 6 inches (15 cm) or lower.
- Pinch will be off the heel of your lead foot.
- Practice only one shot at a time, 15 or 20 times, and keep track.

Reverse Pinch

- Drop the ball approximately ankle high or lower, or 6 inches (15 cm) or lower.
- Reverse pinch will be off the little toe of your lead foot.
- Practice only one shot at a time, 15 or 20 times, and keep track.

Off the Back Wall

Level: Intermediate

Drop and Hit

- Start square to the side wall, with racquet up.
- Be within 1 to 1.5 feet (.3 to .5 m) from the back wall so your racquet can touch the back wall.
- Drop the ball at full extension, hard enough so it hits the floor first and then the back wall, going a little beyond where you stand.
- Shuffle with the ball and hit it on a fly before it hits the floor again.
- Practice different shots off the back wall, such as pass-kills and passes (down the line and crosscourt), pinches, reverse pinches, and so on.
- Your ball drop is the only thing that changes, based on what shot you want to practice off the back wall.
- Practice only one shot at a time, 15 or 20 times, and keep track.

Toss, Turn, and Hit and Toss, Turn, Shuffle, and Hit

- Start square to the front wall, with racquet in ready position.
- Be within 2 feet (.6 m) of the back wall.
- Toss the ball at full extension, hard enough so it hits the floor first and then the back wall, going a little beyond where you stand.
- Turn by pivoting on the heel of the foot on the side you are turning to and shuffle with the ball; hit it on a fly before it hits the floor again.
- The above practice remains the same as the drop and hit except you toss the ball, you do not drop it.

Set Up and Hit With a Bounce Into the Back Wall

- Set the ball up from different distances, 35, 30, 25, and 20 feet (10.7, 9.1, 7.6, and 6.1 m). Let's use 35 feet (10.7 m) as an example.
- Stand at 35 feet, and hit the ball high enough and hard enough off the front wall so it bounces and then comes off the back wall.
- You want to judge the ball so that when it comes off the back wall, you are 1 to 1 1/2 steps behind the ball, moving with it, then set your feet and hit. Keep in mind when you are taking the ball off the back wall that you still want the ball to drop into your hitting zone off your lead foot, based on the shot you want to hit.
- Practice only one shot at a time, 15 or 20 times, and keep track.
- Practice different shots by calling them out, 15 or 20 times, and keep track.
- Repeat the sequence for 30, 25, and 20 feet (9.1, 7.6, and 6.1 m).

Set Up and Hit With No Bounce Into the Back Wall

- Repeat all distances from the previous drill, hitting the ball high enough and hard enough off the front wall so it does not bounce but rather hits the back wall on a fly and then comes off the back wall.

Wide-Angle Pass

Level: Intermediate

Drop and Hit: Target Hitting

- Place your racquetball bag on the floor on either side wall, with one edge on the dotted line and the rest of the bag pointing toward 30 feet (9.1 m).
- Be square to the side wall, approximately 5 feet (1.5 m) from the opposite side wall.
- Drop the ball at full extension so it ends up in between the big toe and little toe after the step.
- Try to hit the bag on a fly, which is in the exact wide-angle position.
- Do this 15 or 20 times, and keep track.

Toss, Turn, and Hit and Toss, Turn, Shuffle, and Hit: Target Hitting

- Place your racquetball bag on the floor on either side wall, with one edge on the dotted line and the rest of the bag pointing toward 30 feet (9.1 m).

- Be square to the front wall, approximately in the middle of the court, with racquet in ready position.
- Toss the ball at full extension so it ends up in between the big toe and little toe after the step and shuffle.
- Turn by pivoting on the heel of the foot on the side you are turning to, shuffle and try to hit the bag on a fly, which is in the exact wide-angle position
- Do this 15 or 20 times, and keep track.

Set Up and Hit: Target Hitting

- Place your racquetball bag on the floor on either side wall, with one edge on the dotted line and the rest of the bag pointing toward 30 feet (9.1 m).
- Set the ball up from different distances, always winding up 30 feet (9.1 m) and up when you hit the ball.
- You want to judge the ball so that when it comes off the front wall or side wall, you are 1 to 1 1/2 steps behind the ball, moving into it, then set your feet to hit the ball into the bag. Keep in mind when hitting a wide-angle pass that you still want the ball to drop into your hitting zone off your lead foot, based on the shot you want to hit.
- Do the same setup over and over, 15 to 20 times, and keep track.
- Practice different setups, 15 to 20 times, and keep track.

Overhead and Sidearm Pass

Level: Intermediate

Drop and Hit

- Start square to the side wall, with racquet up.
- Be somewhere in the back part of the court, approximately 35 feet (10.7 m) for overhead passes and 30 feet (9.1 m) for sidearm passes.
- Bounce the ball at full extension, hard enough that the ball is above eye level for an overhead pass and at approximately waist to shoulder high for a sidearm pass.
- Step into the shot and swing.
- Practice different shots for each of the overhead and sidearm passes (down the line and crosscourt).
- Your ball bounce is the only thing that changes, based on what pass shot you want to hit.
- For down the line, bounce the ball approximately at the arch of your lead foot.
- For crosscourt, bounce the ball approximately at the big toe of your lead foot.
- Practice only one shot at a time, 15 to 20 times, and keep track.

Toss, Turn, and Hit and Toss, Turn, Shuffle, and Hit

- Start square to the front wall, with racquet in ready position.
- Be somewhere in the back part of the court, approximately 35 feet (10.7 m) for overhead passes and 30 feet (9.1 m) for sidearm passes.
- Toss the ball at full extension, hard enough that the ball is above eye level for an overhead pass and at approximately waist to shoulder high for a sidearm pass.

- Turn by pivoting on the heel of the foot on the side you are turning to, shuffle and hit the shot.
- The above practice remains the same except you toss the ball, you do not bounce it like you do in the drop-and-hit drill.

Set Up and Hit

- Set the ball up from different distances, 35 feet (10.7 m), 30 feet (9.1 m), then anywhere in between for both overhead and sidearm passes. Let's use 35 feet (10.7 m) as an example.
- Stand at 35 feet and hit yourself a short ceiling ball.
- You want to judge the ball so that when it comes off the ceiling, you are 1 to 1 1/2 steps behind the ball, moving into it, then set your feet and hit an overhead pass. Keep in mind when hitting an overhead or sidearm pass that you still want the ball to bounce into your hitting zone off your lead foot, based on the shot you want to hit.
- Practice only one shot from one position at a time, 15 or 20 times, and keep track.
- Practice different shots by calling them out, 15 or 20 times, and keep track.
- Repeat the sequence for 30 feet and anywhere in between.

Cutting the Ball Off

Level: Advanced

Drop and Hit

- Start square to the side wall, with racquet up.
- Be in one of the nine positions (eventually start from all nine).
- Drop the ball at full extension, step into the shot, and hit the ball before it bounces. Your ball toss will determine the shot you are practicing. Always do the basic shots first: kill (shin high and lower), pass-kill (shin high and higher), pass (knee high and lower), and so on.
- Practice different shots when cutting the ball off, such as pass-kills and passes (down the line and crosscourt), pinches, reverse pinches, splats, and so on.
- Your ball drop is the only thing that changes, based on what shot you want to practice when cutting the ball off.
- Practice only one shot at a time, 15 or 20 times, and keep track.

Toss, Turn, and Hit and Toss, Turn, Shuffle, and Hit

- Start square to the front wall, with racquet in ready position.
- Be in the middle of the court, using only positions 4, 5, and 6.
- Toss the ball at full extension, turn by pivoting on the heel of the foot on the side you are turning to, shuffle into the shot, and hit the ball before it bounces. Your ball toss will determine the shot you are practicing. Always do the basic shots first: kill (ankle high and lower), pass-kill (shin high and lower), pass (knee high and lower), and so on.
- The above practice remains the same except you toss the ball, you do not drop it like in the drop-and-hit drill.

Set Up and Hit

- Set the ball up from different distances, 35, 30, 25, and 20 feet (10.7, 9.1, 7.6, and 6.1 m). Let's use 35 feet (10.7 m) as an example.
- Stand at 35 feet, and hit the ball high enough off the front wall so you can move into the ball and cut it off before it bounces. Keep in mind when cutting the ball off that you still want the ball to drop into your hitting zone off your lead foot, based on the shot you want to hit.
- You want to judge the ball so that when it comes off the front wall, you are 1 to 1 1/2 steps behind the ball, moving with it, then set your feet and hit.
- Practice only one shot at a time, 15 to 20 times, and keep track.
- Practice different shots by calling them out, 15 to 20 times, keeping track.
- Repeat the sequence for 30, 25, and 20 feet (9.1, 7.6, and 6.1 m).

Splat

Level: Advanced

Drop and Hit

- Start square to the side wall, with racquet up.
- Be within 1 foot (.3 m) of the side wall.
- Drop the ball at full extension, within inches of the side wall.
- Ball should be ankle high or lower and off the heel of your lead foot.
- Practice one shot at a time, 15 to 20 times, and keep track.
- Practice the splat shot from positions 3, 6, and 9 for forehand and 1, 4, and 7 for backhand.

Toss, Turn, and Hit and Toss, Turn, Shuffle, and Hit

- Start square to the front wall, with racquet in ready position.
- Stand approximately 5 feet (1.5 m) from the side wall.
- Toss the ball at full extension, within inches of the side wall, turn by pivoting on the heel of the foot on the side you are turning to, and shuffle into the shot.
- Ball should be ankle high or lower and off the heel of your lead foot.
- Practice one shot at a time, 15 to 20 times, and keep track.
- Practice the splat shot from positions 3, 6, and 9 for forehand and 1, 4, and 7 for backhand.

Set Up and Hit

- Set the ball up from different distances, 35, 30, 25, and 20 feet (10.7, 9.1, 7.6, and 6.1 m), all setups close to side wall. Let's use 35 feet (10.7 m) as an example.
- Stand at 35 feet, and hit the ball high enough off the front wall and close enough to the side wall so you can move into the ball so it drops into your hitting zone off the heel of your lead foot.
- You want to judge the ball so that when it comes off the front wall, you are 1 to 1 1/2 steps behind the ball, moving with it, then set your feet and hit.
- Practice only one shot at a time, 15 or 20 times, and keep track.
- Repeat the sequence for 30, 25, and 20 feet (9.1, 7.6, and 6.1 m).

Short Hop and Mid Hop

Level: Advanced

Drop and Hit

- Start square to the side wall, with racquet up.
- Be in one of the nine positions (eventually start from all nine).
- Drop the ball at full extension, step into the shot, and hit the ball immediately after it bounces. Your ball toss will determine the shot you are practicing. Always do only the higher percentage shots, pass and pass-kill, not kills, pinches, or reverse pinches.
- Your ball drop is the only thing that changes, based on what shot you want to practice when hitting the short hop and mid hop.
- Practice only one shot at a time, 15 or 20 times, and keep track.

Toss, Turn, and Hit and Toss, Turn, Shuffle, and Hit

- Start square to the front wall, with racquet in ready position.
- Stand in the middle of the court, using positions 4, 5, and 6.
- Toss the ball at full extension, turn by pivoting on the heel of the foot on the side you are turning to, shuffle into the shot, and hit the ball immediately after it bounces. Your ball toss will determine the shot you are practicing. Always do only higher percentage shots, pass, pass-kill, down the line, and crosscourt.
- The above practice remains the same except you toss the ball; you do not drop it as you do in the drop-and-hit drill.

Set Up and Hit

- Set the ball up from different distances, 35, 30, 25, and 20 feet (10.7, 9.1, 7.6, and 6.1 m). Let's use 35 feet (10.7 m) as an example.
- Stand at 35 feet, and hit the ball high enough off the front wall so you can move into the ball and short-hop or mid-hop it before it bounces. Keep in mind when you are hitting these shots that you still want the ball to be in your hitting zone off your lead foot, based on the shot you want to hit.
- You want to judge the ball so that when it comes off the front wall, you are 1 to 1 1/2 steps behind the ball, moving with it, then set your feet and hit.
- Practice only one shot at a time, 15 or 20 times, and keep track.
- Practice different shots by calling them out, 15 or 20 times, and keep track.
- Repeat the sequence for 30, 25, and 20 feet (9.1, 7.6, and 6.1 m).

The short hop and mid hop are the most difficult shots in the game of racquetball because they take the most perfect timing to hit the ball and hit it well. We do not recommend adding these shots to your game and practicing them until the other shots are consistent.

COMMON MISTAKES: AGGRESSIVE OFFENSIVE SHOTS

Kill

ERROR: You try to roll the ball out, therefore hitting too low and skipping too much.

CORRECTION: Hit the ball approximately 6 inches (15 cm) or higher.

SOLUTION: By hitting the ball slightly higher on the front wall and not going for the bottom board or rolling the ball out all the time, you will skip the ball a lot less. Skipping the ball less takes the floor out of the game, and the floor is your enemy. The lower you go on the front wall, the greater the chance of skipping the ball.

ERROR: You swing the racquet down, high to low, rather than level.

CORRECTION: Swing flat and level.

SOLUTION: By swinging flat and level, you will hit the front wall more, with the ball being in play, and you will not skip as many balls. Skipping the ball less takes the floor out of the game, and the floor is your enemy.

Pass: Down the Line

ERROR: You are hitting the ball too close to your body, thus jamming yourself.

CORRECTION: Hit the ball at full extension from your body.

SOLUTION: By hitting the ball at full extension from your body, you will hit flat and level. If the ball is too close to you, it will hit the front wall and then the side wall, setting up your opponent. Hitting the ball too close to your body will also ensure the development of a pendulum swing, hence bringing the floor into play more often since it will be impossible to swing level.

Pinch

ERROR: You hit the ball too high because the contact point is above the ankle.

CORRECTION: Let the ball drop to ankle high or lower.

SOLUTION: By letting the ball drop low enough, it will hit the side wall and then the front wall and bounce two times before hitting the second side wall, therefore not coming off the second side wall for a setup.

Off the Back Wall

ERROR: You move out ahead of the ball and wait for it (camping out).

CORRECTION: Move in and out with the ball; do not camp out and wait for it.

SOLUTION: As you learn to move like a wave in the ocean, in and out with the ball, you will hit off your lead foot, generating the most power, consistency, and accuracy. If you camp out and wait for the ball to come to you, the ball usually winds up too far behind you when you are hitting it. Therefore you lose power and control and will often hit the side wall for a setup.

Wide-Angle Pass

ERROR: You hit the ball too far back in your hitting zone.

CORRECTION: Hit the ball between your big toe and little toe.

SOLUTION: By contacting the ball in the right spot, you will be able to hit the side wall on a fly slightly behind your opponent, which moves your opponent out of the middle so he can spin to get to the ball. If you hit the ball too far back, the shot becomes a crosscourt pass rather than a wide-angle pass.

ERROR: You hit the ball too far forward in your hitting zone.

CORRECTION: Hit the ball between your big toe and little toe.

SOLUTION: By contacting the ball in the right spot, you will be able to hit the side wall on a fly slightly behind your opponent, which moves your opponent out of the middle so she has to spin to get to the ball. If you hit the ball too far forward, it will hit the side wall in front of your opponent and be a setup.

Overhead Pass

ERROR: You don't hit the ball high enough, letting it drop too low.

CORRECTION: Hit the ball at eye level to drive a solid pass shot.

SOLUTION: Contacting the ball at approximately eye level will give you the most consistent overhead, with the ball hitting the front wall at 12 to 18 inches (30 to 46 cm) high. If you let the ball drop too low, it skips.

ERROR: You hit the ball too high, with the racquet facing toward the front wall.

CORRECTION: Contact the ball at eye level to drive a solid pass shot.

SOLUTION: Contacting the ball at approximately eye level will give you the most consistent overhead, with the ball hitting the front wall at 12 to 18 inches (30 to 46 cm) high. If you hit the ball too high, it will lead to a setup off the front wall.

Sidearm Pass

ERROR: You hit the ball too high, with the racquet facing toward the front wall.

CORRECTION: Hit the ball chest to shoulder high, with the racquet at a slight downward angle.

SOLUTION: Contacting the ball at chest to shoulder level will give you the most consistent sidearm pass, with the ball hitting the front wall at 12 to 18 inches (30 to 46 cm) high. If you don't let the ball drop and you hit it too high, it will lead to setup after setup off the front wall.

Cutting the Ball Off

ERROR: You hit the ball too high, above waist to shoulder, before it bounces.

CORRECTION: Contact the ball waist high and lower.

SOLUTION: When you make contact below the waist and you swing flat and level, you will have so much more power and control and hit the ball where you want to.

Splat

ERROR: You try to guide or push the ball into the side wall, and your wrist is stiff.

CORRECTION: Contact the ball with a relaxed grip, off the heel of your front foot at full extension, within 1 foot (.3 m) of the side wall.

SOLUTION: Hitting the ball correctly will generate more power, with the ball coming off the racquet face with natural spin, putting more action on the ball. If you try to push the ball into the corner, the ball will probably not make the front wall, resulting in a side-out or a point being awarded.

ERROR: You hit the ball too far back in your hitting zone.

CORRECTION: Contact the ball with a relaxed grip, off the heel of your front foot at full extension, within 1 foot (.3 m) of the side wall.

SOLUTION: Hitting the ball correctly will generate more power, with the ball coming off the racquet face with natural spin, putting more action on the ball. If you make contact with the ball too far back, it will probably not hit the front wall, likely resulting in a skip.

Short Hop and Mid Hop

ERROR: You try to hit a kill shot off the short hop rather than a pass.

CORRECTION: You want to pass off the short hop, not kill (the percentage is too low).

SOLUTION: By hitting the pass, you will probably put lots of pressure on your opponent. If you try to kill, you will probably skip lots of balls.

Aggressive Offensive Shots Checklist: Core, Intermediate, and Advanced

Core	Intermediate	Advanced
Kill • Contact point in your hitting zone is shin high and lower off the lead foot. • Ball hits 6 in. (15 cm) and lower on front wall. • Bounces 2x before short line.	Off the back wall Footwork: • Move back with ball and then shuffle forward with ball. • Attacking forehand and penetrating backhand mechanics used. Judgment: • The height at which you hit the ball. • The speed at which the ball comes off the racquet and then the front wall.	Cutting the ball off • Take the ball out of the air before it bounces. • Contact point is the same as for whatever basic shot you are attempting to hit.
Pass-kill • Contact point in your hitting zone is shin high and lower off the lead foot. • Ball hits 12 in. (30 cm) and lower on front wall. • Bounces 2x before dotted line.	Wide-angle pass • Contact point is knee high and lower. • Ball hits 18 in. (46 cm) and lower depending on how hard you hit it on the front wall. • Contact point is off your lead foot and is in between the big and little toe depending on where you are hitting from. • Ball hits front wall, then side wall, on a fly, even with or slightly behind opponent. • Opponent on or in front of dotted line. • Based on where you are standing to hit your shot will determine where on the front wall and how close to the side wall the ball hits. • When you are hitting the shot, you are 30 ft. (9.1 m) and up.	Splat • Contact point is ankle high and lower off the heel of your lead foot. • Ball hits 6 in. (15 cm) and lower on side wall deep, about 1-2 ft. (.3-.6 m) from your body. • Ball hits side wall (closest to you), then front wall, then bounces 2x before 2nd side wall. • You hit the ball when you are inches from the side wall.

(continued)

Aggressive Offensive Shots Checklist: Core, Intermediate, and Advanced *(continued)*

Core	Intermediate	Advanced
Pass • Contact point in your hitting zone is knee high and lower off the lead foot. • Ball hits 18 in. (46 cm) and lower on front wall. • Bounces 2x before back wall.	Overhead pass • Hitting arm is at full extension above your head. • Contact point is eye level as ball is coming down, with racquet face angled slightly down off lead foot. • Ball hits 18 in. (46 cm) and lower on the front wall and then bounces 2x before the back wall. • Only forehand, not backhand.	Short hop and mid hop • Hit ball immediately after it hits the floor. • Ball contact for the short hop is ankle to shin high. • Ball contact for the mid hop is shin to knee high. • Racquet gets down faster to hit the aggressive shot, thus quicker swing speed. • Passes, not kills.
Pinch • Contact point is shin high and lower off the heel of your lead foot. • Ball hits 6 in. (15 cm) and lower on side wall, as close to the corner as possible. • Ball hits side wall (closest to you), then front wall, then bounces 2x before 2nd side wall. • You hit the ball when you are 2-3 ft. (.6-.9 m) from the side wall.	Sidearm pass • Hitting arm is at full extension from your body. • Contact point is waist to shoulder high, with racquet face angled slightly down. • Ball hits 18 in. (46 cm) and lower on the front wall and then bounces 2x before the back wall. • Only forehand, not backhand.	
Reverse pinch • Contact point is shin high and lower off the little toe of your lead foot. • Ball hits 6 in. (15 cm) and lower on side wall. • Hits side wall (farthest from you), then front wall, then bounces 2x before 2nd side wall.		

Aggressive Defensive Shots

Core Techniques

The ceiling ball is the foundation of the entire defensive game. You need to develop this standard shot in order to gain racquet control and consistency during rallies and on the return of serve to move up in level. Without this shot, you will be left in the dust and wondering why your game is not progressing. Do not take the ceiling ball lightly.

The ceiling ball shot does exactly what its name indicates—it hits the ceiling, drawing your opponent out of the middle and putting him 35 feet (10.7 m) back, which is the most difficult position to score from because it is the farthest from the target, the front wall. It also gives you time to get back to good center-court position, a must in the game of racquetball. The ceiling ball is a shot that you want to have lots of confidence in, both when you are returning serve and playing a rally. If your opponent knows you lack confidence in your ceiling ball, she will pick on it by serving you lob serves and will hit ceiling balls to you during a rally. What often happens is you will get very frustrated and try to shoot more balls and be too offensive from your shoulder rather than just go back up to the ceiling and start a ceiling ball rally. This can lead to a deteriorating play and more points for your opponent.

Let us show you how to hit the ceiling ball correctly since it is the number one defensive shot in the game of racquetball. Having this shot in your arsenal is absolutely necessary to be a solid intermediate and advanced player. The mechanics of the ceiling ball are almost the same as for the attacking forehand and penetrating backhand, although there are a few differences.

Forehand Ceiling Shot

Grip—the same as forehand

Stance—the same as forehand except that your knees are only slightly bent at approximately 170 degrees because you are not hitting the ball below your knees but above your shoulder (4.10a).

Step and swing—the same as forehand except for the following:

1. Your step is short, 1 to 2 feet (.3 to .6 m), because you are not looking to get low to generate power.

2. The racquet and the elbow start to go up simultaneously.

3. The butt of the handle is pointing up.

4. The face of the racquet is pointing up toward the ceiling.

5. Wrist is cocked back at approximately a 45-degree angle (4.10b).

Figure 4.10a Forehand ceiling ball stance.

Figure 4.10b Forehand ceiling ball step and swing.

Contact point—the same as forehand except for the following:

1. In your hitting zone:
   - Wrist is cocked back at a 45-degree angle.
   - The face of the racquet is pointing up at a 45-degree angle toward the ceiling and front wall.
   - Ball is hit off lead shoulder and lead foot.
   - Hitting arm is slightly to fully extended above your head (4.10c).
2. On the ceiling:
   - The ball should hit the ceiling before the front wall, approximately 5 to 8 feet (1.5 to 2.4 m) back, so that on its second bounce it hits as close to the back wall as possible (ideally in the crotch of the back wall).
   - Where the ball hits on the ceiling is based on how hard you hit it: The harder you hit it, the closer to 8 feet from the front wall. The softer you hit it, the closer to 5 feet from the front wall.
   - Two key factors to keep in mind are that all surfaces play differently, and altitudes affect the flight of the ball. Just remember, if the ball is coming off the back wall for a setup, bring your contact point on the ceiling back farther from the front wall or hit softer; if the ball is dropping short for a setup, bring your contact point closer toward the front wall or hit harder.

Follow-through—the same as forehand except that the racquet comes across the body and points down (4.10d).

Figure 4.10c Forehand ceiling ball contact point.

Figure 4.10d Forehand ceiling ball follow-through.

Backhand Ceiling Shot

Grip—the same as backhand

Stance—the same as backhand except that your knees are only slightly bent at approximately 170 degrees because you are not hitting the ball below your knees but above your shoulder (4.11a).

Step and swing—the same as backhand except for the following:

1. Your step is short, 1 to 2 feet (.3 to .6 m), because you are not looking to get low to generate power.
2. The racquet and elbow begin to move forward and across the shoulder.
3. Wrist is cocked back at approximately a 45-degree angle as you start to swing (4.11b).

Contact point—the same as backhand except for the following:

1. In your hitting zone:
   ○ Wrist is flat upon contact.
   ○ The tip of the racquet is pointing to the side wall.
   ○ The face of the racquet is pointing up at a 45-degree angle toward ceiling and front wall.
   ○ Ball is hit off lead shoulder and lead foot.
   ○ Ball is contacted approximately chest to shoulder high.
   ○ Hitting arm is at full extension (4.11c).

Figure 4.11a Backhand ceiling ball stance.

Figure 4.11b Backhand ceiling ball step and swing.

Figure 4.11c Backhand ceiling ball contact point.

2. On the ceiling:

- The ball should hit the ceiling before the front wall, approximately 5 to 8 feet (1.5 to 2.4 m) back, so that on its second bounce it hits as close to the back wall as possible ideally in the crotch of the back wall (4.11d).

- Where the ball hits on the ceiling is based on how hard you hit it: The harder you hit it, the closer to 8 feet (2.4 m), the slower you hit it, the closer to 5 feet (1.5 m).

- Two key factors to keep in mind are that all surfaces play differently, and altitudes affect the flight of the ball. Just remember, if the ball is coming off the back wall for a setup, bring your contact point back farther from the front wall or hit softer; if the ball is dropping short for a setup, bring your contact point closer toward the front wall or hit harder.

Follow-through—the same as a regular backhand stroke, pointing to the back wall when you are done (4.11e).

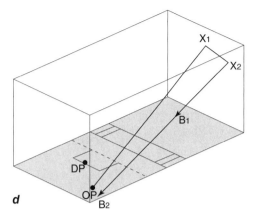

Figure 4.11d Ceiling ball, side view.

Figure 4.11e Backhand ceiling follow-through.

Intermediate and Advanced Techniques

When you get into the intermediate and advanced levels of play, you need to have shots to hit when you are off balance or out of position and you need to buy yourself time. Your goal is to move your opponent out of the middle and put her in the most difficult position to score from, the last 3 to 5 feet (.9 to 1.5 m) of the court, while you regain center-court position. The following shots will accomplish just that.

Higher-Level Ceiling Ball Shot

Instead of hitting the basic ceiling shot from chest high to full extension above your head, you will be hitting from low to high, generally waist high and lower.

Use the higher-level ceiling shot only when you are off balance or out of position or returning a tough serve. The shot uses the same techniques as the basic ceiling shot except for the following:

Grip—the same

Stance—the same except that your knees are bent as much as necessary to push off and lunge at the ball (4.12*a*).

Step and swing—the same except for the following:

1. Your step is big and can be straight ahead or at an angle as you are lunging for the ball (4.12*b*).
2. You are bent at the waist as you are reaching forward.
3. The racquet and elbow move quickly to get under the ball.
4. The racquet head is at an angle facing the ceiling/front wall corner because you are now under the ball to get it up to the ceiling.

Contact point—the same except for the following:

1. In your hitting zone:
   o Ideally off of lead foot, but the contact point can be anywhere since you are off balance and reaching, lunging desperately just to save the point and keep the ball alive (4.12*c*).
   o Ball is contacted approximately ankle to waist high.
2. On the ceiling:
   o The same as the basic ceiling ball shot, but ball contact can be anywhere since you are off balance and reaching, lunging desperately just to save the point and keep the ball alive.

Follow-through—The same as a regular follow-through: try to make sure your racquet comes around, as best as possible, since you are off balance and reaching, lunging desperately just trying to save the point and keep the ball alive. The one thing you do not want to do is poke the ball.

a

Figure 4.12a Higher-level ceiling ball stance.

b

Figure 4.12b Higher-level ceiling ball step and swing.

c

Figure 4.12c Higher-level ceiling ball contact point.

Z Shot

The Z shot is a more advanced shot than the ceiling ball shot, but it accomplishes exactly the same thing (figure 4.13). Too many players just want to keep shooting even though they are off balance and reaching for the ball. Usually they skip the ball completely, an easy point for the opponent, or float it up and leave a setup for the opponent instead of using the Z shot to keep the ball in play and move the opponent back. Here's how to hit it.

Trajectory   The Z shot makes the letter Z. It hits the front wall approximately two-thirds to three-quarters of the way up, then the first side wall and the second side wall on a fly and comes out angled to the back wall. The higher and harder you hit the ball, the deeper it goes in the court. This makes it very difficult for your opponent to retrieve.

Position to hit the ball   You want to hit the ball from in front of the dotted line, preferably from one extreme side of the court or the other, not in the middle because you do not have the correct angle from the middle to hit all three walls.

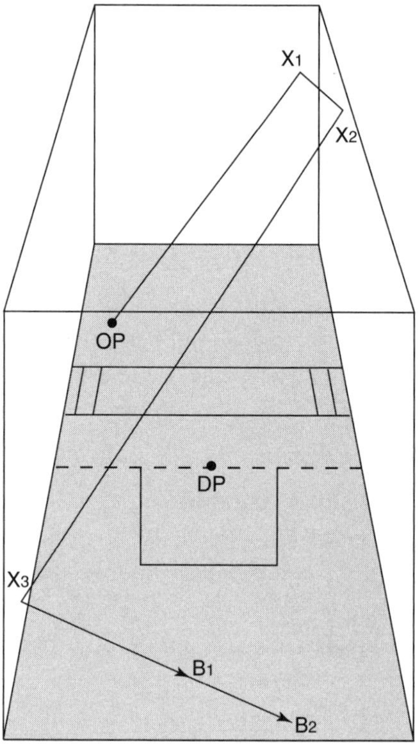

Contact point

Figure 4.13   Z shot.

1. You want to hit the ball off your lead foot, approximately by the little toe.

2. The racquet head is facing the front wall and aimed at the corner. You're tilting the racquet up slightly so as to hit the front wall first about two-thirds to three-quarters of the way up the wall.

3. The ball should hit the front wall within approximately 2 to 4 feet (.6 to 1.2 m) of the first side wall, depending on how hard it is hit.

You don't want to give away easy points by skipping or leaving the ball up, so try to incorporate the Z shot into your game because at the advanced level it is a very powerful tool. The natural spin created by the pace and trajectory of the ball makes it more difficult to return than just a regular ceiling shot.

Aggressive Defensive Shot Drills

To rely on the defensive shots to buy you time, draw your opponent out of the middle, and get you out of trouble when you are off balance or out of position, you need to practice them just like any of the offensive shots. Most players do not like to practice the defensive shots because they really don't like them or want to use them. They would prefer to rock and roll, rip and shoot, and turn and burn, using only offensive shots—but then they will get caught when a defensive shot is needed in a particular situation in a match. To be a well-rounded player, you need to be able to call on these defensive shots.

Jason was instrumental in bringing the defensive shots back to professional racquetball in the early 1990s when he returned to the game after breaking his back. The pro game at the time was primarily a power game (the low game), which was harder for Jason to play because of his injury. For a year after he came back, he studied all the pro players' games and determined that most of the pros played a power game and did not really like or excel at a controlled power game (the high game). So Jason went on a mission to bring the ceiling ball back to the pro game and began to use the Z shot in his matches.

As we did in the first three chapters, we recommend you have regular drill sessions to develop the consistency level needed for you to win more matches at your appropriate skill level on the road to becoming a champion.

Ceiling Ball Shot

Level: All

1. Square to the side wall, with racquet up.
2. Stand approximately at 35 feet (10.7 m), within 5 feet (1.5 m) of the back wall and within 5 feet of the side wall.
3. Bounce the ball high, off your lead shoulder and fully extended from the body.
   - Forehand ceiling shot: Ball ends up slightly to fully extended above your head.
   - Backhand ceiling shot: Ball ends up chest to shoulder high.
4. Practice one ceiling ball at a time, 15 or 20 times, and keep track until you get some good racquet control and consistency.
5. Now practice two ceilings in a row, then three in a row, and so on, and keep track.

Higher-Level Ceiling Ball Shot

Level: Intermediate and Advanced

Toss, Turn, Shuffle, and Hit

1. Stand square to the front wall in the down and ready position in the middle of the court, with feet more than shoulder-width apart, knees bent, waist slightly bent, shoulders level, and weight on the front part of the foot, ready to push off.
2. Toss the ball up from different distances, 35, 30, 25, and 20 feet (10.7, 9.1, 7.6, and 6.1 m). Let's use 35 feet (10.7 m) as an example.
3. Stand at 35 feet and toss the ball low, approximately ankle high or lower, and far away from you. In the beginning, toss it forward; as you get better, toss the ball even with you, and finally toss the ball behind you.
4. Cross over by pivoting on the heel of the foot on the side you are turning or crossing over to and lunge and reach, getting under the ball and hitting to the ceiling.
5. Practice only one shot at a time, 15 or 20 times, and keep track.
6. Practice different shots, tossing the ball forward, even with, and then behind you, 15 or 20 times, and keep track.
7. Repeat the sequence for 30, 25, and 20 feet (9.1, 7.6, and 6.1 m).

Set Up and Hit

1. Set the ball up from different distances, 35, 30, 25, and 20 feet (10.7, 9.1, 7.6, and 6.1 m). Let's use 35 feet (10.7 m) as an example.

2. Stand at 35 feet and hit the ball low off the front wall and far away from you. In the beginning, hit it forward; as you get better, hit the ball even with you, and finally hit the ball behind you.

3. You want to judge the ball so that when it comes off the front wall, you know where it is going so you can get there and lunge and reach to get under the ball.

4. Practice only one shot at a time, 15 or 20 times, and keep track.

5. Practice different shots, hitting the ball forward, even with, and then behind you, 15 or 20 times, and keep track.

6. Repeat the sequence for 30, 25, and 20 feet (9.1, 7.6, and 6.1 m).

Z Shot

Level: Intermediate and Advanced

Toss, Turn, Shuffle, and Hit

1. Stand square to the front wall in the down and ready position in the middle of the court, with feet more than shoulder-width apart, knees bent, waist slightly bent, shoulders level, and weight on the front part of the foot, ready to push off.

2. Toss the ball up from different distances, starting at 25 feet (7.6 m) and up.

3. Stand at 25 feet and toss the ball low, approximately ankle high or lower, and far away from you and forward from where you are positioned. Toss it out by your big toe on your backhand side or little toe on your forehand side. Toss it to one side of the court or the other, but not the middle.

4. Cross over by pivoting on the heel of the foot on the side you are turning or crossing over to and lunge and reach, getting under the ball and hitting to the front wall.

5. Practice only one shot at a time, 15 or 20 times, and keep track.

6. Repeat the sequence from anywhere on the court as long as the ball winds up farther up in the court than 25 feet (7.6 m) when you toss it and hit it.

Set Up and Hit

1. Set the ball up from 25 feet (7.6 m) first, and then you can set it up from anywhere on the court as long as the ball winds up farther up in the court than 25 feet when you set it up and hit it. Let's use 25 feet as an example.

2. Stand at 25 feet and hit the ball low off the front wall and far away from you and forward from where you are positioned. Hit it out by your big toe on your backhand side or little toe on your forehand side. Hit it to one side of the court or the other, but not the middle.

3. You want to judge the ball so that when it comes off the front wall, you know where it is going so you can get there and lunge and reach to get under the ball.

4. Practice only one shot at a time, 15 or 20 times, and keep track.

5. Repeat the sequence from anywhere on the court.

COMMON MISTAKES: AGGRESSIVE DEFENSIVE SHOTS

Ceiling Ball

ERROR: You hit the ball too hard and too close to the front wall off the ceiling, within 1 to 4 feet (.3 to 1.2 m).

CORRECTION: Hit the ball so it contacts the ceiling 5 to 8 feet (1.5 to 2.4 m) back from the front wall.

SOLUTION: By hitting the ball in the correct position on the ceiling and without a lot of pace, your ball should end up in the crack of the back wall on its second bounce. This will not allow your opponent an offensive opportunity but rather force a defensive return because the ball will not come off the back wall on one bounce.

ERROR: You hit the ball too far back on the ceiling, beyond 8 feet (2.4 m).

CORRECTION: Hit the ball so it contacts the ceiling 5 to 8 feet (1.5 to 2.4 m) back from the front wall.

SOLUTION: By hitting the ball in the correct position on the ceiling and without a lot of pace, your ball should end up in the crack of the back wall on its second bounce. This will not allow your opponent an offensive opportunity but rather force a defensive return because the ball will not drop short and be a setup for your opponent.

Higher-Level Ceiling Ball

ERROR: You do not get completely under the ball.

CORRECTION: The racquet head should be at an angle facing the ceiling/front wall corner because you are now under the ball to get it up to the ceiling.

SOLUTION: This angle gets the ball up to the ceiling, giving you time to get back to center court while pulling your opponent out of the middle and putting him deep. If you don't angle the racquet properly, the ball winds up hitting the front wall and does not hit the ceiling, creating a setup for your opponent.

Z Shot

ERROR: The ball hits the side wall before the front wall.

CORRECTION: The ball should hit the front wall, then the side wall, and then the second side wall high and deep, making the letter Z.

SOLUTION: By making the letter Z, this shot pushes your opponent deep as well as adds natural spin to the ball as it hits all three walls, making it tough for your opponent to return the ball. If the ball hits the side wall first, you have a greater chance of giving your opponent a setup shot, meaning she can then hit an offensive return rather than defensive return.

Aggressive Defensive Shots Checklist: Core, Intermediate, and Advanced

Core	Intermediate and Advanced
Ceiling ball Forehand: • You are 35 ft. (10.7 m) back in the court. • Contact point in your hitting zone, with your hitting arm slightly to fully extended above your head off lead shoulder and lead foot. • Wrist is cocked back at a 45-degree angle. • Racquet is pointing toward the front wall and ceiling. • Ball hits the ceiling before the front wall, approximately 5-8 ft. (1.5-2.4 m) back, and bounces on its second bounce as close to the back wall as possible, in crotch of back wall. • Racquet comes across body on the follow-through and points down. Backhand: • Same except for contact point and follow-through. • Contact point in your hitting zone, with your hitting arm chest to shoulder high off lead shoulder and lead foot. • Wrist is flat upon contact. • Racquet is pointing toward the side wall and ceiling. • Hitting arm is at full extension from the body. • Follow-through is pointing toward the back wall, not the floor.	Higher-level ceiling ball • Big step because you are lunging and reaching for the shot. • Racquet head is facing the ceiling as you are under the ball. • Contact point is made ankle to waist high off of lead foot, if possible, or anywhere since you are off balance and reaching for the shot. Z Shot • The ball hits the front wall two-thirds to three-fourths of the way up, then it hits the first side wall and second side wall on a fly. • Contact point in your hitting zone is off your little toe off the lead foot. • Ball should hit the front wall approximately 2-4 ft. from the first side wall.

ERROR: The ball does not hit close enough to the side wall.

CORRECTION: The ball needs to hit close to the side wall after hitting the front wall to make it possible for the ball to hit the second side wall on a fly.

SOLUTION: Hitting the front wall and then the two side walls on a fly high brings the ball back deep and parallel to the back wall, making it nearly impossible to return. If the ball is not hit close, it will not be a Z shot because the ball will hit only the front wall, then the side wall, and bounce for a setup rather than hit the third wall on a fly.

Summary

To be a well-rounded intermediate and advanced player and a force to be reckoned with, you must have a balanced combination of the offensive and defensive shots. As you move up in level, you need to be aware that there is a time and place for each type of shot you choose to use. In this chapter, we give you the shots you need for any situation.

Too many players get caught up in hitting only offensive shots and shy away from defensive shots, which leads to what we call survival racquetball. This type of playing usually does not lead to any sort of consistency or success on a regular basis. By using the defensive shots, the ceiling ball in particular, as well as the offensive shots, you will be able to play any type of game like the pros. The pros do not just shoot and try to kill everything; they use their heads to determine which is the best strategy for winning the match, which you will learn in chapter 7. By using your head as well as your body and having good aggressive offensive and defensive shots in your arsenal, you will be on your way to the next level in developing a championship game.

Part II

The Tactics

Part I of the book covers the skills of the game. We give you an in-depth look at the mechanics and the technical parts of the game, namely the strokes, shots, and serves; how to relocate after the serves; and how to return any serve. You will need this information to succeed at the intermediate and advanced levels of play. In part II we focus on the tactics of racquetball.

We pay more attention to game strategy. Strategy involves your perceptions regarding how to play the game and how to attack your opponents. In racquetball, we call this the tactics of the game.

Perceptions provide an unlimited number of interpretations, such as how you remember information you have learned in practice and its application; how you access and use your knowledge under the stress of the game; how you reason when mapping out a game strategy; how you solve problems during the game to outwit your opponent; and how you make intelligent decisions when playing from behind or closing out a game.

Intelligent decisions involve looking ahead and predicting outcomes in a split second. You need to make bold guesses as to how things are going to turn out during the game when you are involved in competition. These factors are all part of game tactics, human behavior, and game strategy.

In addition, we demonstrate how to utilize the techniques you have been exposed to. Experience will give you a great advantage in applying what you know to a game situation. However, sometimes we are afraid to use a new technique because we have doubts. Doubt can be a powerful weapon that we use against ourselves. All of us have experienced fear of failure at one time or another, which makes us somewhat reluctant to try something new. But in the end, as is often the case, high-percentage racquetball becomes the calming element that elevates us to control these fears. If you play the percentages, you make it harder on your opponents by putting them in difficult positions to score from, which will cause them to make more mistakes and lead to easy points for you. These difficult positions deeper in the court with the ball farther away create more pressure on their shots while forcing them to hit on the run.

In part II of the book, we explain why it is important to combine two concepts: playing racquetball from the neck down, which is the physical side of the game, and playing from the neck up, which is the mental side of the game. We also examine one of the most critical parts of the game: court position.

Most successful athletes in racquetball as well as other sports have a clear understanding of the physical and mental aspects of their sport. If you want to succeed in racquetball, remember the mind–body connection.

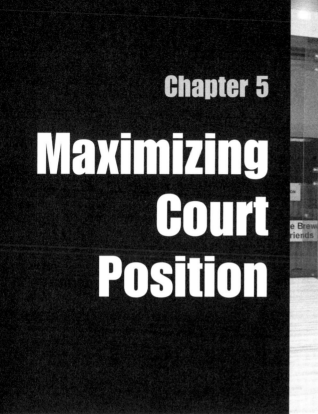

Chapter 5

Maximizing Court Position

In every sport, positioning is everything. In racquetball, being in the right place at the right time is critical to give yourself the best chance of getting to the ball and doing something with it once you get there, whether to defend or to score. Throughout this chapter we emphasize the importance of center-court position.

We touch on court position in chapter 3 when we discuss regaining center-court position after the serve and after the return of serve. Now we will discuss center-court position in detail. You want to be in the best position possible on the court to cover a majority of the shots your opponent is likely to hit.

Center-Court Position

What you should know about the racquetball court:

- The court is 40 feet (12.2 m) long.
- The short line cuts the court in half at 20 feet (6.1 m).
- At all levels, 80 to 90 percent of balls that are hit end up in the back half of the court.
- Center court is in the middle of the back half of the court, just behind the dotted line, and is a box that is approximately 6 feet by 6 feet (1.8 m by 1.8 m) (see figure 5.1).

Once you have a sound foundation, you will begin to improve. Improvement is measured by levels, and as a result of that improvement, a player's shots become more skillful and more precise, and therefore the center-court box will shrink ever so slightly.

COMMON MISTAKES: COURT POSITION

ERROR: You are playing too far forward between the short line and the dotted line.

CORRECTION: No matter whether it is during a rally, after the serve, or after the return of serve, you want to get back to good center-court position, inside that 6 by 6 feet box, and float up and back (based on your opponent's court position and the ball) using the eight positions we discuss later in this chapter.

SOLUTION: By being in the proper position in the center-court box you give yourself the best opportunity to get to a majority of the balls. If you are too far forward, in front of the dotted line, you will have much less time to react to the ball, you will be vulnerable to the pass shot, and you will get jammed often. Also if a ceiling ball is hit, you have to run back to get to it. Because the ball is behind you, you may not have enough time to get back far enough, making your return inconsistent and weak, which would probably result in a scoring opportunity for your opponent.

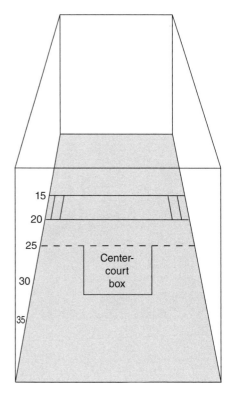

Figure 5.1 Center-court position.

How to Be Down and Ready and Use Proper Footwork

It is not okay to just be in good center-court position—you need to be down and ready. Having your knees bent between 130 and 150 degrees and your legs spread about 1 to 2 feet (.3 to .6 m) wider than shoulder-width apart (the more advanced, the wider the stance) lowers your center of gravity, which will help in returning shots hit by your opponent. Unfortunately, most players are not in center court, having a tendency to shade to the side the ball is on, and are not down and ready. If you are not down and ready, you cannot move to the ball quickly, which will result in a weak return and setups for your opponent. We cannot stress enough the importance of wanting to win, but you cannot win if you have not acquired the habit of being down, ready, and able to get to the next shot.

The following statistics will help you see why you need to be down and ready:

1. Approximately 70 percent of all balls hit by your opponent will pass through the center-court box. If you are down and ready, you can retrieve most of these balls with one step and a reach.

2. The 30/40/30 principle says that
   ○ 30 percent of all balls hit by your opponents are winners, which of course goes in their favor;
   ○ 40 percent of all balls hit by your opponents are left up, called an unforced error, and you can hit them—this goes in your favor; and
   ○ 30 percent of all balls hit by your opponents skip—this is a gift that goes in your favor.

When you add up all those percentages, you will see that whenever your opponent hits the ball, it goes in your favor 70 percent of the time. Being in the right position and down and ready enables you to return a majority of those shots. Having the proper footwork in center court involves exactly the same movements you make when you are returning serve.

Let's review:

1. Down and ready (figure 5.2):
   ○ Legs are spread 1 to 2 feet (.3 to .6 m) wider than shoulder-width apart.
   ○ Knees are bent to between 130 and 150 degrees.
   ○ Waist is bent to between 140 and 160 degrees.
   ○ Racquet is up about waist high to go forehand or backhand.
   ○ Grip should be a relaxed backhand because 90 percent of shots go to the backhand side.
   ○ Your eyes are on the ball.
   ○ Weight should be forward on the front part of your foot, ready to push off and pivot.

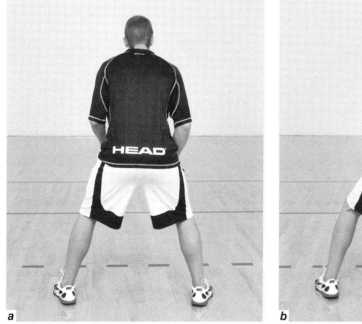

Figure 5.2 Down and ready position for *(a)* intermediate and *(b)* advanced players.

2. Pivot (figure 5.3):
   ○ Pivot your foot on the heel on the side the ball is going to. If the ball is going to the left side of the court, pivot off the heel of your left foot. If the ball is going to the right side of the court, pivot off the heel of your right foot. This opens your hips so you can move in that direction.
   ○ Move toward the ball.
   ○ Racquet begins to come up (ERP).

Figure 5.3 Pivot position.

3. Crossover and lunge step (figure 5.4):
   ○ Push off on the ball of your opposite foot.
   ○ Cross over the pivoted foot if the ball is close by, and add a shuffle step if the ball is farther from you.
   ○ Cross over with a lunge step if the ball is really far from you, almost out of your reach.
   ○ Racquet comes up completely before your opposite foot hits the floor.
   ○ Racquet fully extends out before your opposite foot hits the floor if the ball is almost out of your reach.

Figure 5.4 Crossover and lunge step.

The down and ready position and the footwork for center court look no different from the return of serve (see chapter 3, page 93). With the ball traveling in excess of 100 mph (161 km), you will undoubtedly have even less time to think and react while in center-court position than when returning serve because you are closer to the front wall. As a result, crossing over and getting square to the side wall is even more important so you can engage your legs and hips in the stroke to generate power on a passing shot or when getting the ball to the ceiling. Unfortunately, at all levels of play, if the ball is hit directly at you and you are jammed, you will not have time to cross over and square up to the side wall; therefore, you will hit these shots with an open stance rather than a closed stance square to the side wall.

Do not develop bad habits or get lazy and hit the ball with an open stance when you have time to cross over and hit with a closed stance facing the side wall. Many things can go wrong when players use an open stance. It will cost you power, control, and many weak returns because the racquet does not get up all the way. Hitting in an open stance makes it more difficult to adjust to unexpected bounces the ball will take, and it does not allow you to follow through with good mechanics.

However, at the highest level of racquetball, it is not uncommon to see the pros use the open stance, if and only if the situation dictates it, given the speed of the game and height of the ball.

COMMON MISTAKES: DOWN AND READY POSITION AND FOOTWORK

Down and Ready

ERROR: Your feet are too close together.

CORRECTION: Feet should be a little wider than shoulder-width apart, about 1 to 2 feet (.3 to .6 m) wider based on level of play, to get center of gravity lower.

SOLUTION: With your feet wider than shoulder-width apart, you get to the ball faster because you can take one step instead of two and you have a lower center of gravity. If your feet are too close together, your first step will be to widen your stance, and then your second step will be a crossover, which takes more time because you are adding another step. If your feet are the correct distance apart to begin with, your first step will be the crossover.

ERROR: You are standing up straight instead of being down and ready.

CORRECTION: Be down and ready, with knees bent between 130 and 140 degrees and feet wider than shoulder-width apart, 1 to 2 feet (.3 to .6 m) wider depending on your level of play.

SOLUTION: Being down and ready brings your center of gravity lower and allows you to push off more, with greater knee bend. Both will effectively help you return shots hit by your opponent.

Pivot

ERROR: You take a side step to the right or left and then a pivot instead of just a pivot right to the ball.

CORRECTION: Pivot without taking a side step.

SOLUTION: This extra step slows you down, so just pivot right to the ball; you will be pleasantly surprised by how many more good returns you will make. If you take a side step out of habit instead of pivoting right to the ball, you will get to the ball slower.

Crossover Step

ERROR: You shuffle sideways, and you are not square to the side wall.

CORRECTION: Cross over to get square to the side wall.

SOLUTION: By being square to the side wall you will have greater hip rotation and thus be able to generate more power and better control over the ball. If you do not cross over, you will probably lose power, control, and accuracy on all your shots.

Where to Stand in the Center-Court Box

Where you position yourself in the center-court box is completely dependent on where the ball is and where your opponent is located.

During the Rally

Keep the 30 percent principle in mind at all times when determining where you should position yourself—30 percent of all balls can be killed from the dotted line. A kill shot is defined as a shot that hits 6 inches (15 cm) and lower on the front wall and bounces twice before the short line. The farther back in the court a player shoots the ball, the less likely he will be able to effectively kill the ball, so the percentages go down drastically.

With these statistics in mind, let's take a look at eight positions so you can clearly see where to stand based on where the ball and your opponent are. This is an easy-to-follow snapshot of where the offensive player and defensive player are on the court.

Position 1 Offensive player is deep in the court, approximately 35 feet (10.7 m) and back off to one side of the court, not in the middle.

Defensive player is down and ready, watching the ball by looking over the right or left shoulder, and in the middle of the back half of the center-court box. Keeping the 30 percent principle in mind, the player is protecting against the pass and giving up the kill and pinch (figure 5.5).

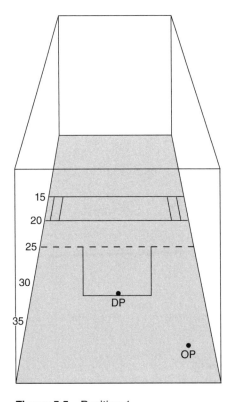

Figure 5.5 Position 1.

Position 2 Offensive player moves up to approximately 25 feet (7.6 m), or the dotted line, off to one side of the court, not in the middle.

Defensive player is down and ready, watching the ball, and moves up to the middle of the center-court box. Keeping the 30 percent principle in mind, the player is protecting against the pass and giving up the kill and pinch (figure 5.6).

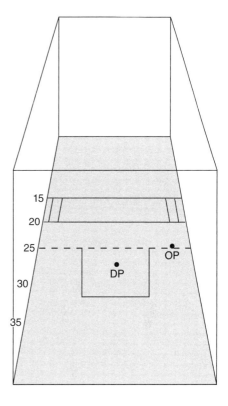

Figure 5.6 Position 2.

Position 3 Offensive player moves up to short line, off to one side of the court, not in the middle.

Defensive player is down and ready, watching the ball, and moves up toward the dotted line in the middle of the front half of the center-court box. The defensive player is still protecting against the pass, but because the offensive player is closer to the target (front wall), his or her odds of effectively killing the ball go up (figure 5.7).

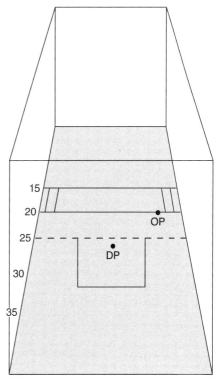

Figure 5.7 Position 3.

Position 4   Offensive player is anywhere at the front wall, approximately 1 to 2 feet (.3 to .6 m) away.

Defensive player is down and ready, watching the ball, and moves up to the middle of the dotted line but no farther. The defensive player is protecting against the pass and giving up the kill and pinch. She already made one mistake by letting the offensive player get within 2 feet (.6 m) of the front wall. If the defensive player moves up beyond the dotted line, she would be making a second mistake and would be vulnerable to the pass, which is an easier shot than the kill or pinch. Stay back on the dotted line (figure 5.8).

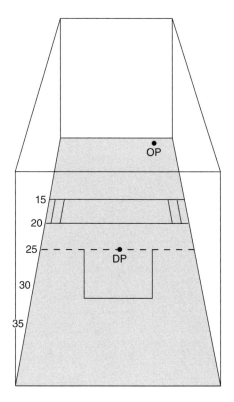

Figure 5.8   Position 4.

Position 5   Offensive player is at the short line in the middle.

Defensive player is down and ready, watching the ball, and is on or slightly behind the dotted line in the middle, protecting against the pass and giving up the kill and pinch (figure 5.9).

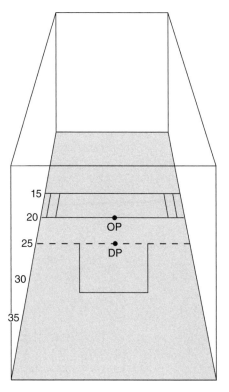

Figure 5.9   Position 5.

Position 6 Offensive player is at the dotted line in the middle.

Defensive player is down and ready, watching the ball, and drops back to the back half of the center-court box in the middle to protect against the pass and gives up the kill and pinch (figure 5.10).

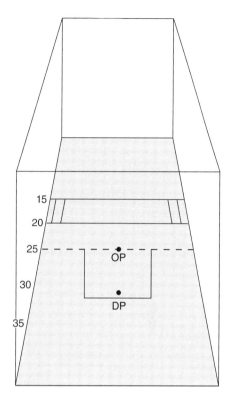

Figure 5.10 Position 6.

Position 7 Offensive player is deep in the court, approximately 35 feet (10.7 m) and back in the middle.

Defensive player is down and ready, watching the ball, and has one foot in the center-court box on one side of the court, approximately a step and a swing away from the offensive player, protecting against the pass and giving up the kill and pinch (figure 5.11). Ideally, the right-handed defensive player wants to be on the left side of the box to have a greater reach to the ball hit to the open court.

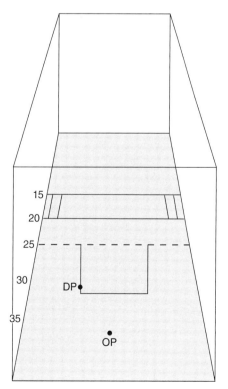

Figure 5.11 Position 7.

Position 8   Offensive player has the defensive player trapped off to one side of the court, not in the middle.

Defensive player is trapped on the wall because he didn't move back to center court after he hit the shot. He is vulnerable to everything, giving up 95 percent of the court—the biggest mistake you can make in court positioning (figure 5.12).

This is the one of the few times the offensive player should run around the backhand to hit the forehand because it puts the opponent in the worst position possible—a great strategic move.

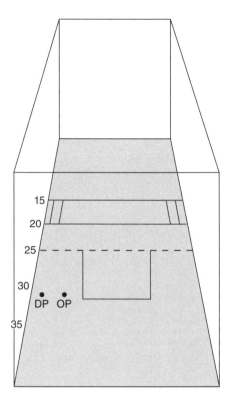

Figure 5.12   Position 8.

Rules of Thumb

Here are a few simple but smart rules you should follow in order to put more wins in the win column and fewer losses in the loss column.

- If your opponent (offensive player) is shooting the ball from closer than 30 feet (9.1 m), you want to be behind her in the middle of the center-court box.

- If your opponent (offensive player) is shooting the ball from beyond 30 feet, you want to be somewhere in front of him:

  ○ In the middle if he is shooting from one side or the other

  ○ Off to the left or right of him, with one foot in the center-court box, if he is shooting from the middle

- If your opponent (offensive player) is shooting the ball from exactly 30 feet, you need to decide whether to position yourself in front or behind her. If your opponent is a great shooter, then go up slightly in front of her; if the player leaves the ball up a lot, then stay back.

COMMON MISTAKES: DURING THE RALLY

Position 1
Offensive player (your opponent) is at 35 feet (10.7 m) off to either side.

ERROR: You are too far up at the dotted line.

CORRECTION: Defensive player should be in the middle of the back half of the center-court box.

SOLUTION: Being in the back half of the center-court box gives you more time to react, and you will be less likely to get passed or jammed.

Positions 2 and 6
Offensive player (your opponent) is at 25 feet (7.6 m) off to either side or in the middle.

ERROR: You are too far up, trying to go up and around and thus in front of the offensive player.

CORRECTION: Defensive player should be in the middle of the center-court box.

SOLUTION: Staying in the middle makes it tougher for your opponent because he has to kill or pinch the ball to beat you. If you are out of position, you will get passed or jammed, which are easier shots to hit.

Position 3
Offensive player (your opponent) is at the short line off to either side.

ERROR: You are directly behind the offensive player, on the same side of the court.

CORRECTION: Defensive player should be up toward the dotted line in the middle of the front half of the center-court box.

SOLUTION: Make sure you are in the middle if the offensive player is off to one side of the court, which allows you to get to more balls. If you are on the same side as the offensive player, you are out of position and will get passed on the other side.

Position 4
Offensive player (your opponent) is anywhere at the front wall, approximately 1 to 2 feet (.3 to .6 m) away.

ERROR: You run up with the offensive player.

CORRECTION: Defensive player needs to stay on the dotted line in the middle.

SOLUTION: You need to protect against the pass, giving up the kill and pinch. If you go beyond the dotted line, you are way out of position and vulnerable, especially to the pass.

Position 7
Offensive player (your opponent) is at 35 feet in the middle.

ERROR: You move right in front of the offensive player and duck to get out of his way.

CORRECTION: Defensive player needs to be approximately a step and a swing away from the offensive player or slightly to either side.

SOLUTION: This court position puts pressure on the offensive player and puts you in the best position possible to cover an unforced error. If you are directly in front of the offensive player, you are out of position and at risk of creating a penalty hinder.

After the Serve

As discussed in chapter 3, relocating out of the service zone after you serve is just as important as the serve itself. You might have a great serve, but you cannot just stand there expecting to win the point. You must get back into the center-court box and be down and ready so you are in the best possible location to respond effectively to your opponent's return of serve (figure 5.13).

On any of the low and hard drive serves, your goal is to get back to at least the dotted line—a little farther, if time permits—to be in the front half of the center-court box. Just remember that when you get back, you want to be down and ready, with your feet stopped and set to respond to your opponent's return of serve. Where you stand in the center-court box depends on where your serve ends up.

On any of the soft and high lob serves, your goal is to get back to at least the middle of the center-court box because you are protecting against the ceiling or pass shot, giving up the kill and pinch. Just remember that when you get back, you want to be down and ready, with your feet stopped and set to respond to your opponent's return of serve. Again, where you stand in the center-court box depends on where your serve ends up.

For example, let's say you just served a drive or a lob serve to the back left corner of the court. When you relocate after the serve, you move in between the short line and dotted line and not to the dotted line or farther

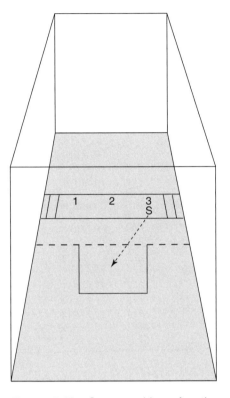

Figure 5.13 Court position after the serve.

back. This position puts you too far forward and vulnerable to both a passing shot and a ceiling ball. If your opponent returns the serve with a passing shot, you will not have enough time to react, and either the ball will go by you for an easy point or you will barely get your racquet on the ball, hitting a weak shot and creating a setup. If your opponent returns the serve to the ceiling, you will be way out of position because you will be so far forward you would have to scramble back and then jump to get the ball behind you. As a result, your shot will not hit the front wall at all for a side-out for your opponent, or your ceiling shot will be short, creating a setup for your opponent. In both cases, playing too far forward would be disastrous.

COMMON MISTAKES: AFTER THE SERVE

ERROR: You do not come back all the way to the dotted line or beyond after the serve.

CORRECTION: Come back to at least the dotted line or beyond based on the serve you hit.

SOLUTION: Moving immediately to the right position protects against a majority of the returns. If not, you will get passed or jammed.

ERROR: You go back only as far as the dotted line on a good lob serve.

CORRECTION: Get back to the middle to back half of the center-court box.

SOLUTION: Getting back deeper puts you in position to hit a good ceiling ball off the lob serve. If you don't get back far enough, you will be late getting back, and your ceiling ball will likely clip the side wall for a setup.

After the Return of Serve

One of the objectives of the return of serve is to get yourself back into center court by moving forward as quickly as possible to regain control of center court and the match (figure 5.14, page 151). Basically, your returns should be the ceiling ball and passes to get the server out of the middle; thus you want to move up and ideally be in the back half of the center-court box to cover one of the two shots you just hit. Where you stand in the center-court box depends on where your return ends up.

COMMON MISTAKES: AFTER THE RETURN OF SERVE

ERROR: You hit the return of serve and just stand there, not moving back to center court.

CORRECTION: Immediately move into good center-court position.

SOLUTION: By moving up, you are ready for any shot. If you stay back and do not move, you will be out of position and always scrambling to make a good shot.

ERROR: You hit the return of serve, and no matter what the return is, you run to the dotted line, which is too far forward.

CORRECTION: Move back to the proper position in the center-court box based on the return of serve.

SOLUTION: Always move after you hit the return or you will be out of position and scrambling to make a good shot.

What to Look for in Center Court

When you are in the center-court box, down and ready, you are on defense and your opponent who is hitting the ball is on offense. You have put yourself in the best possible position to get to whatever ball your opponent hits. To enhance your ideal position and excellent footwork that you learned earlier in this chapter, there are a few things you can do to get a quicker jump on the ball and anticipate the shot your opponent is about to take. This will help you get to more balls than you can imagine, even ones you think are unreachable. Remember to never give up on the ball. The only time you should acknowledge that you can't get to the ball is after its second bounce.

Watch and Read the Ball and Your Opponent
- Look at the height, speed, and angle of the ball.
  - Height: If the ball is high, your opponent is probably going up to the ceiling. If the ball is lower, your opponent is probably going to shoot either the pass, pass-kill, kill, or maybe a pinch. Familiarize yourself with the shots of the game in chapter 4, and look at the exact heights.

- Speed: If the ball is hit hard and fast, there is less time for racquet prep; therefore your opponent will spray the ball and not be very consistent.
- Angle: If the ball is hit close to the side wall, there will be a lot of straight in and out shots or maybe a splat shot. If the ball is coming off a side wall, it will probably be hit back to that same side wall. Also, when you hit a ball to your opponent, she is most likely to hit the ball back at the same angle as the ball coming in. If you hit a crosscourt shot, your opponent is likely to hit a crosscourt back. It is more difficult to change the ball's angle, and therefore a player is likely to take the easy route. The only time this changes is when a ball kicks off the side wall when you miss a pass or pinch. In this case, when the ball comes off the side wall and jams your opponent, she is most likely to hit the ball in the direction it is already moving because of the difficulty of changing its direction.

- Look at the racquet and contact point.
  - If the racquet is behind your opponent, expect a pinch or a splat.
  - If the racquet is way out in front, expect a crosscourt shot.
  - If the racquet is up above your opponent's head on the forehand side, expect either a forehand ceiling ball or, if it drops a little, an overhead pass.
  - Refer to the contact points outlined in the first three chapters for more detailed options.
- Look at your opponent's body position.
  - Look at your opponent's feet because players usually step in the direction they are going to hit the ball.
  - If your opponent is standing straight up, expect a higher shot that ends up deeper in the court.
  - If your opponent is low, expect a lower shot such as the kill or pinch shot that ends up in the front of the court.

Analyze Your Opponent

- Know what level of player you are facing and what shots he is capable of making. Focus on the shots he makes more often because most players are predictable.
- Be aware of your opponent's patterns. Look at each position she is shooting from, and determine whether she hits only one shot from each position. Do this exercise all over the court. Take mental notes of what your opponent does in different situations.
- Look at your opponent's habits, such as an exaggerated backhand grip that will force a lot of high-to-low balls, or a pendulum swing that lofts the ball high in a lot of instances. Be alert at all times.

Too often we see players giving up on the ball prematurely—before it bounces twice—because they think they can't get to it in time. We encourage you to go after everything. By watching and reading the ball and your opponent, you will get a better jump on the ball, and you will get to more balls than you ever thought you could.

Where to Stand When Returning the Serve

Having the right mechanics is only part of a good return of serve. Knowing where to stand is another key element. Ideally, you want to put yourself in the best position possible to return a majority of the serves and return them well (figure 5.14).

1. Be in the down and ready position, approximately 2 to 3 feet (.6 to .9 m) from the back wall, not any farther up. By being farther back, you will not be vulnerable to serves hit too deep in the corners or jammed off the wall. This deeper court position buys you time to react and think. Be careful not to play too far forward on the return of serve because two things can happen:

   o Going farther up—what we call "cheating up"—gives the server an open invitation to hit low and hard serves because being too far forward greatly diminishes your reaction time.

   o If the ball is hit deep in the corners, you will be reaching and hitting the ball behind you where you have no leverage; if the serve comes off the side wall right at you, you will be jammed and handcuffed and will just flail at the ball. Stay back because it is easier to move up than back.

2. Be centered between the two side walls at 10 feet (3 m). This position enables you to return a shot hit from either your forehand or backhand. You do not want to shade to one side because if the server is paying attention and is aware of your poor position, it makes you vulnerable on the other side; the server can and will take advantage of that mistake. Stay in the middle so you can protect both sides.

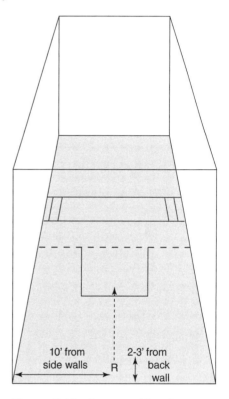

Figure 5.14 Court position for return of serve.

3. Your weight should be on the front inner part of your feet, not on your heels, so you are ready to push off and explode toward the ball with a crossover step.

4. Your racquet should be waist high and in the middle of your body, with a relaxed backhand grip. Be ready to bring your racquet up (i.e., use ERP) to hit a forehand or backhand return of serve.

COMMON MISTAKES: COURT POSITION FOR RETURN OF SERVE

ERROR: You are playing too far up at 5 feet (1.5 m) or more from the back wall rather than 2 to 3 feet (.6 to .9 m) up from the back wall.

CORRECTION: Be down and ready approximately 2 to 3 feet (.6 to .9 m) from the back wall.

SOLUTION: By staying back, you will have more time to react and get to balls before they go into the back corners, creating more leverage to hit the ball off your lead foot.

ERROR: You have a tendency to shade to one side of the court, especially if you have an injury.

CORRECTION: Be in between the two side walls at 10 feet (3 m).

SOLUTION: This position enables you to return a shot hit from either your forehand or backhand side. You do not want to shade to one side because it makes you vulnerable to the opposite side.

ERROR: Your weight is on your heels rather than the front part of your feet.

CORRECTION: Your weight should be on the front inner part of your feet.

SOLUTION: Having your weight correctly balanced makes you ready to push off and explode toward the ball with a crossover step. If your weight is back rather than forward, you will not be able to explode to the ball as quickly on your return of serve, and therefore you will have weaker returns.

ERROR: Your racquet is down instead of up by your waist.

CORRECTION: Your racquet should be at least waist high in the middle of your body.

SOLUTION: If your racquet is up in the proper position, you can get your racquet to the forehand or backhand side more quickly with one motion. If your racquet is down when the serve is hit, you have to lift your racquet up and then to the ball using two motions, taking more time.

What to Look for When Returning Serve

Pay attention to the server because you can pick up many clues that will help you anticipate the serve about to be hit. This information gives you an extra jump on the ball so you know what's coming as opposed to being caught off guard, which usually results in a weak return of serve.

When returning serve, you should be focused on the ball because the ball never lies. The spot the server drops the ball can determine the direction it's going. If the ball is in the front of the server's stance, it will likely go to the left; if the ball is farther back in the server's stance, it will likely go down the line (to the right). Move only after you know exactly where the ball is going—never guess. Anticipation happens in your mind, utilizing information to determine likely outcomes. Guessing happens when your body moves before you know exactly where the ball is going, which is one of the biggest mistakes you can make when returning shots.

1. Watch the server's position in the service zone. Most servers are very predictable because they have particular serves from position 1, 2, or 3 and never deviate. Here are some examples:

- ○ They serve only a low and hard Z from position 1.
- ○ They serve only a drive serve to the left from position 2.
- ○ They serve only a drive serve to the right from position 3.

2. Watch where the server drops the ball, what position she is serving from, and where she makes contact. Knowing where the server is standing in the service zone and where she drops the ball helps you anticipate where she is going to hit the serve based on contact with the ball.

Here are some examples:

- ○ If the server drops the ball deep in her stance, close to her heel from position 1, she is going to hit a drive Z serve.
- ○ If the server drops the ball too close to his body and not at full extension from position 3, by the arch, he will wind up hitting the front wall and then the side wall for a setup instead of a clean drive serve down the line.

3. Watch the server step into the ball because that motion can give away what serve is coming.

Here are a few examples:

- ○ Usually if the server steps at an angle to the front right corner, from any position, she is going to serve down the right side of the court.
- ○ Usually if the server steps at an angle to the front left corner, from any position, he is going to serve down the left side of the court and will serve to the left side if he or she steps toward the front left.
- ○ Usually if the server steps at a sharper angle to the front left corner, from position 1 or 3, he is going to serve a Z serve to the right side of the court.

4. Be aware of any patterns the server develops because these will give you even more information about what serve is coming.

- ○ The server serves two drive Z serves from position 1 to the left.
- ○ Then the server hits a lob nick to the left from position 2.
- ○ Then the server looks up at the front wall to where he is going to hit the next lob serve.
- ○ Then the server might touch her sleeve before hitting a lob Z to the right from position 3.

COMMON MISTAKES: WATCHING THE SERVER

ERROR: You are watching the front wall rather than the ball.

CORRECTION: Keep your eye on the ball—watch the server drop it out of his hand.

SOLUTION: Watching the ball as your opponent's racquet hits it gives you the most educated guess as to where the ball is going. If you are not watching the ball, you will undoubtedly lose a second or two of reaction time, resulting in a weak return.

ERROR: You are unaware of certain patterns the server has developed.

CORRECTION: Pay close attention to the server's pattern of serves.

SOLUTION: By being aware of the server's patterns, you will have valuable information to anticipate what serve is coming, thus getting a jump on the ball and resulting in a better return of serve.

Court Position Drills

We just discussed how important it is to get into the correct court position, which places you in the best position possible to get to a majority of the shots your opponent hits. Getting to that position as quickly and efficiently as possible is the key, and the first step to the ball is critical.

The following drills will help you get to center court quickly and efficiently. We recommend having a good conditioning base, with no lingering injuries and no knee or back problems, before attempting these drills. If you have any questions, see your physician. Remember to keep track of what you are trying to accomplish.

During the Rally

Off the Court

1. Use a diagram of a blank court.
2. Place an *O* for the offensive player somewhere in the court.
3. Now figure out where the defensive player should be best positioned and place a *D* there.
4. Keep repeating these two steps until you are very proficient at knowing where you, the defensive player, should be positioned based on the position of the offensive player.

On the Court

1. Grab a towel or your racquetball bag.
2. Place the towel somewhere in the court to represent the offensive player.
3. Now figure out where the defensive player should be best positioned and stand there.
4. Keep repeating these two steps until you are very proficient at knowing where you, the defensive player, should be positioned based on the position of the offensive player.

After the Serve

Down and Ready

To improve on relocating after the serve and being in the down and ready position, here is a chair drill.

1. Grab a low chair.
2. Tape a center-court box on the court, 6 feet by 6 feet (1.8 m by 1.8 m), using painter's tape.

Drive Serve

1. Place the chair in the center-court box on the dotted line.

2. Visualize yourself serving a drive serve, with no ball. After you finish the motion, relocate to the center-court box, squaring up to the front wall, legs spread and knees bent. Lightly touch the chair with your butt, and hold that position for several seconds. Do not sit on the chair.

3. Repeat steps 1 and 2 by moving the chair to the front half of the center-court box and visualizing different drive serves, working on one serve at a time, and then relocating.

Lob Serve

1. Place the chair in the center-court box in the middle.

2. Visualize yourself hitting a lob serve, with no ball. After you finish the motion, relocate to the center-court box, squaring up to the front wall, legs spread and knees bent. Lightly touch the chair with your butt, and hold that position for several seconds. Do not sit on the chair.

3. Repeat steps 1 and 2 by moving the chair to the back half of the center-court box and visualizing different lob serves, working on one serve at a time, and then relocating.

After the Return of Serve

Down and Ready

Use the same chair drill, but instead of pretending to serve, pretend to return serve, and then relocate to the center-court box.

Footwork for Center Court

No Ball

1. Tape a center-court box on the court, 6 feet by 6 feet (1.8 m by 1.8 m), using painter's tape.

2. Place yourself inside the center-court box, and get into the down and ready position.

3. Cross over to the left, get your racquet up, step or lunge (whichever you are practicing), and then set your feet and swing.

4. Hustle back to the center-court box and get down and ready, pretending you are waiting for the next shot. Repeat 15 or 20 times on the left side.

5. Repeat the drill to the right side and continue alternating sides.

Add a Ball

1. Now repeat the drill with a ball, practicing all passes to the left, then all passes to the right, and then alternate.

2. Now practice all ceilings to the left, then all ceilings to the right, and then alternate.

Court Position Footwork Checklist: Core, Intermediate, and Advanced

Core	Intermediate	Advanced
Down and ready • Legs are spread shoulder-width apart. • Knees are bent 150-160 degrees. • Bend a little at the waist, about 160-170 degrees. • Racquet is up about waist high to go forehand or backhand. • Grip is a relaxed backhand grip as 90 percent of shots go to the backhand side. • Keep your eyes on the ball. • Weight is forward on the front part of your foot, ready to push off and pivot.	Down and ready • Legs are spread 1 ft (.3 m) wider than shoulder-width apart. • Knees are bent 140-150 degrees. • Bend a little more at the waist, about 150-160 degrees. • Weight is a little bit forward on the front part of your foot, ready to push off and pivot.	Down and ready • Legs are spread 2 ft (.6 m) wider than shoulder-width apart. • Knees are bent 130-140 degrees. • Bend even more at the waist, about 140-150 degrees. • Weight is even more forward on the front part of your foot, ready to push off and pivot.
Pivot • Pivot your foot on the heel on the side the ball is going to. This opens your hips so you can move in that direction. • Move toward the ball. • Racquet begins to come up (ERP).	Pivot • All the components happen more quickly.	Pivot • All the components happen even more quickly.
Crossover and lunge step • Push off on the ball of your opposite foot. • Cross over the pivoted foot if the ball is close by, and add a shuffle step if the ball is farther from you. • Cross over with a lunge step if the ball is really far from you, almost out of your reach. • Racquet comes up completely before your opposite foot hits the floor. • Racquet fully extends before your opposite foot hits the floor if the ball is almost out of your reach.	Crossover and lunge step • All the components happen more quickly and a bit more smoothly. • Crossover step is slightly bigger.	Crossover and lunge step • All the components happen even more quickly and more smoothly. • Crossover step is even bigger.

Core	Intermediate	Advanced
Swing and contact point	Swing and contact point	Swing and contact point
• Hitting arm is extended.	• Hitting arm is fully extended.	• Hitting arm is fully extended.
• Racquet head is flat on contact if the ball is within reach or up if the ball is out of reach.	• Racquet head is flatter on contact if the ball is within reach or farther up if the ball is out of reach.	• Racquet head is the flattest on contact if the ball is within reach or farther up if the ball is out of reach.
• Hit off of lead foot.	• Ball contact is slightly lower for all the shots except kill shot.	• Ball contact is even slightly lower for all the shots except kill shots.
• Ball contact is approximately knee high for pass shots.		
• Ball contact is approximately shin high and higher for pass-kill shots.		
• Ball contact is approximately shin high and lower for the kill or re-kill shots, unless the ball is out of your reach, in which case you should go up to the ceiling to save the ball.		
Follow-through	Follow-through	Follow-through
• The racquet head is pointing to the back wall.	• The racquet head is pointing to the back wall or as far around as it can possibly go based on whether you are off balance.	• The racquet head is pointing to the back wall, and when it comes around it should be completely exaggerated.
• Chest and belly button are facing the front wall.	• All components are the same, with quicker head speed.	• All components are the same, with even quicker head speed.
• Eyes are looking up at the ball.		

Summary

Court position is truly the start of your thought processes on the court and of allowing yourself to move up to the intermediate and advanced levels of play. You are no longer just running around without purpose. Instead, you are positioning yourself in the most strategic location possible based on the ball and where your opponent is standing in relation to the ball. Being in center court puts you in the best position possible to get to a majority of the balls, and you will probably win more matches if you are in the box more than your opponent.

Being down and ready and shifting up and back in the box based on where your opponent is hitting the ball is crucial. Once you are down and ready and in the proper position, you can utilize the correct footwork to get you to the ball quickly and efficiently.

You are well on your way to becoming a champion, but remember to be aware of where you are on the court, where your opponent is on the court, and where you need to be on the court.

It is time to use your head, not just your body. This separates the good from the bad, the great from the good, and the champions from the nonchampions. Court position sets the mental tone of the game, so make sure you know where home is—center court.

Chapter 6

Improving Shot Selection

Chapter 5, "Maximizing Court Position," is the first chapter in the book that incorporates the thinking part of the game: the tactics. In chapter 6, we continue to teach you to use your head and to think on the racquetball court as you make conscious decisions of what shots to take in any given situation. In this chapter we cover which shots to take based on where the ball and your opponent are located on the court. This is called shot selection.

Shot selection is defined as taking the right shot at the right time and making your opponent run the farthest distance to get to the ball. It is the offensive player's choice of shots based on himself, the ball, the opponent, and the score. When many of us get into the heat of the battle, we don't think about our shots. You may be guilty of hitting the shot you like or that you feel comfortable with rather than the most effective shot that will win the point. By taking the right shot at the right time and hitting the most effective shot in a given situation, you are playing the percentages. No matter what level of player you are—pro, advanced, or intermediate—playing the percentages is a philosophy we teach, preach, and live by. This basic philosophy will help you reach your goal of moving from the intermediate to advanced level of play.

Playing the Percentages

Playing the percentages, in other words, playing high-percentage racquetball, gives you the edge. When you play high-percentage racquetball, you make more shots than you miss; when you play low-percentage racquetball, you miss more shots than you make. If you play the percentages, you're making it more difficult for your opponent, which will cause her to make more mistakes, leading to easy points. Jason has told me, "I can't tell you how many intermediate and advanced players I play that have trouble scoring points against me without forcing me to kill a ball. I hit them hundreds of passes, and eventually they skip the ball because I put them in difficult positions, which frustrates them and then forces them to make a low-percentage shot." Playing the percentages forces your opponent to take difficult shots and allows you to earn the right to kill. Earning the right to kill means you put your opponent in a difficult position, forcing a weak return into the middle of the court.

Playing high-percentage racquetball is one of the keys to being consistent and moving up in your level of play. So many great players and great athletes never reach their potential because they play low-percentage racquetball. Whether their feet are stopped and set or whether the ball is in or out of their hitting zones, they try to shoot and kill everything from everywhere on the court, no matter what. High-percentage racquetball is the philosophy that will win you more points, more games, and more matches.

COMMON MISTAKES: PLAYING THE PERCENTAGES

ERROR: The number one mistake most people make is having their dials on kill all the time instead of pass.

CORRECTION: Think of the percentages, and remember the 30 percent principle.

SOLUTION: There is a time and place for every shot, and when you are in front of your opponent is the time when you should think *kill*. When you are deep in the court, off balance, or out of position, use the pass, ceiling, or Z—not the kill—or you will give your opponent unnecessary setups or just give free points when you skip the ball.

Now that we have established what shot selection is, we break the chapter into four parts and help you develop the best shot selection possible. This is what can make you or break you as you move up in levels of play.

1. Shot selection formula
2. When to go offensive or defensive
3. Shot selection during the rally
4. Shot selection during the return of serve

If the strokes are the foundation of your racquetball dream house, we are building the frame with your shot selection and good court position. Let's get started.

Shot Selection Formula

Here is a simple formula that summarizes how to determine what shot to use in any given situation, during the rally as well as return of serve. All four of these factors are important for deciding your shot selection.

$$A \quad + \quad B \quad + \quad C \quad + \quad D \quad = \quad E$$

A = You (court position and skill level)
B = Ball (height, speed, and angle)
C = Opponent (court position and skill level)
D = Score (of the game or match)
E = Shot selection (which shot to take)

A = You   Ask yourself, *Where am I located on the court?* and *What is my skill level shooting this shot from this position?* Be honest with yourself, and hit only the shots you are capable of making. Don't get fancy and try something you haven't hit before or are not good at.

B = Ball   What is the height, speed, and angle of the ball coming off the front wall, back wall, or side wall? Is the ball jamming you, or are you running forward to save the ball because it is almost out of your reach? Remember from chapter 4 what the best shots are given these elements.

- If the ball is coming off the front wall, you can wait for it to drop and go offensive, but if it is too high on your body, then you can go defensive.
- If the ball is coming off the back wall and you have a setup, go offensive and put the ball where your opponent is not.
- If the ball is coming off the side wall, back away from the ball so you don't jam yourself, and then you can wait for it to drop and go offensive. But if it is too high on your body, then you can go defensive.
- If for some reason you do get jammed, hit defensive.
- If you are running forward to save the ball because it is almost out of your reach, hit a defensive shot; do not try to go offensive and force a winner.

C = Opponent   Be aware of your opponent's position at all times, and know his skill level so you know what he can and cannot handle.

- You want to hit the ball where your opponent is not, making him run the farthest distance to get to the ball and hitting on the run. When your opponent hits on the run, he will make more mistakes than if his feet were stopped and set.
- By paying attention to your opponent's skill level, you can give him something he cannot handle, leading to mistakes. More mistakes means more opportunities for you to take advantage of these setups and go offensive for scoring opportunities or to put your opponent on the defense again.

D = Score   Knowing the score is important because it gives you valuable information as to when you can go offensive or defensive and when to play higher-percentage racquetball. Here are a couple of examples:

- If you won the first game and are leading in the second game, continue to do what you are doing to win the next game and match.
- If you lost the first game and are behind in the second game, play smarter and higher percentage to work your way back into the match to force a tiebreaker.

E = Shot Selection   If you add all four of these factors together, it will give you a great indication of what shot to hit in order to move up in your level of play. The higher you go, the more shot selection plays a critical part in your winning or losing a match and becoming the champion you want to be. We have a sample scenario below to show you how the formula works:

A. You: You are at the dotted line in the middle of the court.

B. Ball: The ball is below your knee in your hitting zone.

C. Opponent: Your opponent is trapped on the left wall at the short line because she did not move back into good center-court position after she hit.

D. Score: You won the first game and are ahead in the second game, and you want to extend the lead with a good high-percentage shot.

E. Shot selection: Your choice of shots should be to hit the ball with your forehand and take a down-the-line passing shot. This blocks your opponent out. By hitting to the right side of the court, you are hitting the ball where your opponent is not, making her run the farthest distance to get to the ball and forcing her to hit on the run.

COMMON MISTAKES: SHOT SELECTION FORMULA

ERROR: You are unaware of your opponent's position and just hit the shot you like and that feels most comfortable instead of hitting the shot that's most effective in that situation.

CORRECTION: Hit the shot that will make your opponent move the farthest distance to get to the ball. Hit as far away from him as possible.

SOLUTION: Making your opponent hit on the run will force more errors and give you more scoring opportunities. You will have much less success if you hit the ball right back to your opponent for an easy setup and an offensive shot.

ERROR: You are unaware of the ball position and just hit the ball even though it is out of your hitting zone.

CORRECTION: Be aware of the height, speed, and angle of the ball, and take the appropriate shot.

SOLUTION: Take the right shot for where the ball is in your hitting zone and you will be more consistent. If you force your shots, you will tend to skip the ball, giving your opponent an easy point or leaving the ball up for an easy setup. Either way, it is a costly mistake.

ERROR: You are unaware of the score and just hit your favorite shot, not the shot most effective in that situation.

CORRECTION: Know the score and take the appropriate shot (more about this in chapter 7).

SOLUTION: If you are behind, you must go higher percentage to work your way back into the game or match, otherwise you may skip away the game or match. If you are ahead, you have a greater margin of error, so you can continue to use the shots that have been working rather than just play survival racquetball.

Shot Selection Checklist: Core, Intermediate, and Advanced

Core	Intermediate	Advanced
You Where are you located on the court? • Knowing how far you are from the front wall, back wall, and side walls plays a factor in taking the right shot. What level player are you? What shot are you capable of making from that position? • You should be hitting shots such as the pass, pass-kill, kill, pinch, reverse pinch, and ceiling.	You • Start to be aware of where you are located on the court (the 8 positions) so that you become more comfortable. • Start to think more on the court. • Hit off the back wall; use wide-angle, overhead, and sidearm passes; and introduce the Z shot.	You • Use all 8 positions proficiently. • Think more clearly and more often. • Cut the ball off; use a variety of shots such as splat, short hop, and mid hop; and perfect the Z shot.
Ball • Height: Learn to let the ball drop waist to knee high and lower. • Speed: Learn how to handle the different speeds. • Angle: Learn how to handle the different angles.	Ball • Height: Feel more comfortable with the ball dropping closer to knee high and with reading the ball. So if a ceiling ball is short, take advantage with an overhead or sidearm pass. • Speed: Feel more comfortable. • Angle: Feel more comfortable.	Ball • Height: Feel more comfortable with the ball dropping knee high and lower and with taking the appropriate shots. Also be totally comfortable reading the ball so you can make split-second decisions on what shot to take in any given situation. • Speed: Feel even more comfortable. • Angle: Feel even more comfortable.
Opponent Where is your opponent positioned on the court? • Watch where he is located in the center-court box or if he is in the box at all. What level player is your opponent? What shots is he capable of making? • He should be able to handle shots such as the pass, pass-kill, kill, pinch, reverse pinch, and ceiling.	Opponent • Be more aware of where he is located on the court. • Start to look at the 8 positions. • He is able to handle more of the intermediate shots.	Opponent • Be the most aware of where he is located on the court. • Know the 8 positions proficiently. • He is able to handle more of the advanced shots.
Score • Know the score.	Score • Know the score, and start utilizing it to take the appropriate shot in that situation.	Score • Know the score, and use it to your advantage while choosing a shot to hit.

When to Go Offensive or Defensive

Now that we have discussed the shot selection formula, let's take the confusion and guesswork out of when to go offensive versus defensive. Too often players do not know whether to take an offensive shot or a defensive shot in particular situations.

Let's define offensive shots and defensive shots again:

offensive shot—Ends the rally, scores a point, or puts your opponent on the defense.

defensive shot—Draws your opponent out of center court or buys you time.

We've made it easy for you to see when you should go for what shot. We've broken the court into three clearly marked zones (figure 6.1).

In zone 1 you want to go offensive whenever possible (95 percent of the time) because you are closest to your target, the front wall, where it is easier to score a point. But if you are off balance, jammed, or running forward to try to get your racquet on the ball, you want to go defensive (5 percent of the time).

In zone 2 you want to go offensive about 80 percent of the time because you are moving farther from the target. Your chances of making a good offensive shot drop a little, but you still want to be offensive and shoot the ball when it is in your hitting zone, especially as you move up to the advanced level of play. This keeps the pressure on your opponent. Remember, 20 percent of the time you are going to go defensive when your feet aren't stopped and set and you are unable to rip a good offensive shot consistently because you are off balance, reaching, or jammed. The last thing you want to do is try to make something out of nothing and force an offensive shot when you should be going with a defensive shot to buy yourself time and put your opponent in the deep part of the court.

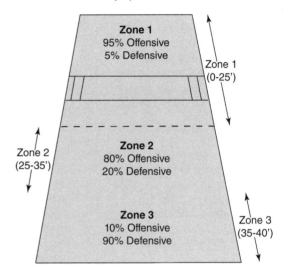

Figure 6.1 Zone diagram.

In zone 3 you want to go offensive the least (10 percent of the time) because you are in the deepest part of the court, the farthest from your target (the front wall), making it a low-percentage shot. Only when the ball comes off the back wall or a ceiling ball drops short should you attempt to go offensive (probably a pass); otherwise you should be defensive, which probably occurs 90 percent of the time.

Jason likes to have a trigger when playing. He defines his trigger as the shot he's most likely to take based on his opponent's habits as well as where he is on the court and where the ball is in his hitting zone. He typically has one offensive and one defensive trigger.

If Jason is in the front court (zone 1) and the ball is not in his hitting zone or he's off balance, his defensive trigger against all players is the Z shot.

If Jason is on the front right side of the court (zone 1) and his opponent is in the back left side of the court (zone 3), and his opponent has a habit of not moving back quickly into center-court position, his offensive trigger is a down-the-line pass-kill. Conversely, if Jason's opponent has the habit of moving back very quickly into center court, then Jason's offensive trigger will be to pass the ball back to the same side his opponent just hit the ball from.

If Jason is on the front left side of the court, near the side wall (zone 1 and 2), and his opponent likes to hit the ball down the line and stays on the left side after hitting the ball, Jason's offensive trigger is to splat the ball. If Jason's opponent cheats, or moves up too quickly, then Jason's offensive trigger is to hit the ball right back down the line (pass).

We are confident that the diagram in figure 6.1 will take the confusion out of going offensive versus defensive. If you understand this principle off the court, you will have more success on the court when the ball is traveling at different speeds and coming off the wall at different angles and spins.

COMMON MISTAKES: OFFENSIVE VERSUS DEFENSIVE

ERROR: In zone 1 you go offensive no matter what, even if you are off balance and reaching for the ball.

CORRECTION: In zone 1 when you are off balance and reaching for the ball, you need to go to the ceiling or hit a Z ball.

SOLUTION: Go up to the ceiling or hit a Z shot because it keeps you in the rally and buys you time to recover. If you try to shoot you may skip the ball, giving your opponent the gift of an easy point or leaving the ball up for any easy setup for your opponent because you are out of position with no time to recover. Either way it is a costly mistake.

ERROR: In zone 2 you hit too many defensive shots because you have poor footwork, are not watching the ball, or just do not know what to do so you play it safe and go up.

CORRECTION: If your feet are stopped and set and you have an opportunity, then go offensive more (80 percent of the time).

SOLUTION: Think offensive more than defensive so you do not lose prime opportunities. This is where drilling and practice come in so you have the confidence to take advantage of those offensive opportunities.

ERROR: In zone 3 you go offensive too much. Not only that, you try to kill the ball from zone 3 time after time, no matter what. It almost feels as if it feeds your ego.

CORRECTION: Keep the 30 percent principle in mind and think *pass, pass-kill,* or *ceiling* from zone 3. Remember, the farther back you go in the court, the less likely you will be able to effectively kill the ball, so the percentages go down drastically to maybe 20 percent, or 15 percent, or even 10 percent.

SOLUTION: Do not think *kill* from zone 3. Use the pass shot because it will put pressure on your opponent rather than give her easy points she did not have to earn.

Shot Selection During the Rally

You just learned when to go offensive versus defensive, based on where you are located on the court. Now we are going to tell you what shot choices you have during the rally as well as on the return of serve. In chapter 5 we cover the eight court positions. Here we are going to cover the particular shot choices you have from each of those positions.

The shot you hit is completely dependent on the four factors that determine shot selection. The two most important factors are where the ball is and where your opponent is positioned on the court.

Keep the 30 percent principle in mind at all times when you are determining what shot to hit. Remember that 30 percent of all balls can be killed from the dotted line. A kill shot is defined as a shot that hits 6 inches (15 cm) and lower on the front wall and bounces twice before the short line. The farther back you go in the court, the less likely you will be able to effectively kill the ball, so the percentages go down drastically.

With this in mind, let's take a look at all eight positions we have given you. For all these positions, we share our top three choices, with number one being the high-percentage shot, so you will be less predictable and more deceptive—the key to smart shot selection. These examples illustrate high-percentage racquetball based solely on you, your opponent, and the ball.

Position 1   Offensive player is deep in the court, approximately 35 feet (10.7 m) from the front wall, off to one side of the court, not in the middle (figure 6.2). Defensive player is down and ready, watching the ball over her right or left shoulder, and positions herself in the middle of the center-court box. Keeping the 30 percent principle in mind, the offensive player should be going for one of these three shots:

1. Down-the-line pass—number one choice of the pros because it covers the shortest distance, giving the opponent less time to react, and it pulls the opponent out of the middle
2. Crosscourt pass
3. Pinch

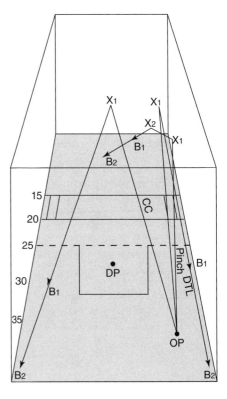

Figure 6.2   Position 1.

Position 2 Offensive player moves up to approximately 25 feet (7.6 m), or the dotted line, off to one side of the court, not in the middle (figure 6.3). Defensive player is down and ready, watching the ball, and moves up to the front half of the center-court box. Keeping the 30 percent principle in mind, the offensive player should be going for one of these three shots:

1. Down-the-line pass—places offensive player between the ball and the opponent, which gives the offensive player an advantage
2. Crosscourt or wide-angle pass
3. Down-the-line kill

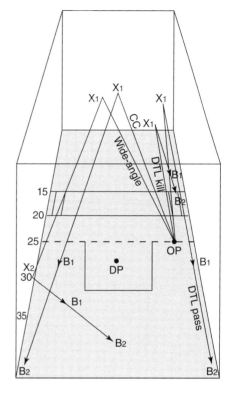

Figure 6.3 Position 2.

Position 3 Offensive player moves up to the short line, off to one side of the court, not in the middle (figure 6.4). Defensive player is down and ready, watching the ball, and moves up toward the dotted line in the middle of the front half of the center-court box. Keeping the 30 percent principle in mind, the offensive player should be going for one of these three shots:

1. Down-the-line kill
2. Pinch
3. Crosscourt kill

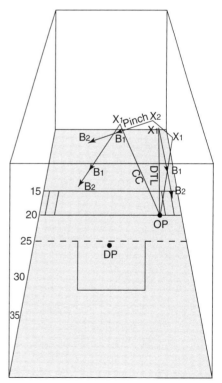

Figure 6.4 Position 3.

Position 4   Offensive player is anywhere at the front wall (figure 6.5). Defensive player is down and ready, watching the ball, and moves up to the middle of the dotted line, but no farther up. Keeping the 30 percent principle in mind, the offensive player should be going for one of these three shots:

1.   Down-the-line kill
2.   Pinch
3.   Crosscourt kill

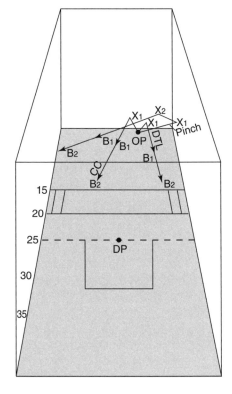

Figure 6.5   Position 4.

Position 5   Offensive player is at the short line, in the middle (figure 6.6). Defensive player is down and ready, watching the ball, and is on or slightly behind the dotted line in the middle. Keeping the 30 percent principle in mind, the offensive player should be going for one of these three shots:

1.   Down-the-line kill
2.   Crosscourt kill
3.   Pinch

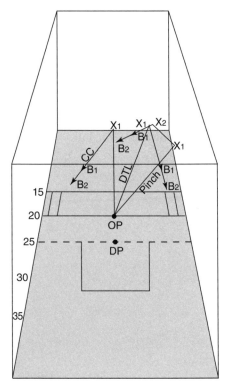

Figure 6.6   Position 5.

Position 6 Offensive player is at the dotted line, in the middle (figure 6.7). Defensive player is down and ready, watching the ball, and drops back to the back half of the center-court box in the middle. Keeping the 30 percent principle in mind, the offensive player should be going for one of these three shots:

1. Down-the-line kill or pass-kill
2. Crosscourt kill or pass-kill
3. Pinch

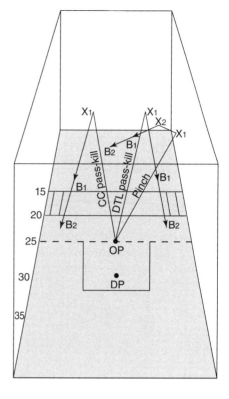

Figure 6.7 Position 6.

Position 7 Offensive player is deep in the court, approximately 35 feet (10.7 m) and back, in the middle (figure 6.8). Defensive player is down and ready, watching the ball, and has one foot in the center-court box on one side of the court, preferably on his backhand side. Keeping the 30 percent principle in mind, the offensive player should be going for one of these three shots:

1. Down-the-line pass
2. Crosscourt pass, hitting behind him as he commits
3. Pinch

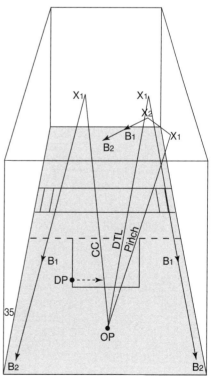

Figure 6.8 Position 7.

Position 8 Offensive player has the defensive player trapped, off to one side of the court, not in the middle (figure 6.9). Defensive player is trapped on the wall because she didn't move back to center court after she hit her shot. She is vulnerable to everything, giving up 95 percent of the court—the biggest mistake you can make in court positioning. Keeping the 30 percent principle in mind, the offensive player should be going for one of these three shots:

1. Crosscourt pass
2. Crosscourt pass-kill
3. Pinch

This is one of the few times the offensive player should run around the backhand to hit the forehand because it puts the opponent in the worst position possible.

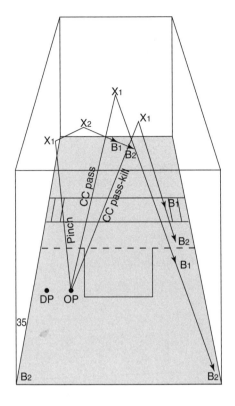

Figure 6.9 Position 8.

We designed the following chart as yet another way to make it easy for you to check your shot selection based on your position and your opponent's position.

Shot Selection Chart

OPPONENT'S POSITION (DEFENSIVE)	YOUR POSITION (OFFENSIVE)		
	Front court	Center court	Back court
Front court	Use a pass, ceiling, or Z shot. Do not kill.	Use a DTL pass, CC pass, wide-angle pass, ceiling shot, or Z shot. Do not kill.	Use a DTL pass, CC pass, or ceiling shot. Do not kill.
Center court	Use a kill, pinch kill, reverse pinch, or DTL pass-kill.	Use a pinch kill, DTL pass, wide-angle pass, ceiling shot, or Z shot.	Use a DTL pass, CC pass, or ceiling shot.
Back court	Use a kill, pinch kill, reverse pinch, or DTL pass-kill. Do not pass.	Use a kill, pinch kill, reverse pinch, or DTL pass-kill. Do not pass.	Use a DTL pass-kill, CC pass kill, or splat if close to wall. Do not pass.

COMMON MISTAKES: SHOT SELECTION DURING A RALLY

Position 1

Offensive player (you) is at 35 feet (10.7 m), off to one side or the other.

ERROR: You shoot the kill shot from too deep.

CORRECTION: Offensive player should shoot the pass if there is an offensive opportunity.

SOLUTION: The pass is the best choice because the odds of shooting an effective kill shot from the back court are substantially lower than 30 percent.

Positions 2, 3, and 6

Offensive player (you) is at 20 or 25 feet (6.1 or 7.6 m), off to one side or the other or the middle, and the defensive player is in good position behind you.

ERROR: You shoot the pass.

CORRECTION: Offensive player needs to kill or pinch.

SOLUTION: A pinch or kill keeps the ball up front because your opponent is behind you and deeper.

Position 4

Offensive player (you) is anywhere at the front wall, approximately 1 to 2 feet (.3 to .6 m) away. Defensive player runs up with the offensive player.

ERROR: You dink or tap the ball right to the defensive player.

CORRECTION: Offensive player should go for the pass, taking advantage of the defensive player's poor positioning.

SOLUTION: By hitting the pass, you are putting the ball where your opponent is not.

Position 7

Offensive player (you) is at 35 feet (10.7 m), in the middle.

ERROR: Defensive player moves right in front of you and ducks to get out of your way. You hit around your opponent and go up to the ceiling.

CORRECTION: Offensive player should hold up and get the penalty hinder because the defensive player cannot move in front of the offensive player and take away the offensive shot.

SOLUTION: You must be able to take your shots without hitting around your opponent. Take the penalty hinder created by the defensive player (see USA Racquetball rules for details).

During the Return of Serve

While you are receiving serve, your thought process should be, What did I do to put myself in this position of returning serve? I would rather be serving because then I can possibly score points. Once you figure out what mistake you made to put you in the back court, you want to store it away in your mind so you do not keep repeating that same mistake over and over again. With this information, you are now ready to focus on the return of serve strategy, which has two objectives:

1. Get the server out of center court and move him back to the deepest part of the court, which is the toughest to score from. This is accomplished with the ceiling ball and passing shots.
2. Get yourself back in center court by moving forward as quickly and efficiently as possible to regain control of the match. When you are in good center-court position, you are in position to cover a majority of the shots your opponent hits.

While thinking of the two objectives of your return of serve, you also want to keep the 30 percent principle in mind. You know that 30 percent of all balls can be killed from the dotted line, and the farther back in the court that players shoot the ball, the less likely they will be able to effectively kill the ball, so their percentages go down drastically; therefore, the pass and the ceiling ball are the two predominant shots to hit when you are returning serve. The pass and the ceiling ball returns are discussed in detail in chapter 3.

Shot Selection During for Return of Serve

Just as shot selection during a rally is dependent on certain factors, so is your shot selection on the return of serve. Before you can determine what shot you should hit on your return of serve in any given situation, you need to answer the following questions.

How Well Was the Serve Hit?

Here are a few sample questions to get you started:

Question: Did the serve come off the side wall or back wall for a setup?

Answer: If the answer is yes, be aggressive and shoot the pass. If the answer is no, go to the ceiling.

Question: Did the serve end up deep in the back corners because you didn't attack?

Answer: If the answer is yes, then become defensive and hit a ceiling shot. Do not force the shot. Be smart and respect the server's serve. If the answer is no, go for the pass.

Question: Did the lob serve bounce between the short line and dotted line?

Answer: If the answer is yes, then attack and take it up to the ceiling. If the answer is no and the ball comes off the back wall, then shoot the pass; if the ball bounces beyond the dotted line, step up and cut it off and shoot the pass or go up to the ceiling.

We suggest you analyze each and every serve on its own merit and then decide whether you should go offensive or defensive with the return. Too often players try to make something out of nothing and get in trouble. Play the percentages and you will experience much more success on a consistent basis.

What Does the Server Do After the Serve?

Question: Does the server look back as he is getting out of the box?

Answer: If the server does not look back at all or not long enough, he is vulnerable to pretty much any kind of return (ceiling or pass) because reaction time is cut in half. The server can react only as the ball is coming off the front wall; if he had watched his opponent hit the ball, the server could have reacted as soon as the ball was hit.

Question: Does the server backpedal, meaning her back is square to the back wall, or does she come out leading with her shoulder?

Answer: If the server backpedals she will not be able to watch the ball completely, and the server will not be able to get back into good center-court position as quickly and efficiently as possible because her weight would be too far back. In this instance, you want to return the serve with a ceiling or a pass shot because your opponent would not be able to change direction quickly to run down the ball you hit.

Question: Does the server relocate, or shade, to one side of the court or the other rather than back to the middle?

Answer: If the server shades to the right or left side of the court, he is left open to being passed to the opposite side. If the server shades more aggressively to one side of the court, he will create a penalty hinder by taking away your crosscourt pass shot, resulting in a side-out. So without a doubt, pass in this situation.

Question: Does the server not get back far enough, positioning in front of the dotted line?

Answer: Again, in this scenario you would always go for the pass.

What Is Your Skill Level?

Knowing your skill level and what shots you are capable of executing in any given situation is important so you take only those shots you can make and make well. Most players force the return of serve and hit returns they are not capable of making, trying to get a side-out. Unfortunately, they inadvertently create a lot of unforced errors such as outright skips (gifts for opponents because they do not have to do anything to earn the point) or setups (easy opportunities for opponents to hit offensive shots).

What Is Your Opponent's Return of Serve and Skill Level?

Does your opponent like ceiling balls to his backhand?

Does your opponent like down-the-line pass shots to her backhand?

Does your opponent have a difficult time with crosscourt passes because he has a bad knee and cannot move well to the right?

Give your opponent a return of serve she does not like and cannot handle because it will frustrate your opponent into taking more weak shots, which just means more opportunities for you to be aggressive and go offensive.

What Is the Height, Speed, and Angle of the Ball?

Question: Is the ball in or out of your hitting zone?

Answer: If the ball is in your hitting zone, go for the passing shot.

If the ball is out of your hitting zone, go for the ceiling.

Question: Is the ball jamming you?

Answer: If so, return the ball to the ceiling.

Question: Do you have to lunge to return a well-hit drive serve?

Answer: If so, return the ball to the ceiling.

Pay attention to what the ball is doing based on its height, speed, and angle, and make the appropriate return of serve based on the information you have gathered.

Return Policy

You need to know what your return of serve will be based on what serve your opponent is hitting to you. We will go through all the serves from chapter 3 and give you the different scenarios and what shots to hit with each given serve.

There are two very important things to keep in mind when you are returning serve:

1. Approximately 30 percent of all balls can be killed from the dotted line (25 feet [7.6 m] from the front wall). The odds of killing the ball go down the farther back you go. Your return position is 2 to 3 feet (.6 to .9 m) from the back wall (37 to 38 feet [11.3 to 11.6 m] from the front wall), so your odds of killing the ball go down drastically to 20, 15, or maybe even 10 percent.

2. The purpose of the return of serve is to get the server out of the middle and put your opponent in the most difficult position to score while regaining center court yourself.

With this in mind, think *pass* when you have an offensive opportunity and think *ceiling* when you have a defensive opportunity. Let's examine the returns:

Drive Serves

1. Standard drive serve
   - Good serve: Cross over and lunge toward the front wall or side wall, and go up to the ceiling.
   - Bad serve: If the serve hits the side wall or comes off the back wall for a setup, go for the pass.
2. Intermediate drive serves
   - Drive Z serve
     - Good serve: Hit the ball before it hits the second side wall, and go up to the ceiling.
     - Bad serve: If the serve comes off the side wall short, around 25 to 30 feet (7.6 to 9.1 m) instead of 35 feet (10.7 m) from the front wall, let it hit the side wall and then shoot the pass. If the serve comes off the back wall, hit the pass.
   - Drive jam
     - Good serve: The ball is coming right at your body, so go up to the ceiling.
     - Bad serve: The ball comes across your body for a setup, so shoot the pass.

3. Advanced drive serves
   - Drive wrap serve
     - Good serve: Turn with it as you follow the ball, and go up to the ceiling.
     - Bad serve: Move with the ball, and shoot the pass.
   - Drive nick serve
     - Good serve: Cross over and lunge forward, and pop ball to the ceiling.
     - Bad serve: The ball comes across your body and is high, creating a setup, so shoot the pass.

Lob serve

1. Standard lob serve
   - Good serve: Try to hit it before it goes into the back corner or hits the side wall, and go to the ceiling.
   - Bad serve: If the ball comes off the side wall or back wall, shoot the pass. If it comes long, beyond the dotted line on a fly, cut it off and shoot the pass. If it hits on or near the dotted line, attack and hit an overhead pass only on the forehand side or a short hop or mid hop, based on your level of play.

2. Intermediate lob serves
   - High and half lob nick serves
     - Good serve: After the ball hits the side wall between knee and waist, go up to the ceiling.
     - Bad serve: If the ball comes off the side wall or back wall, shoot the pass.

3. Advanced lob serves
   - Half lob kick serve
     - Good serve: Before the ball hits the side wall, move up and hit the ball to the ceiling.
     - Bad serve: If the ball comes off the side wall or back wall as a setup, shoot the pass.
   - Three-quarter lob Z serve
     - Good serve: Hit the ball before it hits the second side wall, and go up for a ceiling or a more aggressive overhead pass only on forehand side.
     - Bad serve: If the ball comes off the side wall or back wall, shoot the pass.

When Jason is returning a drive serve, he concentrates on the ball, looking for patterns, ball toss, contact point, and unnecessary motions. This helps increase his reaction time and get a better jump on the ball.

When Jason is returning a lob serve, he moves up and attacks the ball. He looks to take the ball to the ceiling and move toward center court, cut the ball off if it is floating over the dotted line, or hit an overhead or sidearm pass if serve is near the dotted live. All of these shots put extra pressure on his opponent.

COMMON MISTAKES: SHOT SELECTION DURING THE RETURN OF SERVE

ERROR: You try to kill the ball.

CORRECTION: Shoot the pass or ceiling on the return of serve.

SOLUTION: Playing the percentages when returning serve is very important because the odds of killing the ball go down the farther back in the court you go, and you are 37 to 38 feet (11.3 to 11.6 m) back. Remember, you are trying to get the server out of the middle and put her in the most difficult position to score from, and you also want to regain center-court position.

COMMON MISTAKES: DETERMINING SHOT SELECTION FOR RETURN OF SERVE

ERROR: You hit the return you like rather than the return that is most effective in that situation.

CORRECTION: Look at all the factors such as how well the serve was hit; what the server does after the serve; your skill level; what your opponent likes or dislikes; your opponent's skill level; and lastly the height, speed, and angle of the ball or the type of serve, and use these factors to determine the return of serve.

SOLUTION: A smart return gets your opponent out of the middle and puts him in the last 3 to 5 feet (.9 to 1.5 m) of the court. Otherwise you wind up hitting too many skips or weak returns because you are forcing your return, which results in easy points for the server.

COMMON MISTAKES: SHOT SELECTION FOR THE RETURN OF SERVE

ERROR: You think *kill* rather than *pass*.

CORRECTION: Start to hit more passes.

SOLUTION: Hit the pass or else you will skip too many balls, resulting in too many gifts for the server.

ERROR: You wait for the lob serve in the back corners and get trapped.

CORRECTION: Move up on the lob serve, and take it early.

SOLUTION: By moving up on the lob serve and taking it early, you accomplish these three things:

1. You put yourself in better court position.
2. You put pressure on the server.
3. You give the server much less time to relocate into good center-court position.

ERROR: When you get jammed with a serve, you try to shoot the ball.

CORRECTION: Go up to the ceiling to buy yourself time.

SOLUTION: Hit a ceiling ball or else you will wind up hitting too many skips or weak returns because you are forcing your return, which results in easy points for the server.

ERROR: You try to return the lob nick before the side wall rather than after.

CORRECTION: Let the ball hit the side wall, and then take it to the ceiling after the bounce.

SOLUTION: Do not cut the ball off before it hits the side wall; if you do, you will make mistakes because you have to hit the ball too high or too far up.

ERROR: You return the drive or lob Z after it hits the second side wall rather than before.

CORRECTION: Hit the ball before it hits the second side wall when possible.

SOLUTION: Once the ball hits the second side wall, anything can happen because more natural spin is imparted on the ball, making it harder to return. Also if the Z serve is hit well and you let it hit the second side wall, it will end up too deep in the court, making it almost impossible to return.

Return of Serve Shot Selection Checklist: Core, Intermediate, and Advanced

Core	Intermediate	Advanced
Core drive serve • Good serve: Cross over and lunge, and go up to the ceiling. • Bad serve: On a setup off side or back wall, go for the pass.	Drive Z serve • Good serve: Hit the ball before it hits the 2nd side wall, and go up to the ceiling. • Bad serve: If it sets up short off second side wall or comes off the back wall, shoot a pass.	Drive wrap serve • Good serve: Turn, follow the ball, and go up to the ceiling. • Bad serve: Move with the ball and shoot the pass.
	Drive jam serve • Good serve: Ball is coming at body, so go up to the ceiling. • Bad serve: Ball is coming across the body for a setup, so shoot the pass.	Drive nick serve • Good serve: Cross over and lunge, and go up to the ceiling. • Bad serve: Ball is hit too high and is a setup, so shoot the pass.
Core lob serve • Good serve: Hit the ball before the side wall or back corner, and go up to the ceiling. • Bad serve: If it is a setup off the side or back wall, shoot the pass. • If it is beyond the dotted line, hit it out of the air (cut the ball off) and shoot the pass. • If it hits near the dotted line, attack and hit a short hop, mid hop, or overhead pass.	High and half lob nick serves • Good serve: Hit the ball after the side wall, and go up to the ceiling. • Bad serve: If it is a setup off the side or back wall, go for the pass.	Half lob kick serves • Good serve: Hit the ball before it hits the side wall, and go up to the ceiling. • Bad serve: If it is a setup off the side or back wall, go for the pass.
		Three-quarter lob Z serve • Good serve: Hit the ball before it hits the second side wall and goes up to the ceiling, or hit an overhead pass for a more aggressive return. • Bad serve: If it is a setup off the side or back wall, go for the pass.

Rules of Thumb

Here are a few simple but smart rules you should follow in order to put more wins in the win column and fewer losses in the loss column.

1. Hit where your opponent is not.
    - When your opponent is in the front court, in front of the dotted line, hit the ball deep in the back court with a ceiling, Z, or pass shot based on the height of the ball.
    - When your opponent is behind you in deep court, behind the dotted line, then hit the kill, pinch, or reverse pinch if the ball is in your hitting zone.
    - When your opponent is on the right side of the court, shoot to the left side with a pinch to the right corner, or hit a pass or pass-kill to the left side of the court based on the height of the ball.
    - When your opponent is on the left side of the court, shoot to the right side with a pinch to the left corner, or hit a pass or pass-kill to the right side of the court based on the height of the ball.
2. Make your opponent run the farthest distance to the ball because more mistakes occur when hitting on the run rather than having your feet stopped and set.
3. Pass first, kill second. If you can win a rally with a pass shot, why kill the ball? The pass is a higher-percentage shot.
4. Keep your body between the ball and your opponent when possible (use your body as a pick, like in basketball).
5. Minimize your skips, and capitalize on your opponent's mistakes.
    - Don't skip away the game (or more important, the match) by going for a low-percentage shot when the ball is out of your hitting zone, or you are off balance, or you are out of position, or you do not have that shot in your repertoire, or any other situation in which you are at risk of not making the shot. Be aware of the shot selection formula because that will help you tremendously in deciding what shot to take in any given situation.
    - If you are skipping a lot, it means you are going for the bottom board too much—hitting too many kills. The more you kill, the more you skip. If this is happening, raise your contact point and go for the pass-kill or pass, not the kill.
6. When you are off balance or out of position, are being jammed, or can barely get to the ball, go up to the ceiling or hit a Z shot. Do not shoot the ball.
7. When you are returning serve, you are approximately 37 to 38 feet (11.3 to 11.6 m) from the front wall, and your chances of effectively killing the ball are extremely low. Remember, 30 percent of all balls can be killed from the dotted line, and it is even lower the farther back you go in the court. Playing the percentages when you are returning serve is extremely important because if you take a low-percentage shot such as a kill or pinch two things can occur:
    - You could skip the ball and give your opponent an easy point.
    - You could leave the ball up, and since your opponent is up in the front court after serving, he can take advantage of your mistake and score an easy point.

Don't get suckered into taking a low-percentage shot, because you are doomed from the start. Take a high-percentage shot such as a ceiling or pass shot to accomplish your goals of pulling your opponent out of center court and allowing you time to regain good center-court position.

Shot Selection Drills

As we talked about earlier, often players hit shots in a game without thinking; they just bang the ball, hitting the shot they like or feel comfortable with, but not the shot that is most effective in that situation. Shot selection involves hitting the right shot at the right time. To effectively raise your level of play, you must not only learn the four factors that determine shot selection (you, the ball, your opponent, and the score) but also execute the choice of shots based on those factors. You have already drilled the different shots, and hopefully you have become somewhat proficient and consistent at the pass, the ceiling, the pinch, the reverse pinch, the off the back wall, and so on, but now you need to be able to make these shots in a game situation. The following drills will progressively get you ready for the thinking part of the game. Do not forget to keep track as you have done in all the other chapters.

Alone Setup Drills

Put your bag on the court to represent where your opponent is located, and practice the correct three choices of shots based on your opponent's position and the ball's position. Once you take 15 or 20 shots from that position, move the bag to a different location and repeat the drill. Keep doing this for as many scenarios as you want to practice.

1. Practice only one particular shot off of the same setup shot 15 or 20 times, and keep track as suggested in chapter 8. Do only one setup at a time.

Example:

Set up a short ceiling ball, shoot the following 15 or 20 times: pinch, pass crosscourt, pass down the line, and overhead pass.

Off the back wall, hit the following 15 or 20 times: pass down the line, pinch, and pass crosscourt.

2. Practice different shots off of the same setup shot, calling out the shot you will be taking, until you hit 15 or 20 shots. Keep track.

Example:

Off the back wall, set up and call out a pass down the line, 1 time.

Off the back wall, set up and call out a splat, 1 time.

Off the back wall, set up and call out a pass-kill down the line, 2 times.

Partner Setup Drills

Once you get proficient alone, you are ready to team up with a partner to test your skills even more and have a little fun in the process. The beauty of working with a partner is that he or she can see things you may not be able to see or may not be aware of and point them out, making your drill session even more valuable. Each person will do both tasks: setting the partner up as well as being the offensive player hitting the shots you are practicing.

1. Your partner hits you the same setup shot 15 or 20 times and you return it with the same offensive shot 15 or 20 times, and you keep track. Hit only one setup at a time.

Example:

Partner makes a shot that hits the front wall and then the side wall for a setup, and you hit a pass down the line, 15 or 20 times.

Partner makes a shot that hits the front wall and then the side wall for a setup, and you hit a pinch, 15 or 20 times.

Partner hits a ceiling ball too hard so that it comes off the back wall for a setup, and you hit a pinch, 15 or 20 times.

Partner hits a ceiling ball too hard so that it comes off the back wall for a setup, and you hit a pass crosscourt, 15 or 20 times.

2. Hit continuous setups one right after the other, always getting back to center court after you hit your shot to wait for the next setup shot.

Example:

Your partner sets up a pinch shot that is too high for a setup, and you hit a pass down the line then you go back to center court. Without catching the ball, your partner keeps setting you up with the same high pinch shot, and you keep hitting a pass down the line always getting back to center court. Do this 15 or 20 times.

3. Your partner hits you different setup shots and calls out the shot you will be taking until you have made 15 or 20 shots, and you keep track. Do this drill two ways:

Hit only one setup at a time.

Example:

Set up off the back wall and call out a pass down the line, 1 time.

Set up along the left side wall and call out a splat, 1 time.

Set up off a short ceiling ball and call out a pass-kill down the line, 2 times.

Hit continuous setups one right after the other, always getting back to center court after you hit your shot to wait for the next setup shot.

Example:

Your partner sets up a splat shot that is too high for a setup, and calls out a pass down the line. Without catching the ball, your partner now sets you up with a side wall/front wall/side wall set up, and calls out a pinch. Do this 15 or 20 times.

Shot Selection Diagram Drill (Situation Analysis)

This is a great practice tool to make sure you know the right shot choices. Using the diagram in figure 6.10 (make copies for each situation you create), put a defensive player in one position and an offensive player in another position. Write down at least three choices of shots you can take in that situation, starting with the highest-percentage shot. If you cannot do this off the court on paper, how can you do it on the court when the ball is traveling in excess of 100 mph (161 km/h)? There are no shortcuts here—you need to know what shot choices you have in any given scenario in order to improve your level of play and build a championship game.

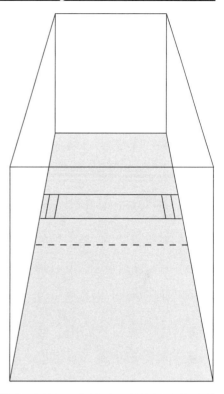

Figure 6.10 Shot selection diagram.

Summary

Smart shot selection is an extremely important part of your game—you cannot just aimlessly hit any shot, anywhere, at any time if you expect to move up the ladder on your way to becoming an advanced player. Whether you are playing a rally and trying to put your opponent on the defense or returning the serve and trying to get your opponent out of the middle so you can regain good center-court position, shot selection needs to be in the forefront of your mind. Every time your racquet hits the ball, you need to have an objective.

Many aspects of racquetball affect each other. None may have greater repercussions than taking the incorrect shot. Being able to not only perform the basic shots associated with your level but also know when to use each shot can dramatically affect the outcome of every match you play. One or two bad choices can lead to a countless run of points for your opponent. Conversely, if you hit the correct high-percentage shots, consistently keeping your opponent off balance and forcing him to take difficult shots, you will set him up to fail and turn the tables to score easy points. The tools we have given to you in this chapter to carry out smart shot selection will help you accomplish this.

Now that we have helped you think more clearly on the court and make better shot choices in any given situation, you are well on your way to raising your level of play and becoming the champion you want to be.

Chapter 7

Developing Game Plans and Match Strategy

We are going to cover two topics that are often overlooked and very much needed as you become an intermediate and then an advanced player: formulating and utilizing game plans and learning how to strategize during a match. Unfortunately, most people don't plan or strategize in everyday life let alone on the racquetball court. When you plan and strategize before a situation gets out of hand, you are being proactive, which is taking control of the match. If you wait until after something happens (i.e., being reactive), you are letting the match control you. People often do not realize that in order to be successful on and off the court, in anything you do, you need to be proficient in game planning and strategizing. Let's define the two:

- **Game plan:** A plan of action based on your strengths and weaknesses as well as your opponent's strengths and weaknesses.
- **Strategy:** A method of achieving a specific goal or end result, which is to play your best to win the match. Your strategy helps you carry out your game plan.

Planning and strategizing holds true for racquetball as well. If you just step out on a court without a plan and a particular strategy, you will be doomed from the start. You will always be reacting to the situation rather than creating the situation. You are in a much better position to win when creating the situation right from the beginning of the match.

Here is an example of planning and strategizing you can relate to in racquetball:

Situation: You are playing in a semifinal match Sunday morning to advance to the finals.

Game plan:

- You watched your opponent play Saturday night.

- Your opponent has a strong drive and drive Z, but he rushes his serve, so you want to take your full 10 seconds when receiving serve.

- Your opponent's forehand is strong, but his backhand is very weak, so you want to hit the ball hard and deep to his backhand side and even serve to his backhand.

- Your opponent plays in front of the dotted line most of the time, so you want to hit lots of passes, not pinches and kills.

- Your opponent doesn't always watch the ball, so he is vulnerable to passes and ceilings, which are balls that are hit behind him, giving him no time to react.

Strategy:

- Slow the game down and take control by using your 10 seconds on the serve and service return.

- Use your time-outs when your opponent runs off points and wants to play fast.

- Make sure you are warmed up and ready to go in your first game; do not use your first game as a warm-up.

- You want to be tough from the get-go and put pressure on your opponent because he likes to play fast.

- Since your opponent likes to rush, play one point at a time and be methodical.

You can't wake up Sunday morning and say, "Oh, I have to be at the club in an hour to play my semifinal match," and expect to win.

In this chapter we will teach you both game plans and strategies in detail and discuss the following:

- Game plans
  - Eight areas to look for when assessing a player
  - How to be a racquetball detective
  - How to develop a game plan
- Strategies
  - Foundational strategies
  - Intermediate and advanced strategies

Incorporating these two topics into your game will help you enter both the intermediate and advanced levels of play more easily. Let's get started.

Game Plans

These are the eight most important areas we recommend focusing on when assessing a player and developing a game plan.

1. Stroke Mechanics: If your opponent has flaws in her mechanics, this is where you can really take advantage so your opponent will fall apart from the get-go.

Poor racquet preparation or none at all (swing too small)—You can hit hard at your opponent because her reaction time has diminished greatly, and she will catch the side walls a lot for setups.

Excessive looping racquet movement (swing too big)—The racquet is up rather than up and set, ready to swing. You can hit hard at your opponent because with this excessive motion of the racquet, he will not have time to get it through and swing flat; therefore the ball will be erratic, creating inconsistency.

Curled backhand—You can hit hard at your opponent because with this excessive motion of the racquet (curling and uncurling), she will not have time to swing flat; therefore the ball will be erratic, creating inconsistency.

Poking the backhand—Since your opponent pushes the backhand with no follow-through, you do not want to hit hard because then he can use your power to get the ball to the front wall. You want to hit softer and higher so your opponent has no power to rely on to get the ball to the front wall.

Stiff wrist—By having a stiff wrist, your opponent will be guiding the ball to the front wall, losing power and control. You do not want to hit hard because then your opponent can use your power to help get the ball to the front wall. You want to hit softer and higher so she has no power to rely on to get the ball to the front wall.

Hammer grip or no change of grip—Loss of control and power creates lots of unforced errors because the ball will float for setups or skip for easy points because of the racquet face. Hit the ball low and hard right at your opponent, keeping the hitting zone small.

No follow-through—The racquet stops prematurely and slows down in the hitting zone. Do not use power against this player because that will help your opponent get the ball to the front wall. Use soft and high shots.

   2. **Court Position:** Here's where you can really exploit your opponent by putting the ball out of reach.Be aware of all these factors not only during the rally but also after the serve and while returning serve.

Too far up—Opponent is in front of the dotted line, so it's easy to pass.

Too far over or shading to one side—This makes it easy to pass to the open court.

Too far back—Opponent is behind the center-court box, so it's easy to pinch, kill, or splat, which keeps the ball in front of the short line and away from your opponent.

Square to the side wall—Opponent is vulnerable to the crosscourt pass because he is facing the side wall. The player will have to take two steps to get to the ball rather than just one if he were facing the front wall, and therefore it takes more time to react to the ball.

Not watching the ball—Opponent's reaction time is cut in half if she does not watch the ball because she does not see the ball coming off your racquet until after it hits the front wall, which is too late.

   3. **Shot Selection:** Look for your opponent's habits.

Goes crosscourt all the time—Look at his feet and look at the contact point, which is based on how he approaches the ball. Since you know he goes crosscourt all the time, you can mentally expect and prepare for that shot, but do not move prematurely.

Runs around her backhand to hit a forehand even if there is no room—If your opponent has no confidence in her backhand and always runs around the shot, she is vulnerable to ceiling balls as well as lob serves right along the backhand wall.

Is predictable—Every time your opponent is in X position he hits a Y shot, so now you can be ready for that shot you know is coming.

Is splat happy—When an opponent is splat happy, she will take splats from all over the court. When you're in trouble, you can hit a ceiling ball and put your opponent as far away from the target as possible, forcing her to either hit you a ceiling ball or go for the splat, which is low percentage from back there. You can therefore expect this mentally. Do not move up prematurely because if she leaves it up, which is highly likely, you are right in position to move up and go on the offensive, taking advantage of that shot left up, or unforced error.

Goes to ceiling—If your opponent lacks confidence to take the balls offensively off the back wall, he will tend to take the ball defensively to the ceiling, leaving no pressure on you.

Has no patience, especially on ceiling balls—Opponent will try to shoot everything. Be ready for shots that are left up. You can also serve lobs.

Does not watch the ball—Opponent's reaction time is cut in half if she does not watch the ball because she will not see the ball coming off your racquet until after it hits the front wall, which is too late.

4. **Serves You Hit:** Serving puts you in the driver's seat and gives you the edge, so pay close attention to your opponent's habits.

Is a power player who loves balls hit low and hard because he likes to rock and roll and rip and shoot—Defuse your opponent's power by hitting serves that are softer and higher, keeping the ball chest to shoulder high and out of his hitting zone.

Has knee problems—If your opponent has knee problems and can't move well, hit low and hard serves into the corners, forcing sudden movement to one direction or the other. Jam serves work here too because typically your opponent will have to change direction when you hit the serve, and the ball is moving away from her toward the side wall.

Plays too far forward on the return of serve, 4 feet (1.2 m) or farther from the back wall—Playing too far up greatly diminishes your opponent's reaction time, so give him anything low and hard such as drives in the corners, jams, wraps, and hard Zs.

Runs around the backhand to hit a forehand on a lob serve—Put the lob serve as close to the side wall as possible, preventing her from turning around and hitting a forehand. This tells you she has no confidence in her backhand or backhand ceiling shot. Frustration will set in big time.

Does not like lob serves (the slower game)—Serve as many lobs as possible. By giving him what he doesn't like, you will see him start talking to himself or even getting upset because of his lack of confidence.

Has trouble returning Z serves—If your opponent does not hit the Z serve before the ball hits the second side wall but instead waits until after the ball will be harder to return because of its natural angle coming off the side wall and the natural spin imparted on the ball, this indicates your opponent cannot return the Z serve effectively. You will get lots of weak returns.

Shades a little to one side or the other on the return of serve—Sometimes a player protecting an injury shades to cover a weakness by moving to one side. This opens up serving to the other side, so pay attention to this.

Shuffles sideways to the ball—If your opponent does not cross over so he is square to the side wall but rather shuffles sideways and is square to the front wall, he is vulnerable to low and hard serves such as the jam and Z serves.

5. **Return of Serve:** What your opponent does and doesn't do gives you lots of information to get back to center-court position after the serve and be ready.

Does not attack the lob serves—If your opponent is passive and does not move up on the lob serves but waits deep in the corners, then all the lob serves will be very effective.

Plays too far forward on the return of serve, 4 feet (1.2 m) or farther from the back wall—Playing too far up greatly diminishes reaction time, and your opponent will have to step back instead of forward. This means the player will be hitting balls behind your opponent rather than out in front of her, catching the side wall a lot for setups and losing power as well.

Shades a little to one side or the other—Sometimes a player protecting an injury shades to cover a weakness by moving to one side. If you serve to the other side, your opponent will get to the serve late and will therefore hit the side wall a lot, so get back into the center-court box quickly to capitalize.

Shuffles sideways to the ball—If your opponent does not cross over to be square to the side wall but rather shuffles sideways to be square to the front wall, she will not have the reach to get the racquet on the ball for a solid hit and will force lots of weak returns. Be ready.

6. **Footwork:** Getting there quickly and efficiently on your first step is critical. So pay close attention to your opponent's footwork—it can tell you what shots to hit.

Steps toward the side wall instead of straight ahead or at a 45-degree angle—You can jam your opponent or hit a ball at an angle off the side wall to handcuff him.

Faces the front wall when hitting a shot—Since she does not turn her body, you can hit right at her or hit a ball at an angle off the side wall to handcuff her. Your opponent will also push the ball and lose power and control.

Steps toward the front wall on his backhand rather than at a 45-degree angle—Your opponent will be going crosscourt on his backhand, so be ready.

Has slow footwork—Your opponent always has to lunge and is truly never set up to hit off her lead foot. She generally hits way out in front for lots of crosscourt shots.

7. **Emotional State:** You want to stay calm and watch your opponent get distracted and rattled. Pick on your opponent's weaknesses because that will usually make her uncomfortable and uneasy. Pay attention to your opponent's comments because they usually are an indication of how frustrated he is and how uncomfortable you are making him feel about his game.

Does not take time on the serve—If your opponent rushes the serve, slow him down by taking the 10 seconds you are allowed to put the ball in play. You are forcing your opponent to play your game. You are in control. Most players like to play fast, and slowing down makes some players upset and causes them to lose their mental focus.

Does not take time on the return of serve—If your opponent rushes the return of serve and gets down and ready immediately, then slow the game down by using the 10-second rule. Once again, you are forcing the opponent to play your game, putting you in control.

Knows the rules and questions close calls—Most players do not like to be challenged and think they know it all. If you have a referee, appeal to him. If you do not have a referee, then agree before the game starts that close calls, or calls you both disagree on, are played over. Be aware of how your opponent handles these rules questions.

Likes a fast and powerful game—Slow the game down because most players cannot adapt to the slower pace and will often get upset. You will force a lot of weak shots.

Gets down on himself and does not have a positive attitude—This negatively affects how your opponent plays.

Gets upset with the referee's calls and loses focus and concentration—This negatively affects how your opponent plays.

8. **Types of Players:** Know your opponent. Is your opponent:

- **a righty or lefty?**

It doesn't matter if your opponent is a righty or a lefty because you need to play to her weaknesses and not which hand she uses to hit the ball. Most people either miss the fact that the opponent is a lefty or righty, or their style of play is simply to hit the shot most comfortable rather than the shot that makes the most sense.

Usually your opponent's backhand is the weaker side, so you should hit to the weaker side. The only difference between a righty and a lefty is which side the backhand is on.

If you encounter a lefty who likes to serve hard drives from position 1, then you can probably expect him to hit a fair amount of Z serves since he has the perfect angle to do so. Watch out for the Zs, and try to jump on them and hit them before the ball hits the second side wall. If you are playing a righty who likes to serve from position 3, do the same thing: Watch for Zs so you can jump on them, giving the opponent fewer options, which usually makes him uneasy.

- **slow or fast?**

Slow—you want to spend a lot of time moving a slow player around the court because they will likely not be able to run down everything.

Fast—There is a common misconception of how to play fast players, which you can use to your advantage. Take it from Jason because he has done this his entire career. "Most people allow the fact that the 'rabbit' gets to everything to affect their shot selection, causing them to hit the ball lower. I fight this reaction by staying patient, and I run the rabbit around. Usually they get tired of running all over the place and start taking low-percentage shots to end the rally, which is to my advantage."

- **tall or short?**

Tall—You want to hit a lot of angles at tall players. A tall player uses her reach to her advantage, so you want to try to handcuff her by hitting the ball at her feet or body, causing her limbs to get in the way.

Short—You want to hit a lot of lines against short players. A short person lacks reach, which makes down-the-line passes a great option because they cover the least distance in the least amount of time, making them difficult for a smaller player to reach.

- **big or small?**

Big—Play a big player the same way you would play a tall player.

Small—Play a small player the same way you would play a short player.

- **a power player or a control player?**

Power—When you play a power player, you want to defuse his power. You can do this by keeping the ball out of his hitting zone on the serve, causing him to hit the ball at his waist, chest, or shoulder, or by changing the pace and slowing the ball down. These two strategies will not allow your opponent to hit at full pace. They also cause him to take more difficult shots, which should make him perform at a lower level, giving you easy points. This is a very similar strategy to one used against a power hitter in baseball: Keep the ball out of his hitting zone, and change the pace.

Control—Playing a control player is about being patient and waiting for the easy setup. You don't want to put the pressure on yourself, which is exactly what most players tend to do. Instead, stay the course and play the percentages in order to earn the right to be offensive in the middle of the court. Don't play into her strategy!

- **in shape or out of shape?**

In shape—Playing someone who is in shape is similar to playing a control player. He's probably not going to get tired, so there's no need to run him around the court. Just play high-percentage racquetball and wait to earn your kill shots.

Out of shape—Playing someone out of shape is simple: You need to move him around. Most of these players play close to the front wall (too far forward), so there are many times you can simply hit ceiling balls and pass shots to move them around. It can't hurt to speed up your service; taking less time to serve will give out-of-shape players less time to recover. Jason likes to spend some time tiring out his opponents, taking pass shots even when kill shots would work a little better. Those extra shots in the rally wear opponents down, and then when he senses this, he tries to put the match away.

- **healthy or injured?**

Healthy—You want to play a healthy player just like you play someone who is in shape, unless she has a glaring flaw, which you would obviously concentrate on and take advantage of.

Injured—Playing an injured player will depend on the injury. If it hurts him to take a backhand, then hit to your opponent's backhand. If he has a knee injury, then hit the ball around him, forcing him to run all over the place. If he has a back injury, then make him bend a lot.

- **a counterpuncher or a ripper?**

Counterpuncher—When you play a counterpuncher (a defensive player who punches your shots back), try not to shoot too many balls into the front court. You need to turn her into an offensive player (a shooter), so you want to use more ceiling balls and down-the-line passes to make her run around and take difficult shots, turning yourself into the counterpuncher. This is usually uncomfortable for your opponent, which should play right into your game.

Ripper—When you play someone who rips the ball, you want to put him in the back court. The farther away from the front wall he is, the slower the ball comes off the wall. Forcing him to hit balls from deep court and above the waist will put him in a difficult position and play into your favor.

- **orthodox or unorthodox?**

Orthodox—Orthodox players are those with the typical habits that you can easily figure out. For example, is the player a power or control player, is she fast or slow, is she tall or short, etc?.

Unorthodox—When you play a person who is unorthodox, you want to do everything you can to stay within yourself and not force shots to conform to her unorthodox style. It is difficult, but you have to remember that if someone can hit a certain shot, that doesn't mean you should take that same shot. One thing that always amazes us is that an unorthodox player usually has "a three-wall boast" (the ball hits three walls consecutively: side wall, side wall, front wall, in that order) in her bag of tricks. We can't tell you how many people try to hit this shot in order to combat their opponent's lousy shot instead of just being ready for it and attacking it. We have given you all the tools you need to be successful, so don't try to mimic an unorthodox person.

How to Be a Racquetball Detective

As a racquetball detective you must analyze your opponent's strengths and weaknesses as well as your own strengths and weaknesses, which will determine the game plan you need to put together in order to beat your opponent. Here's a simple formula:

Game plan = opponent's strengths and weaknesses + your strengths and weaknesses

There are several ways to collect the information you need in order to develop a game plan:

1. Video analysis—If you have time, this is the ideal way to watch your opponent in a match because you can watch the video leisurely as many times as you like to obtain as much information as possible that you might miss with only one viewing.

2. Scout opponent—If you are going to play the winner of a match in an hour or so and there is no time for filming and video analysis, then you could spend time watching and observing your opponent warming up and playing in a live game situation.

3. Talking to someone who has played your opponent before—This is another method you can use to help you get data on your opponent.

On page 191 is a game evaluation form to assist you in collecting the data and facts about your opponent's strengths and weaknesses, as well as your own, helping you become that racquetball detective. The more information you collect, the better prepared you will be when developing the game plan.

How to Develop a Game Plan

Now that we have covered the eight areas for assessing a player and you have seen the game evaluation sheet to determine your opponent's strengths and weaknesses, you are ready to develop a game plan. We suggest you add notes to the evaluation sheet and ask questions. Following are some sample questions, but ask yourself as many questions as possible to obtain the information you need about your opponent.

1. Stroke mechanics: Does your opponent have a stronger forehand or backhand? Does he poke his backhand? Does he follow through? Does he have a stiff wrist on his forehand?

2. Court position: Is your opponent too far up? Does she shade to one side or the other? Is your opponent square to the side wall?

3. Shot selection: Does he go crosscourt too much or kill more than pass? Is he splat happy? What are his tendencies? Is he predictable, hitting the same shots over and over again?

4. Serves: Is she predictable, or does she have good variety? Can she hit an effective Z serve? Can she handle your power? Can she return a lob to her backhand?

5. Return of serve: Is he aggressive, attacking on the return of serve? Can he hit an effective ceiling return? Does he try to kill off the back wall? Does he hit the Z serve before it hits the second side wall?

6. Footwork: Does she square up to the side wall or hit in an open stance a lot? Is she quick on her feet?

7. Emotional state: Is he calm, or does he get upset easily with himself? Is he easily distracted? Does he get rattled when you slow him down?

8. Type of player: Power or control? Rabbit or turtle? Righty or lefty?

Game Evaluation

Area of evaluation	Strength				Weakness	Comments
STROKE MECHANICS						
Forehand	1	2	3	4	5	
Backhand	1	2	3	4	5	
Consistency	1	2	3	4	5	
COURT POSITION						
During rally	1	2	3	4	5	
After-serve relocation	1	2	3	4	5	
During return of serve	1	2	3	4	5	
SHOT SELECTION						
Offensive shots	1	2	3	4	5	
Defensive shots	1	2	3	4	5	
During rally	1	2	3	4	5	
During return of serve	1	2	3	4	5	
Variety or predictable	1	2	3	4	5	
Percentages: playing the odds	1	2	3	4	5	
Consistency	1	2	3	4	5	
SERVES						
Drives	1	2	3	4	5	
Lobs	1	2	3	4	5	
Mechanics/techniques	1	2	3	4	5	
Strategy	1	2	3	4	5	
Variety	1	2	3	4	5	
Quality/consistency	1	2	3	4	5	
Deception	1	2	3	4	5	
RETURN OF SERVE						
Attack serves	1	2	3	4	5	
Mechanics/techniques	1	2	3	4	5	
Quality/consistency	1	2	3	4	5	
Footwork	1	2	3	4	5	
Strategy	1	2	3	4	5	
FOOTWORK						
During rally	1	2	3	4	5	
Return of serve	1	2	3	4	5	
Crossover step	1	2	3	4	5	

(continued)

Game Evaluation *(continued)*

Area of evaluation	Strength			Weakness		Comments
EMOTIONAL STATE						
Positive attitude	1	2	3	4	5	
Calm and in control	1	2	3	4	5	
Stays focused	1	2	3	4	5	
Easily upset	1	2	3	4	5	
Mentally tough	1	2	3	4	5	
TYPE OF PLAYER						
Righty or lefty	1	2	3	4	5	
Slow or fast	1	2	3	4	5	
Tall or short	1	2	3	4	5	
Big or small	1	2	3	4	5	
Power or control	1	2	3	4	5	
In shape or out of shape	1	2	3	4	5	
Healthy or injured	1	2	3	4	5	
Counterpuncher or ripper	1	2	3	4	5	
Orthodox or unorthodox	1	2	3	4	5	
MISCELLANEOUS						
Uses different strategies: adjusts game plan	1	2	3	4	5	
Use of time-outs	1	2	3	4	5	
Knowledge of the rules	1	2	3	4	5	
Warm-up	1	2	3	4	5	
Etiquette/behavior	1	2	3	4	5	
Pace/tempo of game	1	2	3	4	5	
Nutrition	1	2	3	4	5	
Conditioned	1	2	3	4	5	
Watches the ball	1	2	3	4		

Results of game evaluation:

If you scored 1 or 2 in an area of evaluation, then it is a relative strength.

If you scored 4 or 5 in an area of evaluation, then it is a relative weakness.

If you scored 3 in an area of evaluation, then you are in the middle but looking to make it a strength.

From F. Davis and J. Mannino, 2011, *Championship Racquetball* (Champaign, IL: Human Kinetics).

When Jason develops a game plan, he simply asks himself these questions and applies the information to his strengths. Let's take a look at how Jason develops some of the game plans he uses on tour:

1. Stroke mechanics: "If a player has poor stroke mechanics, I try to hit the ball into him and force him to move his feet, hopefully causing him to hit the ball out of his ideal hitting zone. If he has a bad grip or stroke, then the only shots he can hit accurately are ones that line up perfectly. If I can get him to hit balls behind him, too close to him, or in front of him, there is a better chance of him missing the shot."

2. Court position: "If a player has poor court position, I simply hit the ball away from him and play the battle of attrition."

3. Shot selection: "If a player has poor shot selection, then I play the game of patience. I make sure I don't skip the ball. I put him in difficult positions such as deep in the court, keep the ball behind him, keep the ball out of his hitting zone, and make him stretch for the ball and let him fail all by himself."

4. Serves: "I commonly run into players that want to cut off my lob serves. I have devised a service strategy that makes this game plan very difficult to execute. I have many different heights, speeds, and angles that I hit my lobs at, and I feed my opponent a steady diet of all of them. If he tries to short-hop my lob, then I hit half lob nicks. If he tries to shoot my half lob nick from deep, I make sure the ball contacts the side wall when the ball is waist high, therefore making it difficult for him to shoot it successfully."

5. Return of serve: "If a player doesn't have a particularly good drive serve, allowing me to be offensive, I like to do just that. I know players get uncomfortable when you cut off their serve, so I cut off their Z serves, their drive serves, and all their lobs. I try my best to be offensive when it fits the situation, meaning if my opponent is drive serving, but not well, chances are that he is still in the service box—a perfect time for me to be offensive and hit a pass."

6. Footwork: "When I notice my opponent has poor or slow footwork, I jump all over that. If a player shuffles sideways with no crossover step on the return of serve, I will first serve him drives in the corners to bait him and then immediately go to drive jams and Zs. This will handcuff him and force a weak return, which is an opportunity for a setup for me to possibly score. If a player shuffles sideways during a rally with no cross step, I pound lots of wide-angle and down-the-line passes. The power of my shot and my opponent's lack of reach usually results in lots of easy points for me because he has to push the ball a lot."

7. Emotional state: "Every player has what I call a trigger—something he does not like that gets him upset—and I pay very close attention to that. Once I figure out what it is, I go directly after that. It may be a backhand ceiling rally, or a drive serve to the right, or a Z serve, or taking my time, or whatever, but I zero in on it. For every level and every player it is different, but when I see my opponent defeated, I continue to do what made him feel that way, and I do not let up. If your opponent starts talking to himself, pacing up and down the court, or he has a tantrum by hitting the racquet on the wall or floor, you know you have him right where you want him because he will fold and choke big time."

8. Type of player: "Let's say my opponent is getting annoyed with things happening on the court, and it seems that he wants to play a faster game. That's the perfect time to slow things down. I will take my time on the serve and return of serve as well as take more time during the rallies. Conversely, if a player needs time to calm down, I speed things up, forcing him to make as many decisions when he is agitated as I possibly can."

When you are formulating your game plan, keep in mind that each opponent you play possesses a combination of these characteristics, not just one. Here are some examples:

- Tall lefty with a weak backhand who likes to play a fast game and plays too far up in the court
- Power player with knee problems who shades to one side of the court and curls her backhand; has a negative attitude, likes a slow game, and doesn't like lob serves
- Unorthodox rabbit with a predictable shot selection who kills everything and does not switch grips

You are now ready to develop your own game plans.

COMMON MISTAKES: GAME PLANS

ERROR: You don't have a game plan at all.

CORRECTION: Make sure you take the time to develop a game plan.

SOLUTION: In anything you do on or off the court, having a game plan—a plan of action—is critical to your success. If you fail to plan, you plan to fail.

ERROR: You elect to play the game you "like," not the game that is most effective, which is not playing to your opponent's weaknesses.

CORRECTION: Play your opponent's weaknesses coupled with your strengths.

SOLUTION: Pay attention to and exploit your opponent's weaknesses. If the game you like is the same game your opponent likes, it can build your opponent's confidence.

Strategies

- **Control center court:** Being in the center-court box puts you in the best position possible to get a majority of the shots. Remember, the center-court box is the 6 feet by 6 feet (1.8 m by 1.8 m) area behind the dotted line, discussed in detail in chapter 5. The person who owns and controls center court has a greater chance of winning the match. This strategy is key.

- **Keep your opponent out of center court:** If you keep the other player out of your space, she is not in the best position to get to a majority of the shots. You can accomplish this by putting the balls in the corners and hitting lots of down-the-line shots, which definitely keeps her away from center court, a basic strategy that works.

- **Watch the ball at all times:** By watching the ball, you gain valuable information and more time so you can better determine your opponent's shot and react faster to the ball. If your opponent is the offensive player hitting the ball and you are watching it, and you see that he is going to hit the ball behind him, you can probably expect the ball to hit the side wall. If you are the offensive player hitting the ball, you can determine whether to go offensive or defensive and what specific shot to hit based on the ball position and of course your opponent's position too.

- **Hit away from your opponent:** Your goal is to hit where your opponent is not and make her run the farthest distance to get to the ball by going to the open court. The more you make her move and hit on the run, the more mistakes she will make, giving you more opportunities to take advantage of the situation and possibly score or put her on the defensive once again until you can score.

- **Hit to and exploit your opponent's weaknesses:** By hitting to your opponent's weaknesses, you are forcing him to do something he does not want to do. Often the player will then try to make something out of nothing, hitting shots he is not capable of making. This type of strategy causes your opponent to get frustrated, doubt himself, and then usually self-destruct.

- **Avoid hitting to your opponent's strengths:** This will only build his confidence level and make him feel like king of the hill, able to take and make any shot he wants, thus winning the match.

- **Keep your opponent deep in the court:** This strategy keeps him as far away from the front wall, the target, as possible. Remember that 30 percent of all balls can be killed from the dotted line, and the odds go down the farther back in the court he goes.

- **Always stay positive:** When you are positive, you can think more clearly and good things happen. When you are negative, you cannot think clearly and bad things happen. Remember, negativity breeds negativity.

- **Do not use your first game as a warm-up:** Often players don't warm up properly, thinking they can warm up by playing. First off, your chances of getting injured increase if you are not warmed up properly. Ideally, you should be warmed up as if it were 10-10 in the tiebreaker. Second, if you use the first game as a warm-up, there is a greater chance of your losing the game, which puts you in a deficit. If you lose the first game, you have to win both of the remaining games in order to win the match. This is not a good position to be in because the odds are against you. Why put yourself under such tremendous pressure?

- **Carry out your game plan:** If you fail to plan, you plan to fail. A game plan is just as important as your racquet, shoes, and eye guards—you would never enter the court without any one of these three things, and the same should be true for your game plan.

COMMON MISTAKES: CORE STRATEGIES

ERROR: You are not in center court.

CORRECTION: Make sure you are in center court as often as possible.

SOLUTION: Make every effort to get back to center court! If you are struggling and not getting back to center court immediately, you are not putting yourself in the best position possible to get a majority of the balls, which puts you at a disadvantage. If you are not in center court, your opponent probably is, which puts her in a better position to beat you.

ERROR: You are unaware of where your opponent is, and you hit right back to him.

CORRECTION: Hit away from your opponent, and make him move to get the ball.

SOLUTION: Remember you want to make your opponent run the farthest distance to get to the ball because he will make more mistakes when hitting on the run. Hitting the ball to your opponent boosts his confidence level and probably will help him play better.

Intermediate and Advanced

Just because some things may sound elementary doesn't mean they are not important in intermediate and advanced levels of play. Some players get to the intermediate levels while ignoring the core strategies—which is why they plateau. Also, after you reach the intermediate and advanced levels of play, there's more to be cognizant of—little idiosyncrasies such as where in center court to be and what to look for while your opponent is setting up or preparing to return your shot.

- **Wait for the shot to develop, read the ball, and play the percentages:** Do not rush, overrun the ball, and hit out of control. Read the ball coming off your opponent's racquet, and make a decision as to how your opponent hits the ball and where in her stance she contacted it to figure out the height. You need this information so you can let the ball drop into your hitting zone and take a high-percentage shot.

- **Play your game and focus on your strengths:** You certainly want to start out with this strategy because it is a confidence booster, but you must make adjustments if your strengths are also your opponent's strengths or if his strengths counter yours. For example, if you have a dynamite drive serve that works against most players, but you run up against an opponent who can handle your drive serve relatively easily, then it's time to try some different serves.

- **Be in control of the match:** Being in control means playing more methodically and being aware of your surroundings and what's happening out on the court. This is a strategy that clearly separates levels of play, which is needed in order to move you into the intermediate and advanced game. Here are a few tips for controlling the game:

Know the rules—Knowing the rules puts you in a more powerful position where you can challenge calls your opponent makes or the referee makes. When you start understanding the rules, you can use them to your advantage. For instance, you can use the 10-second rule to slow your opponent down. A great example of this is when you are serving and your opponent immediately gets into the ready position after losing the previous rally. He usually wants to receive the serve right away, and this is the time to take your full 10 seconds, making your opponent wait. If your opponent complains about it because he doesn't like it, you can explain that the server and receiver combined have 10 seconds once the score is called before the ball has to be put into play. Another example of using the rules to your advantage is that you can ask for the referee to be replaced if you are playing in a tournament and you think the referee isn't calling a fair match.

Use your time-outs effectively—All amateur matches go two out of three games, the first 2 to 15 and the tiebreaker to 11. You receive three 30-second time-outs in a 15-point game and two 30-second time-outs in a tiebreaker. The pros play three out of five to 11 and receive only one 1-minute time-out in a game. There is more than one reason to take a time-out. You can use a time-out to

- recover from a long rally if you are tired and need to catch your breath;
- change the momentum of the match and stop the flow of points if your opponent is rattling off unanswered points;
- regroup and review your game plan if you lose your concentration so you can get back on track by making adjustments where necessary;
- change your opponent's rhythm and tempo because this makes her uncomfortable; and
- get rid of negative thoughts because negativity breeds negativity, and you will not play at your best.

You should never have any time-outs remaining, especially if you have lost the game, because then you haven't done everything in your power to try to win.

Control the tempo and rhythm—The timing, or pace, of the game is referred to as the tempo and rhythm. Most players unfortunately just rush and put the ball into play without thinking. You need to find your tempo and rhythm as well as your opponent's tempo and rhythm. This information will help greatly when you are in the heat of the battle and wanting to settle into the match. Your goals are twofold:

1. You want to control the tempo and rhythm of the game so that you feel comfortable with the pace because this will allow you to play at your best.

2. You want to disrupt your opponent's tempo and rhythm as much as possible, without disrupting your own, because that will make your opponent uneasy, possibly resulting in a poor performance.

Now let's see how you can control the tempo and rhythm of your racquetball game:

• Utilize the 10-second rule, which is that the server and receiver combined have 10 seconds to serve or receive the ball. If the server is ready to serve, the receiver can put his racquet up and make the server wait 10 seconds. If the receiver is down and ready, the server can make the receiver wait for 10 seconds by delaying her serve. In both cases, the waiting player may get annoyed or anxious and lose focus.

• Use a time-out when your opponent gets 4 or 5 points in a row, whether it is during a rally or when he is serving and seems to be on a roll. This may help break his momentum and give you time to regroup and make appropriate adjustments.

• If your opponent is serving well and you are having trouble returning the serve effectively, take a time-out to possibly break the server's rhythm.

• **Play one point at a time**—Most players think too far back (in the past) or too far ahead (in the future) instead of being in the now (the present).

   The past—If you get a bad call and keep thinking about it and lose 5 points because you can't let it go, you are in the past. Instead of just losing that 1 point from the bad call you lose 5 points, and now you are 4 points in the deficit. Let it go!

   The future—If you are ahead 9-2 in the tiebreaker and begin to celebrate your win in your mind, you are in the future. Because you are not playing in the now, you could end up losing the match.

   The present—Take it one point at a time and be here and now, and you will see the astounding results in your favor.

• **Stay focused and concentrate**—Keep all your attention on the task at hand: the game. If your mind wanders and you start thinking of everything but what you are doing, this is a sign that you have lost your concentration. The flow of points will start to drift in your opponent's direction, and it is hard to get your momentum back. It is easier to keep and maintain your concentration than to let it slip and try to reel it back in. To help you stay focused, pay attention to these simple things: the ball, your opponent, whether you are in center court, how aggressive you are being, and whether you are playing your game. Also, this is a great time for a time-out to get refocused.

• **Play the ball, not your opponent**—This is a strategy that most people don't think about. Often players either do not like their opponent for one reason or another or they are playing a friend whom they like very much. Unfortunately, if they cannot get those thoughts out of their heads, they generally overplay, wanting to win too badly, or play too nice because they do not want to hurt their friend's feelings. These thoughts are crippling. The strategy we advocate is to play the ball. The ball does not have a personality or does not cheat or does not look at you funny or does not talk back. With this thinking, you can play your game without being adversely affected by worrying about your opponent.

COMMON MISTAKES: INTERMEDIATE AND ADVANCED STRATEGIES

ERROR: You rush the ball without letting the play develop.

CORRECTION: Read the ball coming off your opponent's racquet to determine the shot he is hitting.

SOLUTION: If you do not watch the ball come off your opponent's racquet, you cannot make an educated guess as to where he is hitting the ball. As a result, you will probably not hit many high-percentage shots and will set your opponent up too often.

ERROR: You are not in control of the match.

CORRECTION: Take your time, and be more methodical and aware.

SOLUTION: By slowing down, taking your time-outs, and knowing what's happening around you, you stay in control. When you don't take time-outs and are not controlling the tempo of the match, your opponent starts to get into her own rhythm, which makes her feel very comfortable, and she will play better.

ERROR: You are looking ahead in the match.

CORRECTION: Be in the now.

SOLUTION: Be in the present moment, playing one point at a time. The future has not been decided, and when you play ahead, the present rally usually suffers, shot after shot until you lose the point, then the game, then ultimately the match.

ERROR: You lose focus because of a bad call.

CORRECTION: Let a bad call go because one bad call will usually not lose you a match.

SOLUTION: Let it go! If you allow a bad call to affect you negatively point after point, you will ultimately lose the game because of it.

ERROR: You play your opponent, not the ball.

CORRECTION: Play the ball because it does not talk back, cheat, look at you funny, and so on.

SOLUTION: Playing the ball, not your opponent, keeps all the tension off you and allows you to play your best. When you play your opponent, you often get wrapped up in analyzing why he took a double bounce or why he is taking so long to serve, and you get distracted from the task at hand.

COMMON MISTAKES: GAME SITUATIONS

ERROR: When you are behind in the match, you try to kill everything to get some quick points to get back into the match.

CORRECTION: Play high-percentage shots more, such as passes, and don't force a weak return.

SOLUTION: Going for more passes and working your way back into the match gives you the best opportunity to come back. Playing kill shots actually works against you because the more you kill, the more you skip since your target on the front wall for the kill is much lower than the target for the pass shot. By going for the kill in a stressful situation, you are even more likely to skip the ball.

Rules of Thumb

In chapter 6 we shared some simple but smart rules for shot selection. Now we are going to do the same for strategies. These rules of thumb for strategies will put more pressure on your opponent and help you win more matches.

1. Watch the ball at all times. By watching the ball, you gain valuable information and more time so you can better determine your opponent's shot and react faster to the ball.

2. Always stay positive. When you are positive, you can think more clearly and good things happen. When you are negative, you cannot think clearly and bad things happen. Remember, negativity breeds negativity.

3. Carry out your game plan. A game plan is just as important as your racquet, shoes, and eye guards—you would never enter the court without any one of these three things, and the same should be true for your game plan. Adjust game plan, if necessary.

4. Stay focused and concentrate. Keep all your attention on the task at hand: the game. If your mind wanders and you start thinking of everything but what you are doing, the flow of points will start to drift in your opponent's direction, and it is hard to get your momentum back. It is easier to keep and maintain your concentration than to let it slip and try to reel it back in.

5. Game situations. By understanding sample game situations and tactical strategies, you can fully understand how to play the game so you can move up to the advanced level of play.

ERROR: When you are ahead in a match, you sit on a big lead, get complacent, and expect your opponent to make mistakes and give you the match instead of going for your shots and earning the win.

CORRECTION: When you are ahead keep on going, and use the shots that got you the big lead.

SOLUTION: You want to play to win, not have your opponent give you the points to win. When you have the mentality of letting your opponent make mistakes to give you the match, you are setting yourself up to be passive rather than aggressive, and you are no longer in control of the situation.

Game Plan and Strategy Drills

For you to get comfortable and proficient at developing game plans and using the different strategies set forth in this chapter, you need to practice doing them so you will be more apt to use them each and every time you walk on the court, whether it's to play a match or to practice.

Drills for Game Plans

1. Scout your opponent by using the game evaluation sheet.

2. Make a list of the eight areas to look for when assessing a player (page 184), and fill in the strengths and weaknesses of your opponent.

Game Situations and Their Strategies

Game situation	Strategy
You are ahead 10-7 in tie-breaker, and you are serving for the match.	Pressure, pressure, pressure. Don't let up. Go with what got you to 10. Serve your best serve and the one you have the most confidence in.
You are behind 0-7 in the first game.	Play high-percentage shots, and don't force a weak shot. Work your way back into the match. Explore different serves and shots to find your opponent's weaknesses, and then exploit them. You want to try to win the first game to put pressure on your opponent to win the next two games in order to win the match.
You won the first game.	Start the second game with constant pressure, and use what worked in the first game. Stick to your game plan—you were successful.
You won the first game but are down 12-4 in the second game.	Work hard to get your momentum back. Be defensive when your opponent is serving and more aggressive when you get the serve. Adjust your game plan.
You lost the first game.	You need to adjust your game plan and the tempo of the match.

3. Now formulate a game plan, simply by starting with one area at a time and building to two areas, then three areas, and so on, working your way up to all eight areas for the most complex game plans. By using this step-by-step approach, you will be less overwhelmed as you learn how to develop game plans, and you will be more successful.

Game Plan 1 Pick one area and write a simple game plan to utilize the strengths and weaknesses you observed.

Area: Opponent's court position

Facts: Your opponent plays too far up during the rally, and after the serve she is playing only in between the short line and the dotted line, too far up, not in the center-court box behind the dotted line.

Game plan: Since your opponent plays too far up, she is susceptible to passes during the rally and to passes and ceiling balls on the return of serve.

Game Plan 2 Pick two areas and write a simple game plan to utilize the strengths and weaknesses you observed.

Area: Opponent's backhand and return of serve

Facts: Your opponent hates his backhand and runs around the ball all the time to use his forehand, even if he has to put himself up against the wall and way out of position. He plays too far up on the return of serve and stands about 5 feet (1.5 m) from the back wall on the return of serve instead of 2 to 3 feet (.6 to .9 m) from the back wall.

Game plan: Since your opponent has a weak backhand, exploit that by serving to his backhand and hitting as many balls as possible to his backhand until he doesn't get off the backhand wall and then go to his forehand to keep him guessing.

Low and hard drive serves are great choices to hit to an opponent who plays too far up on the return of serve because his reaction is slower, and he will have to retreat back into the corner and hit the ball behind him. With a player like this who also has a weak backhand, you want to hit those low, hard drive serves to the backhand—a double whammy.

Game Plan 3   Pick three areas and write a more complex game plan to utilize the strengths and weaknesses you observed.

Continue until you have covered all eight areas and developed a complete game plan.

Drills for Strategies

1. Pick different opponents to work on different strategies, and arrange games so you get more and more comfortable competing against players, such as the following:
   - Power player
   - Lefty
   - Weak backhand
   - Fast player
   - Emotional player
   - Athletic player
   - Tall player
   - Unorthodox player

2. Pick different game situations, and start playing a simulated game beginning with the following situations:
   - You are ahead.
   - You are serving for the match with the game at 10-7 in a tiebreaker.
   - You are behind.
   - The score is 0-7 in the first game.
   - You won the first game.
   - You won the first game but are down 12-4 in the second game.
   - You lost the first game.

Game Plans and Strategies Checklist: Core, Intermediate, and Advanced

Core	Intermediate and Advanced
• Control center court. • Keep opponent out of center court. • Watch the ball. • Hit away from opponent. • Exploit opponent's weaknesses. • Avoid opponent's strengths. • Keep opponent deep in the court. • Stay positive. • Do not use first game as a warm-up. • Carry out game plan by using one area at a time.	• Play the percentages. • Play your game. • Be in control. • Play one point at a time. • Stay focused and concentrate. • Play the ball, not your opponent. • Be aware of game situations. • Carry out game plan by using all eight areas.

Summary

None of the game plans or strategies we discuss in this chapter will work if you don't play a high-percentage racquetball game, exhibit good mechanics, and play smart. If you are impatient, are inconsistent, have poor mechanics, don't drill, and tire easily, then it is difficult to put pressure on your opponent and execute properly. Work on your overall game first and get comfortable with the techniques and concepts we cover in the earlier chapters of this book. Only then will you be confident enough to carry out the game plans and use the strategies we lay out in this chapter for every situation. Jason has a great way to look at this: "When you're on the court, you and your opponent are at war. Without great weapons and a competent strategy, you stand little chance of winning and being a champion."

Part III

The Competition

Up until this point, we have given you the skills and the tactics you need to compete, but to have the competitive edge over your opponents, we need to make you a more complete player. This requires providing you with additional tools to add to your tool chest to give you that complete game needed to become a champion.

A complete player is someone who has all three sides of the "racquetball sports triangle." We have discussed the skills section of the book in part I (the base of the triangle). We haven't yet addressed mental toughness and conditioning, the right and left sides of the triangle, and we do that in part III.

In part III, we show you how to develop consistency, develop the mind, develop the body, and develop your championship doubles game. All of these important tools will make you a complete player, which is what you will need to be to become the ultimate competitor and the champion you've always wanted to be.

Chapter 8

Practicing Perfectly

Perfect practice makes perfect is a philosophy we feel so strongly about that we play, teach, and coach using this as our guiding light. It is not good enough to say, "Practice makes perfect," because it has to be perfect practice, which means you are practicing the skill—the stroke or shot—100 percent correctly using the drill techniques we taught you in chapters 1 through 4. With this repetition, your body will develop the muscle memory necessary for the skill to be automatic, which will allow you to utilize it when you are playing. If you have to think about how to hit the ball (e.g., *Is my racquet up? Am I square to the side wall? Am I following through all the way? Did I change my grip?*), you will not perform at your best because performing a skill and thinking about the skill don't really mix. The skill should happen automatically because your muscles have memorized that motion from the practice and drill sessions you have done thousands of times. The only things you want to think about when you are playing a game are where you are on the court, where your opponent is on the court, and what the best shot is in that situation. As a result of your practice and drill sessions, this can occur more successfully.

The drill sections in chapters 1 through 7 are designed to help you perfect the particular skills and tactics we are teaching. In this chapter we cover some practice guidelines and combination drills when you are alone as well as with a partner.

Practice Guidelines

As you approach your drill sessions, we want to stress a few guidelines that we think will make your sessions more helpful and more valuable so you will see the direct impact in your game.

Always go from the core drills to the more advanced drills.

Core Drills

1. Use one wall because it is less complicated (only one direction).
2. Slow down the speed so you will have more reaction time and more time to set up.
3. Hit your set ups 1/2 (10 ft) to 3/4 (15 ft) of the way up on the front wall so you will have more reaction time and more time to set up.
4. Practice from one position on the court so you do not have to read the ball, and then move to another spot.
5. Practice one shot at a time only so there is less thinking and decision making involved.
6. Use the same setup, then hit the ball, catch the ball, and repeat; do not use continuous setups.

Advanced Drills

These involve reading the ball, making judgments, and making adjustments.

1. Use more than one wall so you get comfortable with the trajectory of the ball.
2. Hit your shots harder, with more speed, because this gives you less time to react and simulates the game more closely. You should now have muscle memory from the core drilling you have been doing.
3. Mix up heights to high, medium, and low because that is more realistic to the game.
4. Move to different positions on the court because that is more realistic to the game.
5. Combine shots and movements such as hitting ceiling balls to yourself and then hustling into position to shoot an offensive shot when you make a mistake.
6. Combine two shots at a time from the same position, first taking the same shots using continuous setups and then taking different shots using continuous setups.
7. Combine two shots at a time from different positions, first taking the same shots using continuous setups and then taking different shots using continuous setups.

Moving from core to advanced drilling is important, but you must master the core drills first because those are your foundation. Then and only then can you build on the core drills and start combining them to make the drills more advanced and more like a game situation—the key to moving from the intermediate to advanced level of play.

Repetition Is the Key Component of Muscle Memory

By having perfect practice sessions, you will hone your skills by developing muscle memory. The drills in chapters 1 to 4 will help you develop and perfect key skills—your attacking forehand, your penetrating backhand, your serve and relocation out of the service box, your aggressive offensive and defensive shots, and your return of serve. In this chapter, we combine the drills and add movement. This advanced process of drilling will help you transition your skills into a game situation. And as you grow as a player, your skills should become sharper and more consistent so you can call on them in a game when stress is at its peak.

Make Drilling Fun

Often players do not drill because they are bored. Unfortunately, that is a poor excuse; you cannot expect to perform at your very best if you do not put the time in and drill correctly. So here are a few tips to make your drilling sessions fun.

- Listen to your favorite music while drilling because music usually relaxes you.
- Use targets, and count your success. Here are a few examples, but be creative, too, and make up your own, and be sure to keep track of your percentage:
  - Kill shots: Put a ball can (or a couple of cans) at the front wall, and try to hit them on a fly. For intermediate players, attempt 15 and see how many you get. For advanced players, attempt 20 and see how many you get.
  - Pass shots: Put painter's tape on the front wall at 12 inches (30 cm) and 18 inches (46 cm) off the floor, and try to hit in between those lines. For intermediate players, attempt 15 and see how many you get. For advanced players, attempt 20 and see how many you get.
  - Ceiling balls and regular lob serves: Put a garbage can in each back corner, and when you hit your ceiling ball or lob serve, see if the ball lands in the can on its second bounce. For intermediate players, attempt 15 and see how many you get. For advanced players, attempt 20 and see how many you get.
  - Wide-angle passes: Rest one end of your racquetball bag on the dotted line and back so it is 25 to 30 feet (7.6 to 9.1 m) from the front wall. Now stand on the opposite side of the court, anywhere from 30 feet and up, and hit the bag with the ball on a fly. For intermediate players, attempt 15 and see how many you get. For advanced players, attempt 20 and see how many you get.

Using targets gives you a visual aid to shoot for. By keeping score of how you are doing, you can track your progress from week to week and month to month, whether you are drilling alone or with a partner. This is an excellent way to see where you need improvement, and then you can adjust your drilling sessions accordingly.

Maximize Your Time: Develop a Drill Session

Here are a few examples, but be creative, too, and make up your own. Keep track of your percentage.

- One-hour session—Can be divided into two 30-minute segments, four 15-minute segments, or six 10-minute segments. During each segment, practice a different skill and keep track of results. For intermediate players, attempt 15 and see how many you get. For advanced players, attempt 20 and see how many you get.
- 30-minute session—Can be divided into two 15-minute segments, three 10-minute segments, or one 20-minute and one 10-minute segment.
- Work your own amount of time, and divide into your own segments.
- What you practice and drill is based on what's working and not working in your leagues, tournaments, shootouts, or pickup games at the club. You must pay close attention so your sessions are centered around correcting your weaknesses and reinforcing your strengths.
- How long you drill for is based on your goals, commitment level, and desires, which you learn in detail in chapter 9. At a minimum, we recommend drilling for 10 to 15 minutes for every hour you play per week. So if you play three times per week, your drill session should be 30 to 45 minutes. Keep in mind that some practice time, no matter how minimal, is better than no practice at all. Also, the quality of your practice sessions is more important than the quantity of your practices. Our motto is "Don't just do it, do it right."

Check Your Progress

It is not good enough to just get on a court and practice for a specified amount of time. You must qualify your drill sessions by keeping track of your practices using the sample drill worksheet provided in appendix A. Regardless of what technique you are working on, this information holds true.

Decide what shot you are going to practice and how many of that shot you are going to hit. We recommend 15 for intermediate and 20 for advanced.

Count how many you did correctly by using the checklists at the end of the chapters. Did you do what you were supposed to do? Did the ball do what it was supposed to do? For example, if you are practicing a down-the-line pass, did the ball stay between you and the side wall and bounce two times before the back wall?

Here's an example of some points to consider from the checklist for the forehand:

1. Was your racquet up (ERP)?
2. Did you snap your wrist?
3. Did you follow through?
4. Were your belly button and chest square to the front wall?
5. Did you step forward into your shot?
6. Were your eyes on the ball?
7. Did you pivot your back foot?
8. Was your weight properly distributed?

Depending on your level of play, your percentages will change, 10 out of 15, or 67 percent for intermediate and 17 out of 20, or 85 percent for advanced.

These percentages are guidelines and are not definitive—they are benchmarks for you to try to achieve as you move into the intermediate level and then onto the advanced level. When Jason and I are coaching our students and they reach 85 percent, they are convinced more than ever that their hard work is paying off, and they do not want to stop there. As your percentages climb and you move beyond 85 percent, you are moving up into the elite and open levels, the next step in your racquetball journey. Keep in mind it is consistency that separates one level from the next, and it is the drilling sessions that create the consistency needed to move up and win more matches.

Solo and Partner Combination Drills

In the previous chapters, we discuss the five-step approach to drilling for your attacking forehand, your penetrating backhand, and your aggressive shots. We also cover drills for the different shots of the game, utilizing setup drills that call for hitting only one shot at a time.

In this chapter we introduce setup drills combining movement, multiple shots, and continuous setups to simulate more of a game situation.

Progression of Drills

1. Combine two shots at a time from the same position, taking the same shots using continuous setups (no catching the ball), like a game situation. One set equals 15 or 20 reps of the same routine, which you should repeat at least twice, and keep track. Here's an example:
   ○ Hit three to five good backhand ceiling balls in a row from the same position deep in the court. If you can do more than five in a row, great. If you cannot hit three in a row, go back to drop-and-hit backhand ceiling balls.

- Once you reach three to five good backhand ceiling balls in a row, keep going until you make a mistake and get a setup.
- Choose the shot you will be working on for your setup shot, such as a down-the-line pass or a pinch, and hit only that shot off the setup.
- After you take the shot, do not stop and catch the ball—just go to the ball and hit it back to the same position for the backhand ceiling.

2. Combine two shots at a time from the same position, taking different shots using continuous setups (no catching the ball), like a game situation. Do this 15 or 20 times, and keep track. Here's an example:

- Hit three to five good backhand ceiling balls in a row from the same position deep in the court; if you can do more than five in a row, great. If you cannot hit three in a row, go back to drop-and-hit backhand ceiling balls.
- Once you reach three to five good backhand ceiling balls in a row, keep going until you make a mistake and get a setup.
- Choose the shots you will be working on for your setup shot, such as a down-the-line pass, crosscourt pass, or pinch, and hit those shots off the setup by calling out the shot you want to hit.
- After you take the shot, do not stop and catch the ball—just go to the ball and hit it back to the same position for the backhand ceiling.

3. Combine two shots at a time from different positions, taking the same shots using continuous setups (no catching the ball), like a game situation. Do this 15 or 20 times, and keep track. Here's an example:

- Hit three to five good backhand ceiling balls in a row from different positions deep in the court; if you can do more than five in a row, great. If you cannot hit three in a row, go back to drop-and-hit backhand ceiling balls.
- Once you reach three to five good backhand ceiling balls in a row, keep going until you make a mistake and get a setup.
- Choose the shot you will be working on for your setup shot, such as a down-the-line pass or a pinch, and hit only that shot off the setup.
- After you take the shot, do not stop and catch the ball—just go to the ball and hit it back to any position for the backhand ceiling.

4. Combine two shots at a time from different positions, taking different shots using continuous setups (no catching the ball), like a game situation. Do this 15 or 20 times, and keep track. Here's an example:

- Hit three to five good backhand ceiling balls in a row from different positions deep in the court; if you can do more than five in a row, great. If you cannot hit three in a row, go back to drop-and-hit backhand ceiling balls.
- Once you reach three to five good backhand ceiling balls in a row, keep going until you make a mistake and get a setup.
- Choose the shots you will be working on for your setup shot, such as a down-the-line pass, crosscourt pass, or pinch, and hit those shots off the setup by calling out the shot you want to hit.
- After you take the shot, do not stop and catch the ball—just go to the ball and hit it back to any position for the backhand ceiling.

Solo Drills

Before you can bring in a partner to drill with, you need to be somewhat proficient alone and have racquet control. Having good racquet control means being more accurate with the shots and having more consistency. Use the drill progression we just described for all the following drills.

Ceiling Ball Rally Into Setup Shot

Start in the last 5 feet (1.5 m) of the court.

Hit three to five good ceiling balls in a row until you hit a bad ceiling ball, and then shoot an offensive shot. If you do not hit three to five good ceiling balls in a row, stop and start again until you do.

A variation of this drill is to hit good ceiling balls that end up anywhere deep in the court; keep the ceiling ball within the 3-foot (.9 m) drive serve line.

Another variation is to keep the ceiling ball within 1.5 feet (.5 m) of the side wall, within the doubles box.

As your level of play improves, increase the number of ceiling balls in a row from three to five to five to seven, then to seven to nine, and so on.

Set Yourself Up and Hit an Offensive Shot

When setting yourself up, at first use only one wall, then add a second wall, then multiple walls, and work on moving into the proper position to hit a good offensive shot.

A variation of this drill is to add different heights and speeds, which can give you hundreds of different drills.

Serve and Relocate Into the Appropriate Position

Most players underestimate the power of having very consistent and accurate serves with proper relocation into good center-court position. Your serve is only as good as your ability to get into position and ready for your opponent's return.

In chapter 3 we give you drills for both serving and relocating after the serve, but we now want you to make a list of all your serves and tackle them one serve at a time, relocating after every serve.

Short Ceiling Ball Into an Overhead Pass or Sidearm Pass

At every level, your opponent will undoubtedly hit ceiling balls that wind up being short, 35 feet (10.7 m) or so. At the lower levels most players just go back up to the ceiling, not making their opponents pay for their mistakes. At the intermediate and advanced levels of play, you want to make your opponents pay, so you want to hit an overhead or sidearm pass off the short ceiling ball.

Hit yourself a short ceiling ball and set up to hit all overhead passes: first all down the line, then all crosscourt, then mix them up.

Now hit yourself a short ceiling ball and set up to hit all sidearm passes: first all down the line, then all crosscourt, then mix them up.

Long Ceiling Ball Into a Setup off the Back Wall

At every level, your opponent will undoubtedly hit ceiling balls that are overhit and go long, which means the ball comes off the back wall for a setup. At all levels of play, you want to make your opponents pay for their mistakes, so you want to hit an offensive shot off the long ceiling ball.

Hit yourself a long ceiling ball and set up to hit all passes: first all down the line, then all crosscourt, then mix them up.

Now as you become more of an advanced player, hit yourself a long ceiling ball and set up to hit other offensive shots, such as pinches or splats.

Off Balance or Out of Position Ceiling Ball or Z Shot

When you are off balance or out of position, you want to reset the rally by using a ceiling ball or a Z shot. This gives you time to get back into center court and pulls your opponent out of the middle and deep into the court.

From the dotted line, hit yourself a pinch shot or any low shot that ends up in front court. Now move to the ball, and if you can get there in time and set your feet, then go ahead and go offensive, but if not go up to the ceiling or hit a Z shot.

30-Second Reaction

This is a more advanced drill that works on racquet control, footwork, and conditioning all at once. This is ideally used to practice your open-stance forehand and backhand because you often do not have time to turn.

Stand on the dotted line and blast balls back and forth to yourself. Do not let the ball go past you—just keep trying to rekill the ball. You can hit it on one or two bounces. The idea is to be able to react quickly up front and shoot the ball, making your hands and feet fast.

Even Jason, an IRT professional player, knows the importance of practicing drills alone to keep his game sharp: "My typical drill sessions are done alone. I like to drill two different ways.

1. The first way is to simply 'sharpen my sword.' I have a very basic 20-minute session that starts with drop and hit. I like to hit all the shots from about the service line, then move back about 35 feet (10.7 m) from the front wall and then hit all the relevant shots from deep court. Then I give myself setups from the exact same places, again hitting all the shots I normally take. Then I set myself up off of the back wall, making all the shots as well. Whatever I do with my forehand, I do the exact same thing with my backhand. I'm simply looking to develop a rhythm and increase my consistency.

2. The other way I practice is when I'm looking to solve a particular problem. I usually spend a few days dropping and hitting to get comfortable, for at least 45 minutes at a time. Then when I'm comfortable, I start to do set-up-and-hit drills—drilling the particular problem area. I repeat until it's fixed."

Partner Combination Drills

Now that you have more racquet control, you are ready to drill with a partner and add combinations. Drilling with someone usually adds a few elements you do not get when you drill alone—it's more fun, it's more competitive, and it's more like a game situation.

Ceiling Ball Rally Into Setup Shot

1. You start in the last 5 feet (1.5 m) of the court.
2. Your partner is in the back of the center-court box, with eyes on ball.
3. After you hit a ceiling ball, you move back to the center-court box, and your partner moves back to hit a ceiling ball.
4. Hit three to five good ceiling balls in a row combined, until one of you hits a bad ceiling ball. When this happens, the other person shoots an offensive shot, and you play out the point. If you do not hit three to five good ceiling balls in a row combined, stop and start again until you do.

A variation of this drill is to hit good ceiling balls that end up anywhere deep in the court; keep the ceiling ball within the 3-foot (.9 m) drive serve line.

Another variation is to keep the ceiling ball within 1.5 feet (.5 m) of the side wall, within the doubles box.

Another variation is for one person to hit all down-the-line ceiling balls while the other person hits all crosscourt ceiling balls.

As your level of play improves, increase the number of ceiling balls in a row from three to five to five to seven, then to seven to nine, and so on.

Do 15 or 20 repetitions, depending on your level of play.

Set Each Other Up and Hit an Offensive Shot

When setting each other up, at first use only one wall, then add a second wall, then multiple walls, and work on moving into the proper position to hit a good offensive shot. Play out the point.

Start anywhere on the court, and set your opponent up with a particular shot. Your partner is in the center-court box, with eyes on ball. He moves to the setup shot and shoots the offensive shot he is working on. Play out the point.

A variation of this drill is to add different heights and speeds, which can give you hundreds of different drills.

Do 15 or 20 repetitions, depending on your level of play, and then reverse who sets up and who returns the setup.

Pinch and Down the Line

This is a great drill to get proficient at because if your opponent pinches from the left side and leaves the ball up, you want to get into position to shoot the ball down the line on the right side of the court, which is far away from your opponent.

One of you pinches the ball a little high into the left corner while the other person is in good center-court position. The other person moves to hit the ball down the line on the right side.

One of you pinches the ball a little high into the right corner while the other person is in good center-court position. The other person moves to hit the ball down the line on the left side.

Do 15 or 20 repetitions, depending on your level of play, and then reverse who sets up and who returns the setup.

Cut Off Balls Hit Into the Back Wall

Often you hit a good passing shot, but the other player somehow gets her racquet on the ball and hits it into the back wall, making a great save. This is the ideal time to cut the ball off on a fly and go offensive because your opponent is deep in the court and still scrambling to get back into good center-court position.

One of you hits the ball into the back wall while the other person is in good center-court position. The other person moves up to cut the ball off and hits it out of the air. Which offensive shot he takes depends on where his opponent is after he hits that great save into the back wall.

Do 15 or 20 repetitions, depending on your level of play, and then reverse who sets up and who returns the setup.

Z Shot and Return to the Ceiling

Some players do not know how to return a Z shot, and they often lose points because they are unsure of what to do.

One person is in front of the dotted line and will hit a Z shot.

The other person is on the dotted line in good center-court position. Once the Z shot is hit, this person runs back and hits the ball to the ceiling before it hits the second side wall.

Do 15 or 20 repetitions, depending on your level of play, and then reverse who sets up and who returns the setup.

30-Second Reaction

This is the same 30-second reaction drill you practiced alone, except this time you have a partner.

Both players stand on the dotted line, one on the right side and the other on the left side, and blast balls back and forth to each other. Do not let the ball go past you—just keep trying to rekill the ball. You can hit it on one or two bounces. The idea is to be able to react quickly up front and shoot the ball, making your hands and feet fast.

Do 15 or 20 repetitions, depending on your level of play, and then reverse who is on what side.

Game Scenarios

- Play 5-point games—This works on keeping your concentration and staying focused.
- Play an all-backhand game—Both players can use only their backhands on the serve (serve with your backhand, and hit the serve to your opponent's backhand), the return of serve, and during a rally. This is a great drill if you are trying to make your backhand stronger because you have to hit all the shots with your backhand as opposed to only about 50 percent when playing a normal game. If you use your forehand, it can only be a defensive ceiling shot back to the backhand side.

- Play a bonus-point game—Both of you pick a shot you want to work on, such as the pinch, down-the-line pass, wide-angle pass, or overhead pass. If you are serving and you end the rally with that bonus-point shot, you get a point for winning the rally and a bonus point (i.e., you get 2 points instead of 1). If you are the player receiving the serve and you end the rally with that bonus-point shot, it is a side-out for winning the rally plus you get a bonus point (i.e., you get 1 point instead of 0).

Jason uses partner drills when he has trouble with a certain serve. He has his partner continually serve him a particular serve until he is comfortable with it. He also does a timing drill to improve his reaction time. He has his partner blast balls to him, forcing him to react quickly. Jason also plays two against one. He has two other players play against him. They get two serves, he gets one, and they play a full match. These partner drills help prepare Jason for tournaments.

Summary

This chapter adds to the practice sessions you were given at the end of each individual chapter. Up until this point, you have been using the five-step approach to drilling so you could develop your muscle memory.

You now need to start incorporating the movement drills from this chapter that combine setups with different shots. Once your proficiency improves and you begin to move from intermediate to advanced play, add different heights, speeds, and angles as well. This type of drilling is needed to help you transition into game play because these drills simulate a game very closely.

Many players look like A players when they go on the court and warm up, but when the match starts, they fall apart and look like C players. This is typical of players who are great with drop-and-hit stationary drilling but who don't spend time doing any movement drills. Movement drills make you more proficient at reading the ball and then positioning yourself to where you need to be in order to hit a particular shot. We encourage you to practice both types of drills, stationary and movement, so you are not that person who warms up as one level of player and becomes a different player in the game. You want to be the player to be reckoned with, which means you are consistent whether you are standing still hitting a shot or moving into a shot. There is only one way to get there, and it is to practice and practice perfectly!

Chapter 9

Maintaining Mental Toughness

Mental toughness is about mastering your mind and your emotions. Your body acts and reacts to the mental and emotional instructions that it receives. It always wants to be in harmony with your thoughts and feelings. The good news is that we are in control of the thoughts that we choose to focus on, and our emotions, consequently, come from our thoughts. It is this area of control where one has to be pro-active in his or her game plan. You have to plant positive thoughts, strategies, and techniques into your mind first, and then the body will follow.

An athlete's body has to know what it wants before it performs a skill. See the end result in your mind first, then physically follow through with that thought. A mentally tough player is programmed for success mentally, emotionally, and physically. Professional athletes such as Roger Federer, Lindsey Vonn, and Kobe Bryant say that once you have your physical skills mastered, it all comes down to your mental game. Few athletes realize that the mental game can take as long as three years to master, so we need to address your mental game right now.

Mental toughness is the ability to understand and control one's mind in order to optimize performance. Mental toughness is yet another required skill on the road to championship rac-quetball. In sport psychology, we say that an athlete has two brains—one in his head (learning brain) and one in his gut (sports brain).

1. **Learning brain:** This is the brain in your head, where you absorb auditory and then visual information. At first you listen to instructions (auditory), and once you have heard the message, your brain tries to see, or visualize, the message. In this way you have heard it and then seen it and now you are ready to try it.

   ○ Auditory brain: When you first learn a new skill, it enters the auditory brain, the left side of your brain, and you understand the concept. For some athletes this is good enough, and they hear what you say and then do it.

   ○ Visual brain: Most athletes need more than just hearing instructions; they need to add a visual picture of the skill, and this happens in the right side of the brain.

2. **Sports brain:** Once you have performed a skill perfectly at least seven times, it gets imprinted and sent to your "second brain," your gut, or instinct. All muscle memory is stored here and is triggered by sight and sound. James Loehr, a famous sport psychologist, calls it playing in the zone. This occurs when an athlete's mind and body come together and are on automatic pilot for peak performance.

It all sounds so easy. Learn the skill, practice the skill, imprint the skill, and go out there and win, but there is a lot more to it than that. Seeing and believing are two different things. In this chapter, we are going to teach you the latest skills and strategies that players such as Jason use to maintain mental toughness:

Achieving peak play

Using visualization

Developing a pregame psych plan

Controlling your emotions

Having a positive attitude

Playing in the now

Creating and using affirmations

Overcoming adversity

Setting achievable goals

The body acts and reacts based on whatever the mind is thinking and believing. The mind responds to the confidence and energy of your body. The real goal of mental toughness is to enter the ideal performance state (peak play), called the zone, which we cover later in this chapter. Remember, this is when your mind and body become one, and it is as if you are on automatic pilot, doing everything right with no distractions and no disturbances, just pure confidence. Your body creates high-energy endorphins, and you feel invincible. Unfortunately, this state comes and goes, so learning to be mentally tough is the key to playing well no matter how you are playing that day. Anyone can win when playing well, but the sign of a true champion is knowing how to win even when playing poorly. It is mental toughness that pulls you through in the good times and the bad times. The skills and strategies we teach you in this chapter will help you recapture that feeling of playing your personal best.

Achieving Peak Play

Let's take a moment to define peak play. Peak play is when you are playing your best and every-thing feels right. Almost all athletes, once they have the basic skills, techniques, and tactics familiarized, are ready to train to enter the zone.

When you are in the zone, you are one with the ball. You feel as if you are invincible, and no one can stop you. The ball looks bigger than life, and everything is in slow motion. There is no thinking, and you are playing with your gut. Each move, shot, and play just happens automati-cally, and the endorphin rush is amazing. You see the ball and know instantly what shot to make and where to put it and with what kind of speed. There is no time to think, analyze, or change your mind. You just see it and do it—that is peak play! You are on automatic pilot, playing your very best. It is truly amazing what the body and mind can accomplish together.

Body

Start with your body to warm up to the speed, tempo, and timing of the game. We recommend taking a shower, which loosens up your body, and then doing some sports yoga and stretching to work on your core, hamstrings, quadriceps, and so on. Get to the club at least 90 minutes before your match so you can continue to warm up your body with an aerobic workout on a bike, stair stepper, treadmill, or elliptical trainer for 12 to 20 minutes to get your heart rate up and develop a light sweat. Then you can do a few abdominal crunches and stretches to wind down your warm-up. Make sure you drink lots of water all day to stay hydrated because you will be sweating a lot throughout your warm-up and match.

Mind

There are four steps to getting your mind prepared for peak play. Before you start tapping into your mental skills training, find a quiet place, sit down comfortably, and close your eyes.

Step 1: Nostril Breathing

Begin to slowly inhale and exhale through your nostrils. This form of breathing quiets your mind. Nostril breathing opens up the right side of your brain and slows down your brain waves from a beta state to an alpha, or slower, brain wave state. This technique allows you to tap into the visual and memory banks of your brain. When you are playing your best racquetball, you are usually in the visual (right) brain, relying on your muscle memory. When you are playing poorly, it is because you are in the critical (left) brain, thinking too much.

Nostril breathing gets you from your critical (left) brain to your visual (right) brain, so all visualization is done while nostril breathing. Inhale for four deep counts, pause for six counts, and exhale for eight counts. The exhalation is twice as long as the inhalation. When you get uptight on the court, try a nostril breath.

Step 2: Visualization

Now put on your iPod to your favorite music, and start visualizing your perfect performance. Visualization involves creating images in your mind of what you want to reproduce on the court. Your sports brain works through pictures, not words, and does not know the difference between a vividly imagined picture in your head and actual reality. The benefit is that you get a 30 percent neuroelectrical contraction no matter what, so your muscles are being triggered by your brain. As a result, when a shot you visualized comes up during a match, your body will proactively respond to those prior images. Perfect mental practice leads to perfect results.

Step 3: Affirmations

Next you want to add affirmations, or positive personal statements, to your images of what you want to create on the court. For example, *I feel great today! I am a quick, talented, and fearless player!* These sentences imprint the positive images even deeper. These affirmations bring the future into the now. Your mind will believe whatever you put in it as long as your belief system agrees. Therefore put what you want in your mind, and remove what you don't want. More details on affirmations will appear later in the chapter.

Step 4: Cue Words

After you develop your affirmations, you want to add cue words, which are shortened versions of those affirmations. A cue word is a passionate word that releases a positive response. For example, if you say *Yes!* to yourself on the court after you hit a great shot, all the muscles of that shot are memorized as muscle memory. So whenever you say *Yes!* again, you will hit that perfect shot your muscles have memorized.

Spirit

Emotionally you want to get centered, quiet, and still and store all your emotional energy in your gut. The latest research says there is no need to psych up or psych down. You actually want to be quiet on the inside so that you are not distracted on the outside. All great shots come from the still point in your center.

With the body, mind, and spirit all working together, you are ready to turn your whole game over to trust and faith. Believe in yourself, your skills, and your competitive instincts because these are the only things you can genuinely control. Now you are ready to walk onto the court with your head high, your shoulders back, and confidence in your walk.

Using Visualization

The number one technique in maintaining mental toughness is visualization. It is the art of creating images in your mind of perfect technique and performance and allowing these images to become imprinted into your muscle memory, which lives in your gut. The best athletes do this naturally without even knowing it. Every athlete needs to understand that this is the key to perfecting consistent performance.

Steps of Visualization

The number one sports psychology technique is creating mental pictures in your mind of the ideal way you want to play. Visualization is the art of creating images in your mind of the way you want your body to perform. Let us take you through the steps of how to visualize for the deepest and most accurate visualization session.

Step 1: Nostril Breathing

Use the same nostril breathing technique described for peak play (page 217).

Step 2: Muscle Relaxation

Consciously relax all the muscles in your body, from the top of your head to the tips of your toes. As you nostril breathe, think of each muscle group and "see" it actually relaxing and letting go of all tension as you mention that area. Start with your scalp, neck, and shoulders and move to your spine, arms, biceps, triceps, and wrists. Then go to your chest, abdomen, hips, and legs until finally you have "seen" and relaxed every major muscle group in your body. If you have any aches or pains or old injuries or tightness, go to that area and massage the tension and tightness away. Remember that it is from relaxed and loose muscles that the fastest neuroelectrical responses happen, so you are imprinting the perfect physical playing state.

Step 3: Clearing the Mind

Let go of all your thoughts and create a beautiful blue sky, which we call the blue sky of your mind. If any thought enters your head, allow each letter of the word to disintegrate into a white cloud that just floats across the sky and has no meaning. Your mind is attracted to any thought that you focus on, so once a thought is released and not paid attention to, it loses its power of attraction. Continue this exercise until eventually you have no clouds in your blue sky, which means you have created the perfect movie screen in your mind. No thoughts and no clouds means you have now emptied your mind. It is on this beautiful blue screen that you start to visualize.

Step 4: Emotional Control

The latest research suggests that we play our best when we are emotionally calm and centered. High-level athletes are combining Eastern and Western philosophies in order to find their ideal performance state. Dropping to "center" is something all meditators and martial artists do. The calmer you are on the inside, the faster your reflexes and muscular contractions. A great book to read about centering is *Zen in the Art of Archery* by Eugen Herrigel (1999). He gives you an in-depth process to follow, and it really works. There is no more psyching up or psyching out. You act and react best from a calm, still center so that there are no distractions from your eyes to your gut (muscle memory) and then to your arms and legs. Most shots are actually hit between heartbeats or on your strong exhalation. There is no time to think, only to act and react from the still point of your gut. It is from this stillness that your shots are more accurate and precise, and therefore timing is everything. This is why we emphasize strong core abdominal muscles because the fastest electrical current travels through thick, strong muscle tissue.

Types of Visualization

Now that you know how to visualize, let's look at the three types of visualization and visit the movie theater of your mind.

Type 1: From the Outside In

The first way to practice visualization is to pretend you are watching yourself on TV. See yourself on the TV screen of your mind as if you are a spectator looking for perfect technique, strokes, serves, returns, and strategies. Remember, as far as your mind is concerned, seeing is believing. The key is to actually observe and see yourself playing with perfect skills and technique. Your mind thinks this is really you and connects the muscle reactions to each picture. So now you are imprinting perfect technique, and your belief system knows you can perform the skills. Your mind, body, and beliefs become totally aligned. This is very important because if your mind cannot imitate and imagine that you can play this well, it will sabotage you on the court. Visualization helps your body, mind, and belief system to become one and adds faith and trust in yourself and your game when you are on the court.

Type 2: From the Inside Out

Once you can visualize easily from the outside in, it is time to really step into the movie theater of your mind. This time we want you to visualize through your own eyes as if you are actually playing a game. See the front wall, the ball, the image of your opponent, the ceiling, and the back wall, and have a general awareness of what is happening around you in the court. Now your mind and body think you are actually playing a game, so every shot or stroke or move you make perfectly in your mind is getting imprinted into your muscle memory. This is the strongest imprint because it is exactly like the real game. Athletes say it is worth 30 percent of an actual practice just to do perfect game visualizations.

Elite athletes use this technique when they are too tired to practice or when they are injured and also as a pre-match ritual. This style of visualizing gives you the most direct and deepest imprint for hand–eye and foot–eye coordination.

Jason uses both techniques from the outside in and from the inside out. Remember to use each of these techniques last thing at night, first thing in the morning, and one hour before your match, as Jason does. This is a critical part of his pregame psych plan—and probably the most important.

Type 3: Guided Imagery

Guided imagery is a condensed version of visualization. Often there is not enough time for a full or deep visualization session, so athletes use guided imagery instead. Guided imagery is when you tell your mind to create a picture of what you want instead of words. Since athletes perform best from visual cues rather than auditory cues, guided imagery is a great shortcut to success.

In guided imagery, you close your eyes and instantly create an image on the movie screen of your mind, 6 inches (15 cm) in front of your forehead. It is like a 5- by 7-inch (13 by 18 cm) photo of what you want to happen next and how you want to perform. You can do this on the court between points or outside the court in your car, on a plane, or in the locker room. Guided imagery is a mental flash or a visual reminder of what you want to happen next. Desire it, see it, feel it, and hit it. It's as easy as that.

So here is how visualization works. Since your mind does not know the difference between perfect visualizations and perfect practice, you are imprinting perfect muscle contractions and memory instantly. So when you are actually in a game situation and you see the shot you want to hit, your mind automatically brings up the shot from your muscle memory storage (gut). If there is no doubt, no thinking, and no distractions, the perfect image creates the perfect response. Remember, this is called playing in the zone or playing out of your mind, which is something you make happen. You see the shot and instantly hit it because you are on automatic pilot. This is how you become proactive and not only play ahead of your opponent but also stay ahead of your opponent—a position you always want to be in.

Finally, for visualization to be most effective, the latest research suggests it needs to be done in a three-part sequence. Every shot, game, and match is made up of three parts: the beginning, the middle, and the end. It is imperative that you see in your mind's eye each perfect segment of each move. What you don't see won't happen, so make sure you see your kill or pass shot all the way through each aspect of the stroke. You want to see the racquet preparation (the beginning), the contact with the ball (the middle), and the perfect follow-through (the end). It's the same with your serve: Make sure you see the racquet come up as you bounce the ball (the beginning), then step and swing (the middle), and follow through (the end). Exaggerate each aspect of the shot in slow motion so you have all the time in the world to get things done on the court. When you slow things down, you see the ball bigger than life, and you can see perfect technique. Then and only then do you speed it up to game pace. Remember, seeing is believing.

This is true not only for the skills but also for your games, your matches, your tournaments, and your season. You want to break everything up into triads: the beginning, the middle, and the end. It is like learning a new dance; once you have learned all the different steps, you start to put it all together and then visualize perfect performance at the normal tempo, timing, and speed of the actual dance. There is no difference in sports, so train your performer self to do your routine perfectly each and every time.

Everyone is unique, and how you choose to visualize is up to you. Visualization can enhance positive energy endorphins and actually make you feel better and more excited about your match. It is much stronger than just positive thinking—it is positive believing!

Remember that visualization is a learned skill that takes time to master, so make it as colorful, real, and alive as possible. Eventually you won't even know the difference between playing in your mind and playing on the court.

Developing a Pregame Psych Plan

A pregame psych plan prepares an athlete's body, mind, and emotions to be 100 percent in the present moment. The more an athlete is willing to prepare properly, the more that athlete will walk onto the court with total self-confidence, consistency, focus, and concentration.

For elite athletes, the pregame psych plan begins 48 hours before their competition. If they prepare before each match by eating properly, warming up their bodies properly, sleeping enough, visualizing their game plan, having routines, saying their affirmations, and staying calm and relaxed, the easier it will be to get into their zone, which will allow them to play their personal best. Let's look at all the components of a pregame psych plan that help an athlete do just that.

Sleep   An athlete needs six to eight hours of deep sleep. We go through four rapid eye movement (REM) sleep cycles. Jason likes to get nine hours of sleep before a big match to feel fully rested.

Morning of Your Match   As you wake up, visualize perfect performance; see yourself playing exactly the way you want to play that day. After you get up, have an alternating hot and cold shower to wake up your metabolism. First the hot water to loosen your muscles, then the cold water to raise your metabolism and your heart rate, and then go back to hot and get out. Do some yoga stretches on a towel in your room and some core abdominal exercises, which are covered in detail in chapter 10. You want to get in touch with your body to see how it feels and what else it needs in order for you to reach your peak performance.

Mind   The last thing at night and first thing in the morning is when you are in a relaxed state, so this is the prime time to visualize. See yourself performing exactly the way you want to play using the game plan and strategies you learned in chapter 7. Do this as you are ready to drift off to sleep at night and first thing when you wake up in the morning. This sends slight muscle contractions or impulses through your body as if you were actually on the court playing. We have dedicated an entire section in this chapter to visualization because it is so important for every athlete to learn this mental skill.

The key is not mentally or emotionally exhausting yourself before your match, so read a book, watch a funny movie, or listen to music. Keep everything natural, and go with the flow of your rituals. Rest with your legs up, and relax and conserve your energy. Jason likes to watch movies or read magazines to distract himself and take his mind off the match.

Routines and Rituals   Athletes thrive on consistency and routine. We are creatures of habit and perform best when there are no surprises. In order to obtain optimal performance levels, you need a preperformance routine.

How Is a Routine or Ritual Created?

1. Behavior: An athlete chooses certain behaviors that enhance her game (e.g., bouncing the ball three times before serving).

2. Habit: A behavior done over and over again (seven times) becomes a habit. If you bounce the ball three times every time you serve, you will eventually do it unconsciously.

3. Routine: A healthy habit soon becomes a routine. As you are preparing for your upcoming match, you choose specific routines that you think will guarantee consistency and success. Bouncing the ball three times has now become a necessary routine since you stop thinking about your serve and go into it automatically.

4. Ritual: A ritual is a specialized routine. If a routine works and improves your accuracy, consistency, and timing, you move it into a specialized category called a ritual. This means

it is your own personal behavior that you use to play your personal best because it triggers your muscle memory and puts you into automatic pilot. Professional athletes all have unique rituals that get them deeper into their game, their performance, and their ultimate mind–body state (i.e., the zone), and so can you. Remember to always have a plan B just in case you cannot do exactly the same routine each time. The key is to never get flustered; just create and adjust and stay focused. Winners in sports are always prepared for the unpredictable. So trust yourself that you will know what to do at just the right time. This is called confidence.

All successful athletes thrive on rituals and routines that help their mind and body to relax and focus on the essentials of the upcoming competition. Everything in sports is a learned behavior, so each consistent pre-competition ritual that an athlete does automatically sets up an ideal performance state. If these rituals are performed regularly, then the athlete is on automatic pilot and enters each competition in the ideal performance state.

- **Night Before:** Get to bed at a reasonable hour the night before the match to get a minimum of eight hours of rest a night.

- **Morning of the Match:** After your good night's sleep, make sure you eat and hydrate properly with enough time before your match.

- **Driving to the Club on Competition Day:** Put your windows down a little; nostril breathe in the fresh air; have relaxing, nonverbal, alpha-state music on the radio; park all unnecessary thoughts outside of your mind; and begin to compartmentalize for your event. The key is to eliminate all distractions and unnecessary information from your brain so you can fill it up with your match preparation and game strategies.

- **At the Club:** Find your psychological home—or your comfortable place where you can retreat into your head for pregame preparation—stretch, and go over your game plan. This is your safe place to totally get into your competition mind-set. Jason starts with a 10- to 12-minute cycling workout followed by a full-body stretch for each muscle group he will be using. Hydrate and create affirmations, about the way you want to feel and play and be competitive. If you add an affirmation to a visualization, you get the auditory with the visual, resulting in a much deeper imprint. *I feel great today. I am a competitive, strong, and intelligent player. I feel, act, and play like a champion.*

- **In the Game:** Players have very specific routines that ground them and make them feel right at home within themselves and on the court. Let's get into the mind of a champion and see what Jason's routine is for every match and tournament.

Sample Prematch Routine

1. Get a good night's sleep and take a nap during the day, if you play at night.
2. Make sure to eat at least three hours before you play.
3. Try to do something quiet and relaxing in the hours leading up to your match.
4. Get to the club one hour before your match.
5. Warm up by walking, riding the bike, or running for 5 to 10 minutes and then stretch for 20 minutes.
6. Start hitting balls as soon as the court opens, which is as soon as the previous match ends.
7. Warm up your forehand first, starting from the dotted line with drop-and-hit drills. Hit all the shots you will use in the match. Move back to 35-plus feet (10.7 m) and repeat. Go back to the dotted line and do set-up-and-hit drills. Duplicate your warm-up routine on your backhand side. Then hit your serves, and you'll be ready to perform at your best.

Here is a great example of one of Jason's prematch routines in action before winning his first Pro Stop against Sudsy Monchik:

Jason and Sudsy were rooming together in Rochester, New York. On Sunday morning, the morning of the finals, Sudsy took his shower first. When Sudsy was done, Jason went into the shower and Sudsy headed to the club. When Jason got out of the shower, he noticed his clothes that he had laid out on the bed a certain way were now inside out and upside down. Jason at first was surprised, but he quickly took action. He took the clothes off the bed and put them in the dirty laundry even though they were clean. He then proceeded to get back in bed, get out again, take out a whole new set of clothes, and lay them out on the bed "his way." He then went back into the shower and showered again. Once Jason got to the club, Sudsy smirked at him when he noticed Jason had changed his outfit. Sudsy must have thought he was crazy, but Jason smiled at him and went on to win his first ever Pro Stop.

Controlling Your Emotions

As you learned earlier, there is no psyching up or psyching down these days. An athlete wants to be calm, centered, and emotionally still for the purest responses and accuracy. Too much hype is distracting and upsets accuracy and timing, and the fastest responses come from a still, calm, and relaxed body. Watch a cat ready to pounce on a mouse: It is 100 percent calm, centered, and focused. That is exactly how you want to be on the court—physically relaxed, mentally empty of all thoughts, and emotionally calm.

The whole idea is to be as prepared as you can be, physically, mentally, and emotionally, and to enjoy the process. Remember, it is only a game, not life or death. Keep in mind that racquetball is supposed to be a form of relaxation and rejuvenation. The more you put into your sport the more you get out of it.

Having a Positive Attitude

The human mind is duality based, which means things show up as good or bad, positive or negative, happy or sad. The ego does not like to live in any gray areas. The ego loves to be right and hates to be wrong. But we as human beings are 100 percent in control of the thoughts and emotions that we choose to focus on. So whatever we pay attention to and focus on grows. If you are filled with negativity, doubt and fear is what will grow in your mind. If you focus on being positive, happiness and fearlessness is what you will create. All of this is up to you. Everyday thoughts are random, but the ones we keep thinking about become our truth. So ask yourself these very questions. Do you want to be positive or negative? Do you want to be a winner or a loser? The choice is yours.

In sport psychology we say "Act as if," which means act as if you are winning even if you aren't. Your body and your mind love to be in harmony, so if your body language is positive, your mind wants to be positive too. Chris Evert was nicknamed "the Ice Queen" because she was so good at this. You could never tell if she was winning or losing by looking out onto the tennis court. She always held her head high, shoulders back, and had energy in her step. It had an effect on her opponent too because her opponent never felt as if she was ahead. Try it. Act as if you are walking onto the racquetball court convinced that you feel great, that you are going to play well, and that all is going to work out the way you want it too. If you do, that is the scenario you will create before the first game even starts. If you are in awe of your opponent and think he is better than you and start to put yourself down, then that is what you will create. It is plain and simple: Negativity breeds negativity.

Therefore, a positive attitude is a choice, and you are the only one in control of your mind. To take it even deeper, your body loves to respond to the energy and feelings that come from your mind, so if you feel positive and happy and excited about your match, your body responds by being loose, relaxed, and free of anxiety. This is how you get into the zone. You see the end result that you want, and then you act out the winning scenario.

Stress is a psychophysiological response to any thought, word, or action that you feel is threatening. So why see competition as negative? See it as a wonderful challenge or opportunity to practice your skills and strategies at a higher level. Train yourself to find the good in everything, and play from your heart and gut and not your negative head.

We cannot control the thoughts that come into our minds, but we can totally control what thoughts we choose to focus on. Whatever we focus on becomes larger, and whatever we let go of disappears. This is called thought control, and all the best athletes in the world have figured this out.

A positive attitude shows up in many ways. Your body language says a lot about your attitude. Good body language on the court, such as your head up, your chin horizontal, your shoulders back, and a bounce in your step, sends a message to your competitor that you are on top of your game.

Consistent pre-serve and return of serve routines or rituals help you get into your game and maintain a positive attitude. Your mind and body thrive on consistency and routine. See the section on developing a pregame psych plan (page 221) for more details.

Jason's Pre-Serve Ritual

1. Jason picks up the ball on an even number of bounces, steps on the dotted line, and then throws the ball to the front wall.

2. He steps over the short line and the service line without touching the lines.

3. After the ball bounces twice, he hits it around the court (left side wall to front wall to right side wall) on a fly (at which time he tightens his wrist lacer), it bounces once, and he catches it.

4. He takes a step over the service line once again, moves into position at the center of the service box, bounces the ball into the ground, hits it with his racquet into the ground, and then bounces it again.

5. He looks up at the front wall, looks down at the ball, and serves.

6. The entire time he is thinking about nothing other than what his last few serves were, what won the rally, and if there is something his opponent is uncomfortable with at this time.

Jason's Return of Serve Ritual

1. Jason has a statement, or an affirmation, that he says in his head.

2. He tightens his wrist lacer.

3. He pushes his eye guards closer to his face and gets ready.

4. His objective is to be offensive off of the serve whenever possible.

These are key elements for Jason to maintain his positive attitude and not deviate from the course, which helps him continually put pressure on his opponents.

Here is a great example of Jason's positive attitude when he was playing at the Pro Nationals in Las Vegas, Nevada, in 2001:

The Pro Nationals were held at the Sporting House, and the championship court the pros played on had a glass front wall. Jason always hated playing in the court with the glass front wall and never made it past the quarterfinals in that particular event. As Jason's coach, I explained the old sport psychology strategy advocated by Jim Loehr that you have to learn to love what you actually dislike in sports. So I asked Jason to say to himself *I love playing in the glass court and I love this court.* All week long, every time he passed the court, he blew a kiss at it and said he loved it. Jason actually did win the tournament for the first time ever, playing in the court with the glass front wall that he said he hated.

A positive mind creates positive results, and all of this is within your control. Learn to embrace your fears and anxieties and find a way to love them.

There are four components to preparing for a positive attitude: body, mind, emotion, and spirit.

Body

You always start with the body. Shake out your muscles; do shoulder, elbow, and wrist circles; stretch your groin muscles; and bend your knees to lower your center of gravity for quickness and speed. Your body needs to be loose, relaxed, and like a jellyfish. Only through relaxed muscles do you get optimal speed and quickness.

Mind

Next comes your mind—you need to empty your mind of all thoughts and distractions. Let go of any negative thoughts and replace them with positive thoughts and images. We call these thoughts "the little voice inside your head." The ideal playing state is when you have no thoughts, but that does not always happen. So what do you do when that little voice starts telling you what to do?

There is a three-step process. Ask yourself the following:

1. Is this thought true?
2. Is this thought necessary?
3. Is this thought helping me or hurting me?

If your answer is no to any one of these questions, let it all go.

If the answer is yes, then you can use the rubber band technique. Put a rubber band on your wrist, and any time a negative thought enters your mind, snap your rubber band and replace the negative thought with a positive thought. An example is *I can't win! . . .* snap! *. . . Yes I can!* It stings your wrist so badly that you never want to think a negative thought again—it is a muscle memory imprint now!

Emotion

The strongest sense we have is our feeling state. If it feels great, we continue doing it. If it does not feel good, we stop the pattern. So you have to feel great out on the court all the time. The greatest performances come from a state of enjoyment. We take risks, take chances, and are more creative in this state. If you are not enjoying racquetball, why are you playing?

Your ideal state is always happy, calm, relaxed, and in control. No worries. Your passion and love for the game are nestled in your gut, and your positive muscle memory is ready to act and react. You always want to enjoy the process and play from love and not fear. Remember, this is a game of mistakes, so keep your sense of humor and put it all in perspective. Pretend you are a wild animal before it attacks its prey—totally relaxed, muscles loose, and ready to kill. The animal's mind is positive and emotionally calm. This is the perfect ready state.

Spirit

You are now entering the new paradigm in sports. It has evolved to the point that winning consistently takes more than just preparation of the mind, body, and emotion. You have to be filled with self-confidence; you need to believe in yourself, your preparation, and your game. Self-confidence comes from the willingness to prepare and take total responsibility for all aspects of your preparation and your game. Self-confidence is earned from hard work. If you are totally prepared, that is when all your hard work meets with perfect opportunity, and success happens. This can be expressed in a simple formula:

Hard work + opportunity = success

So when all is said and done, just put the time in and then relax and enjoy the outcome. Win or lose, racquetball is supposed to be fun and challenging, so always stay positive and amazing things will happen.

Playing in the Now

In sport psychology, we say there is only one time, and it is now. When are you going to start to focus? Now! When are you going to win your serve? Now! When are you going to start to play well? Now!

In sports the past is gone and the future never comes, so in racquetball you have to learn that there is only one ball, one shot, one serve, and one point at a time, and that time is always now. That is truly the real beauty, that every shot you hit only happens in the now.

The only problem is that your ego wants to hold onto your past mistakes and fear the future. It always wants to be right and take control of the situation. The beauty of totally playing in the moment is that there is no ego and you are 100 percent connected to the ball, the wall, the shot, or the point. Playing in the now erases the ego because your mind can hold only one thought in your head at a time, so focusing on the moment erases all past or future ego thoughts. Do not dwell on the past or worry about the future because that only feeds the ego.

How to Get Into the Now

Try adding a cue word to fill up the auditory space in your mind. A cue word is a condensed version of an affirmation that still triggers all your muscles to do exactly what you want them to do. It is only one word that has passion and power in it, such as *yes* or *now* or *kill*. These words represent what you want your muscles to do. Adding the word *yes* as you see the ball triggers your muscles to act and react to your perfect choice of shots, perfect technique, and perfect touch and speed. Why does this work? The visual cue is the ball, and the auditory cue is *yes*, and your muscle memory in your gut automatically picks and chooses the right shot selection from its memory bank from your gut. All you have to do is see the ball, say *yes*, and trust in the process—that is how playing in the zone works. Remember you are on automatic pilot, playing from sight, sound, and trust.

How to Get Out of the Now

In sports, choking occurs when your mind is stuck in the past (e.g., thinking about mistakes) or worried about the future. If you are worried about the past, then your mind cannot let go of its own negativity, so you are reactive and slow to respond. If your mind is worried about the future (losing), it cannot focus on the shot that is happening now. Your ego always wants to be in control, so it holds onto things such as mistakes and fears, which puts you out of the moment. To get back to the now, incorporate some of these strategies into your game plan: Bounce the ball, say affirmations, take your wrist strap off, adjust your glasses, or do anything to reconnect to what you want to be thinking about right now. This is called on-court preparation, and the athlete who is willing to take the time to get back into the present moment usually wins.

On-Court Rituals to Bring Your Mind and Body Back to the Now

1. Sound. Bounce the ball—listen to it hit the floor—and catch it in your hand. Then say to yourself *I love racquetball* or *I love this* or *I can do this* or *Yes!*

2. Feel. Take your racquet off your wrist. Play with the strings on your racquet, feeling the strength and tension of each string and knowing that this racquet is there to help you and is your perfect weapon. Then feel the ball as you bounce it and catch it, and feel your athletic body ready to play.

3. Monkey slump. Try the famous mind–body connection called the monkey slump. Bend over and put your hands on your bent knees. Exhale on your way down. Close your eyes and let your upper body fall forward over your lower body. Be as loose as a rag doll. Every muscle in your body is loose and relaxed and shaking itself out over your lower body. Come up slowly one vertebra at a time, inhaling with your eyes closed. Once your head is vertical, open your eyes. You have released all your muscular tension, put blood back into your brain, and opened every vertebrae in your spine. You are in a relaxed and energized state, ready to play in the now.

Creating and Using Affirmations

An affirmation is a personal and present statement of what you would like to happen in your game or life. It is as if you are bringing the future into the present moment. Your mind does not know the difference between a self-created statement and reality, so it sends triggers to your body as if it is a reality now. The beauty of the mind is that you really can control so many aspects of the way it works and how it affects your everyday life.

The law of attraction states that whatever we desire and truly believe in the goodness of our hearts, we can achieve. Our strongest desire starts out as a seed thought, and then we pay attention to the desire and decide whether it is within our realm of possibilities. If we think we have a 50 percent chance of accomplishing it, then our minds start to figure out ways to make it happen. Next we create an image (visualization) in our minds of the end result that we want, and we make it as clear and colorful and real as possible. Then we add a feeling of pleasure and decide what price we are truly willing to pay to achieve this goal. For example, if you want to nail your pass or kill shot, then add a great feeling. Once you have nailed this shot or stroke or game strategy, you will be playing at a higher level, which gets you excited about your future possibilities—and then there is no stopping you. Each time you hit the perfect shot, it just deepens your desire and imprints the technique deeper into your muscle memory until all your body remembers is the good feeling, and it will strive for it every time.

Once you have decided on what you truly want and you are able to see the end result, it is time to add an affirmation, or a statement about its truth, such as *I am now a champion racquetball player!* or *I am a winner!* or *I am a quick, powerful, and intelligent player!* Whatever you repeat over and over becomes your mental truth. First comes the desire, then the image, then the thought, and finally your actions. Once you do that, it gets imprinted into your gut, and you literally start to create what you want. Gretchen Bleiler, an Olympic halfpipe snowboarder, sits down at the top of the halfpipe just before she takes off for her ride, and she visualizes her moves, slaps her thigh, and says, "Yes!" Then she gets up and goes for it. It is amazing to watch her focus, concentration, and guts.

So think of anything you want to achieve in your racquetball game and see the perfect end result, whether it is a new shot, strategy, or outcome. Then add the affirmation of exactly how you want it to turn out (e.g., *I have a perfect pass shot*). Then go to the court and take action by practicing, practicing, and practicing some more until it is a consistent and dynamic part of your game. By hitting the shot, using the cue word, and feeling the rush from the perfect technique, you will imprint it into your muscle memory forever, so look, listen, and trust.

It all sounds so simple, but here is the catch. You have to believe in your heart and gut that this is exactly what you want to achieve. You need to have a strong enough desire that no matter what, this is the destiny you want.

Now it's your turn. Create a present and positive statement about what you want in racquetball (e.g., to perfect a new shot). It takes 21 days for an affirmation to become embedded into a new belief system, so start today. Say it the last thing at night and first thing in the morning. Then when you go onto the court, visualize this new shot, say your affirmation, and hit the shot perfectly to embed it into your gut. You will be amazed at how quickly your game improves and how much fun the whole process truly is.

Overcoming Adversity

Nothing in sport or life is 100 percent predictable—the key is to create and adjust through all kinds of adversity. The first step is to change your attitude about what is happening. The optimist sees obstacles as challenges, and the pessimist sees challenges as obstacles. It is all in your perspective. And as an athlete, you always have a choice about how you view things. Jason sees his opponents as key ingredients that will inspire him to play his game at higher levels. He loves adversity and rises to the occasion. He takes all negativity and uses it as a teacher; he learns from every lesson, and it adds to the thrill of the game. He studies every single aspect of the game, his opponent, the situation, and the challenge ahead of him. And he uses every lesson learned as a new weapon in his competition game plan. This chapter will add to your mental skills and strategies so that you too can be prepared for all situations.

Loss of Concentration and Focus

Ideally, you want to get into a state of total concentration and focus on the court because that is when you play your best. Concentration is total awareness, giving your undivided or fixed attention to the game. Focus is the narrowing of concentration onto a specific thought, idea, or object to a central point. In other words, you concentrate on the game and focus on the ball and your opponent.

The more you play, the easier it is to hold your concentration. When you are getting ready for an important tournament, league match, or game, you want to play lead-up tournaments or matches just to get your focus and concentration into shape for the upcoming big event; we call this tournament toughness, or TT. Some matches last more than 90 minutes, and it is great training to get your brain to concentrate on the match and focus on the ball for that length of time. When you are totally one with the ball, we call it the "cocoon of concentration." You use pinpoint focus (seeing the center of the racquetball) and broad focus (seeing the whole court) during your match. Practicing trains your brain to do this more easily.

Different Types of Focus

There are two types of focus: broad and pinpoint. When you have a broad focus, you are taking a 360-degree peripheral check as to what is going on around you on the court; you see the whole court, your opponent, and the shots you want to hit. This takes all doubt out of your mind.

When you have a pinpoint focus, you are focusing on the center of the ball with laser intensity. All distractions are gone, and you are one with your game again. The more precise, intense, and accurate your focus, the more consistent you become. You have to see the shot in your mind's eye before you can unleash the perfect shot. All of this happens when you are 100 percent present in the now. You start with a broad focus to see all of the court and where your opponent is standing. Then once the point starts, you switch instantly to pinpoint focus.

Racquetball is so fast that the more you play, the easier it is for your eyes to act and react quickly. Often it is the "little voice inside your head" that distracts you and makes you lose your focus and concentration; good players learn how to turn off the inner voice by using rituals such as bouncing the ball, nostril breathing with their eyes shut, and visualizing their next shot.

Just like a great forehand shot, focus and concentration are learned mental skills. When you lose your concentration, step back and go to your on-court rituals; tell yourself to relax, and do a monkey slump. Now you are back in the game! Think about other sports too. In basketball, the coach takes a time-out when the players seem to lose concentration, and he tells the players to relax and refocus. In tennis, the players sit in their chairs, towel off, and relax and regroup. Racquetball players can take the time to regroup and refocus as well. There is nothing worse than continuing to play poorly instead of stopping yourself to recommit to your game plan. Take a time out, a water break, re-tie your shoes, anything to STOP the bad momentum!

Injuries

Elite athletes know that injuries are a part of any sport, and if you are pressing the envelope or giving it your all, injuries are bound to happen. It is your attitude and perseverance that will carry you through.

Fear of Failure or Fear of Injury

These fears are common themes in sport. In sport psychology, we say that *fear* stands for *false expectations appearing real*, and it is self-created and personal. It is an interpretation of a situation that you believe is threatening to you. Fear of failure happens when you allow your mind to get out of the now and to project into the future. So every shot you hit is reactive and tight because your mind is not in the flow of the game or the timing of the shot. You have lost 30 percent of your reach and stretch because your mind is constricted and in the future. When your self-esteem rests on your end results in sport and life, you are much too vulnerable. The key is to know you are a champion all the time. It has nothing to do with your win–loss record. Do not personalize your losses, just keep working on your game. Real winners know that when they lose they need to work on specific skills, strategies, or techniques. They are not losers in life because they lost a match; they are winners in life because they are willing to go back to the trenches and work even harder on their game. Every obstacle in your life is offering you a lesson to be learned. The courageous athletes say, "Bring it on!"

F.E.A.R.= False Expectations Appearing Real

In sports, as with life, we all have fears. How you handle your fear is what matters most. A courageous athlete embraces the fear and pushes through it anyway. The real key is to know the difference between an imagined fear and reality. So the athlete asks himself *Is this thought true? Then is it necessary?* And finally, *Is this thought hurting me or helping me?* If all the answers tell the athlete to *Go for it!* then that is just what he needs to do.

Fear is an emotion that comes from negative expectations, so visualize a positive outcome and keep taking baby steps to get there. Never give in or give up, and amazing things will happen!

Fear of Success

Fear of success is also a reality in sport. Some athletes are actually afraid of winning because there will be even more pressure on them to keep winning. They don't think they can handle the pressure or that they are good enough to do it again. So they sabotage themselves during the game. It is lonely at the top, and some athletes can't handle it. One's self-esteem totally determines how much success and failure an athlete can handle. If the underlying core belief is "I am not good enough" or "I am not worthy," then the body finds ways to sabotage the process. High-level sport psychology is all about erasing and changing athletes' belief systems so they can reach their unlimited potential. We all have fears, but the key is to make sure they are not driving our lives and our choices. It is how you handle your fears that makes you a real winner.

Slumps

Slumps are periods of time when some aspect of your game is off, physically, mentally, or emotionally. You may be partially injured and your technique is off or you are overcompensating. Or you are distracted by things happening in your life and cannot keep your focus on the shot or game. Or you might just be too tired and drained to compete. You need to take some time off, rest, figure out what is going on in your life, and take care of it before you keep imprinting negative habits in your game. Take time off and work on other parts of your life or aspects of your game. Maybe you are bringing the past onto the court, and you are fearing the future. Get back into the present moment. Also remember that change is an option. Do something different—visit a friend, take a trip, get a massage. This will break up your work cycle. If your life becomes monotonous, then how can you expect to create the dynamic energy you need on the court? Energy is created by new experiences and living outside the box. Challenge yourself in different ways, and watch how the ripple effect will improve your game. Know when to work harder or work smarter or not work at all. Listen to your body: It always knows exactly what you need.

Burnout

When you are doing too much too often while under too much stress, you may get burned out. Early warning signs of burnout include being short tempered, feeling extremely moody and emotional, crying easily, and feeling lethargic and depressed. Take a break from racquetball, and do something different. If going to the club doesn't seem like fun, then don't go. Pay attention to when you need a break and a change. All work and no play brings on a burnout. As human beings, we thrive on stress and recovery cycles. But the recovery has to be healthy, such as improving your diet, hydrating with water, having a massage, going to a movie, seeing good friends, listening to music, or reading a book. Burnout is the end result of the accumulation of your life choices.

Remember, you are a representation of your habits. Intense mental or physical stress is good for you because it makes you stretch and grow. The key is to match it with the same amount of intense healthy recovery. It is in the recovery period that you actually grow. In weight training, your muscles grow at night after your workout, while sleeping. It is during your deepest sleep cycle that your muscles heal and grow. So take a good look at your recovery techniques, and make sure they are healthy.

Loss of a Match

Losing should be a learning experience. Ask yourself *Did I play well and lose? Or did I play poorly and lose?* The key is to learn from your mistakes and remember your successes. Winning and losing are ultimately out of your control, so relax and learn from the experience and move on. Let go of all the negative thoughts, and remember your great shots. Erase your mistakes from your mind, and visualize the shot you know you should have hit—see it in your mind with the correction made. Too often athletes do not take the time to redo their mistakes and turn them into positives. We learn from winning, but it is in losing that we feel the pain enough to change.

Chris Evert was able to erase her mistakes instantly on the court. She would walk to the net, pick up her ball, and erase the mistake in her mind. She would then visualize the shot or stroke or strategy that she truly wanted to make in her head as she was walking back to the baseline. So by the time she started her rituals before her serve or return of serve, her mind held only the perfect correction because she had already forgotten the mistake. This was part of her genius. She never got down on herself and was always imprinting perfect shots and strategies until her muscle memory was filled only with perfect strokes. So what are *you* doing on the court to help yourself and your game? Remember, you are always in control of your choices.

On-Court Distractions in a Match

Maybe your life is in turmoil at the moment, but the big championship is coming up soon. Elite athletes know how to compartmentalize their lives for each tournament. They can turn their minds on and off and prioritize and focus on what is important right now. All of us can do this; it just takes commitment and practice. Usually we get into the moment by using rituals.

On-court distractions can be eliminated by rituals such as bouncing the ball a certain way, monkey slumps, picking at the strings of your racquet, shoulder circles, shake-outs, and nostril breathing. Every athlete has specific refocusing techniques to get himself back into the game. The key is to be so present in the moment that you know exactly when you are off your game and need to immediately make small adjustments and when to surge ahead. Mental, physical, and emotional awareness is the key. Your ideal performance state is when you are balanced and in control.

When your body starts to break down technically and mistakes are happening, it affects your mind. You start to doubt yourself and react instead of being proactive. You are thinking instead of just feeling, and you are a step behind because you have lost your confidence.

This is when you need to slow down and physically readjust:

1. This is a great time for a time-out so you can regroup and make adjustments where necessary.

2. Take your racquet off your wrist and massage your racquet hand. Do wrist circles and drop your hand lower than your heart to get fresh blood and oxygen into your fingers and grip. Then do elbow and shoulder circles and stretch out your whole body to get the blood and oxygen back into all your muscles, tendons, and ligaments. You are only as good as the oxygen, water, and blood in your body parts.

3. Drink water to hydrate.

4. Slow down your breathing by taking three deep nostril breaths. Your body needs an exact balance of water, oxygen, blood, and glycogen.

5. Your body thrives at a certain body temperature. If you are too hot and sweaty, your brain starts to play tricks on you, and if you are too cold, your body shuts down. If you are too hot, spritz your face, neck, and arms with cold water and towel off so that the cool air can hit the perspiration on your skin and cool down your core temperature. If you are too cold and stiff, start to jog in place, massage muscles, and do knee bends to warm up. You need to know what physical arousal state you must be in for perfect performance and take the time to create and adjust on the court.

Do not be oblivious to what is going on. If you snooze you lose. Remember there is always something you can do to make things better, so take control of the situation. Never give up.

Other on-court distractions players face include bad calls and cheating opponents. Most players get rattled by these and lose focus. Here are two strategies you can use to handle these situations:

1. **Keep a positive attitude.** Just remember what you learned regarding what you have control over and what you don't in the sections on having a positive attitude and playing in the now. Ask yourself *Is this call under my control or not?* Usually it isn't, so you immediately change to a new positive thought, such as *Everything is all right, stay calm, and get back into the moment!* or *I'm okay!*

2. **Prepare for setbacks.** Mentally rehearse all the things that could go wrong during a match, such as the bad calls or a cheating opponent, so there's no need to get upset because you have already visualized them and have your backup strategies to just let them go. In sport psychology, we call this simulation training, and it solves your problem. The key is to find your mental and physical balance again as soon as possible.

All winning players know that the real battle is within themselves. So once you figure out ways to get out of your own negative thoughts, words, and actions, you are all set. Try some of these strategies because we know you will have lots of success.

Setting Achievable Goals

A dream is a commitment made in your mind, and a goal is a commitment made on paper. Your mind is a goal-seeking mechanism, and it thrives on challenges. Your brain has been programmed to set goals and then select appropriate information in order to achieve the end result you want. You need enough mental activity and stress to stay active and healthy, otherwise you lose track of where you are and what you truly want. Goal setting is the easiest way to keep your mind aligned with what you want. You are always setting goals whether you realize it or not. Your subconscious mind is always taking care of your physical needs (e.g., eating when hungry), and your conscious mind loves to be on task as well. So set goals in racquetball and watch how

Goal Setting in Action

Gretchen Bleiler's goal was to win the halfpipe competition at the 2010 X Games in Aspen, Colorado. So last thing at night and first thing in the morning, she would visualize her perfect moves going down the halfpipe, always breaking them into a three-part sequence (see page 220)—the beginning (takeoff), the middle (trick), and the end (the perfect landing). She did this for each and every jump. She could see it, feel it, believe it, and achieve it.

Next she created affirmations for each trick, such as *I am a self-confident and aggressive rider!* and *I love to go big and spin!* Then she added that great gut feeling she would get when she landed each and every jump. Remember, goal setting always starts with a desire: *I want to win the X Games!* Then you have to see yourself winning and going for it perfectly. You add passion and then create and adjust, and you are there.

Gretchen set her goals at the beginning of her season. And guess what? Gretchen Bleiler was the halfpipe champion at the 2010 X Games!

you can create things that you never imagined. Just plant a seed, thought, or goal and then feed it, water it, fertilize it, and pick the weeds—then be patient and watch what happens. With baby steps you can accomplish anything you set your mind on.

How to Set Goals

- Last thing at night and first thing in the morning, visualize what goals you want to manifest in racquetball.
- Ask yourself what steps you need to take to get there. It all starts with an intention and a desire.
- Visualize your process and end result.
- Create positive affirmations, add passion and truth, and then take action. This is the latest in quantum physics and sport psychology. See it . . . believe it . . . achieve it!

Breakdown of Goal Setting

We've created a realistic timeline for you to follow.

- Immediate goals (0 to 90 days): These are things that need to happen right now. It takes 21 days to change a habit or belief. It takes 60 days to get your body in shape, so whatever your main issue is right now, start to take action.
- Short-range goals (three to six months): These are things that are going to require practice and constant vigilance in order to imprint a new behavior. Consistency is the key to imprinting a new behavior.
- Short-term goals (six months to one year): Where do you want to be one year from now? Set goals at the beginning of every season, and monitor your improvement.
- Long-range goals (one to three years): The world championships are every two years, so every elite athlete creates a training program around that timeline. Where do you want to be in one to three years?

- Long-term goals (three to five years): How long do you want to play, compete, and still keep working on your game? What championships do you want to win? A national championship? A regional, state, or club championship? This is called your sports career.
- Ultimate long-term goals (five-plus years): Racquetball is a lifelong sport. If you stay in shape and keep healthy, you can play forever and maybe play in all your age groups as you pass through them. Remember that it is a social activity, great exercise, competitive, and always a challenge. So, what does your future hold?

Make your own goal-setting log. Here are the areas for keeping a goal-setting log for optimizing your racquetball potential:

1. Healthy diet, hydration, and sleep
2. Visualization, guided imagery, affirmations, nostril breathing
3. Aerobic and anaerobic conditioning
4. Strength, flexibility, speed, and coordination
5. Skills, strategies, tactics, and technique
6. Mental skills training (focus, concentration, and pregame psych plan)
7. Motivation, attitude, humor
8. Stress and recovery cycles
9. Playing with passion
10. Competition toughness

Keep a weekly log, and grade each element from A, meaning great, to F, meaning you need to work on this aspect of your game. Then chart what you did when you played well and what was going on when you played poorly. Look for patterns and how to develop consistency.

Points to Remember About Goal Setting

1. Write your goals down or they are just dreams in your head.
2. Make your goals as realistic and specific as possible; you want them to be challenging but still attainable.
3. Pick an end date. When exactly do you want to accomplish this goal?
4. Make sure your goals are balanced and support each other.
5. Use the staircase method to success: short-term leading to long-term goals.
6. Constantly monitor and check your progress, and be willing to create and adjust.
7. Have personal goals, and always point the finger at yourself first.
8. Immediately set a new goal once you have accomplished your last goal.

Keep your goals simple but specific. Once you have written down your ultimate goal, keep in mind your intermediate goals, which help you reach your ultimate goal. Inside each one of those intermediate goals there are baby steps you need to follow in every aspect of the game, from physical skills to mental skills, conditioning skills, nutrition skills, and footwork, in order to get you to that ultimate goal.

Summary

Maintaining mental toughness takes as much time as learning the physical skills and strategies of your sport. When two equally physically talented athletes battle, it's the mental aspect that separates them, and the player who is more mentally tough will win the battle. But regardless of how mentally tough many players are, if they do not possess the physical skills to compete, then they have no chance. The key is to have a repertoire of great physical skills, and then you are ready to tackle the mental skills.

No one prepares more or has a more elaborate pregame psych plan than Jason does. He is meticulous with his visualization, affirmations, positive attitude, and playing in the now rituals. He has made it a science that works for him because the goals he sets for himself are never-ending.

Remember we are all unique. You have to create your own pregame psych plan that works for you. We have given you all our techniques so you can adjust them to your personality, timing, and lifestyle. Once you are good enough to enter the mental game of sports, racquetball takes on a whole new meaning, and there are no limitations on your creativity and imagination.

Chapter 10

Conditioning and Flexibility

Racquetball is often marketed as "fast . . . fun . . . fitness," and many racquetball players are involved for these reasons. They want the competitive element and the fun, but more important, they know that by participating in the sport they will increase their hand–eye coordination, their footwork, and their overall level of conditioning and maybe even shed a few pounds.

At a certain point in their development, though, players realize they need to do more to reach the intermediate and advanced levels of play. Exposure to the higher levels of play makes it obvious that better footwork, agility, speed, power, balance, flexibility, core strength, and cardiorespiratory endurance would make a huge difference in their on-court performance. There are no shortcuts when it comes to getting and keeping your body in shape.

In this chapter, we highlight specific areas or skills that relate to your conditioning, movement skills, flexibility, and training for peak play. We also outline a sample program that has been proven effective for athletes of all ages and skill levels. Our goal is to help you take your game to the next level, with a better overall understanding of how your body can work to benefit your game. Remember, the new paradigm in sports is to condition the entire athlete (mind, body, emotion, and spirit). When it comes to tough matches, you need to be in touch with every aspect of your game.

Our fitness expert, Dan Obremski, developed the Fast Fit Training System about 12 years ago, with an emphasis on helping athletes develop all their movement skills. Fast Fit is an acronym for fitness agility speed training for individuals and teams. From his program, we've chosen exercises and drills that will specifically develop better movement for the racquetball athlete, and we've organized them into an easy-to-follow program.

Before we begin to delve into speed, agility, power and strength, balance, and flexibility, it's imperative that you know the fundamentals of movement—in other words, how your body parts influence your efficiency and speed of movement. This is critical for all athletes who are trying to develop their movement skills. Just think of it in terms of your racquetball game. If we were to teach you the strategy of the game (including shot selection), what serves to use, and the ceiling shot without showing you the proper stroke mechanics of the forehand and backhand, we would be setting you up to be very frustrated, and you would probably not achieve the success that you could if you were fundamentally sound with good mechanics. It is the same philosophy for all the conditioning skills; they must be performed with correct form in order to get the most benefit from them.

Fundamentals of Movement

The following fundamentals of movement for racquetball should be adhered to when performing the program outlined in this chapter.

Dorsiflexion of the Feet   Dorsiflexion is an anatomical term that means having the toes or foot curled up. This movement is the foundation of all racquetball movement skills because it gets you on the balls of your feet. Ankle flips can develop this skill. (Refer to workout program.)

Hip Drive   Downward hip drive is produced by lifting the knee to hip level, with dorsiflexion of the toes, and then applying force down into the ground under your center of mass (COM). This downward application of force produces forward speed. Downward skips can develop this skill.

Arm Drive   Using the arms properly has a huge impact on your running speed and efficiency. Proper arm drive is produced by keeping the elbows at 90 degrees, with your hands relaxed. The proper range of motion for sprinting is to have your hands flow from chin level to hip level, with an emphasis on backward elbow drive. Upward skips, downward skips, butt kicks, and high knees are exercises that develop effective arm drive.

Posture   Proper posture for an athlete is having the shoulders lined up with the ears. Having proper posture allows you to move your arms in the right fashion and will definitely help with all your racquetball strokes. Building a stronger core in the ladder drill rotational exercises will improve posture.

Head Placement   Many athletes drop their heads when running, which weakens their posture and prevents them from using their arms properly. A good tip to remember is to keep your head up in all running drills and your eyes on the ball when playing racquetball.

Speed

Speed can be defined as getting from point A to point B as quickly as possible. Almost every athlete involved in a sport that requires running would love to move faster and more efficiently. Speed in racquetball is imperative but unique because of the nature of the court itself. You must negotiate a 20- by 40-feet (6.1 by 12.2 m) room while watching your opponent, the ball, and the wall.

The techniques and skills of racquetball require five different speed motions:

1. Starting speed helps you attain the highest rate of speed as quickly as possible so you can get into good center-court position or improve your return of serve.
2. Foot speed is needed to negotiate balls that are hit at different angles and come off the wall at different angles, speeds, and trajectories.

3. Hip speed (or rotation) is often necessary to turn and run as well as to generate more power, which we outline in chapters 1 and 2.

4. Backpedal speed is needed to relocate into good center-court position after the serve, or move back to the back court from center court to hit a ceiling ball, or move back from the front court to center court after you retrieve a great pinch or kill shot.

5. Change of direction speed is an often overlooked element of movement skills, but it is the most important in racquetball. There are four types of change of direction speed that we'll work on: side to side, forward and backward, turning and running, and jumping.

Now that we have addressed moving faster, let's talk about moving more efficiently. In this sport, if you move quickly but not efficiently, you will often overrun the ball or jam yourself, which is a major problem since you will not be able to develop consistency, accuracy, or power. The key factor in racquetball is accelerating quickly in order to get to the ball, but when you are getting into position, you need to be able to decelerate. Being able to accelerate and decelerate on demand is the only way you can develop your attacking forehand and penetrating backhand in a game situation where the ball is traveling at speeds of over 100 mph (161 km/h). Dan Obremski, our fitness expert, gives us a great example of this acceleration–deceleration principle. When he was competing at the professional level, one of his peers sought the instruction of a speed trainer. He worked hard and returned a much faster athlete. The problem, however, was that he worked on starting speed only, and so he was off balance and overran many of the shots he used to hit with ease.

Jason, on the other hand, has the ability to work his way around the court such that no ball is out of reach. He may sprint left, hit the ball, and shuffle back to midcourt. In an instant he lunges or dives forward, picks himself up off the ground, and backpedals into center court. The next shot may be behind him, so he has to make a quick hip turn and sprint back to retrieve the ball, again running to center court after the shot. In just one rally Jason is able to change direction forward and backward, side to side, using a quick hip turn, all while staying light on his feet. The more types of speed you can develop in your training program, the more shots you will get to, thus taking your game to another level.

Remember, by getting faster and being more efficient, your chances of getting to the ball increase in every rally. This translates into possibly winning more rallies and more points, and more games and matches.

If we take a look at different athletes, a sprinter in track and field, for instance, is focused on starting speed. A soccer player, on the other hand, must focus on starting speed, foot speed, and hip rotation when turning to run or kick. And a basketball player is constantly changing direction side to side, moving forward and backward, jumping up and down, and turning the hips. A racquetball player is a complete athlete who uses a combination of all these movements.

The following exercises and drills address all the movements that will assist you in becoming faster and more efficient so you have the opportunity to become a more complete racquetball player. Your weekly conditioning program will begin with two exercises from each category.

- Do one or two sets at first, 5 repetitions in each set, based on your fitness level.
- Time each set and write it down in your fitness log.
- Work your way up to three or four sets, 5 to 7 repetitions in each set, for intermediate players and five or six sets, 8 to 10 repetitions in each set, for advanced players. Try to shave off seconds from your time in each set.

Speed Exercises

Starting Speed

- **Get-up sprints forward:** Face the front wall in a push-up or modified push-up position with arms extended straight, then get up and run forward.

- **Split-step and sprint, 45-degree angle:** Position yourself against the back wall with a cone in front of you. Hop over the cone, land with both feet on the ground, then split-step and sprint on a 45-degree angle to both the backhand and forehand side of the court. A split step is a short hop forward, where your feet hit the ground at shoulders' width, allowing you to react quickly to either the forehand or the backhand side of the court.

- **Box jumps, up only:** With both feet together, start by just jumping over a line, then jumping onto an aerobic step, then onto a small box a foot (.3 m) high, then increase to a higher box as you get more explosive and can jump higher. Make sure you jump and land softly with knees bent, not with your knees straight and locked.

- **Stutter-step and sprint forward:** A stutter step involves moving your feet in place, like a tennis player. Start at the back wall facing the front wall, jog forward, stop after three or four steps, stutter-step, and then explode forward.

- **Stutter-step and sprint, 90-degree turn:** Start at the back wall facing the side wall, sidestep toward the front wall, stop after three or four steps, stutter-step, and then explode at a 90-degree angle and run forward toward the front wall. Repeat to the other side wall so you are working movement to both sides, not just one side.

Foot Speed

Most conditioning coaches use ladder drills to increase foot speed. There are many ladder drills out there, and some go by different names. It is too lengthy to explain each ladder drill, so please refer to books or the Internet. One book that contains plenty of training exercises to reference is *Training for Speed, Agility, and Quickness* by Lee Brown and Vance Ferrigno (Human Kinetics, 2005).

Hip Speed

Most conditioning coaches also use ladder drills to increase hip speed. One of our favorite exercises is downward skips—starts with one knee up at belly button level. Emphasize acceleration downward while skipping. This thrust downward builds hip speed and strength.

Backpedal Speed

Safety precaution: Do these drills at 50 to 70 percent rather than all out at 100 percent so you do not strain a muscle or trip and fall backward.

- **Get-up backpedal:** Face the back wall in a push-up or modified push-up position with arms extended straight, then get up and run backward.

- **Backward swivel turn and run:** Facing the back wall, backpedal three or four steps and then turn 180 degrees toward the front wall and run forward. Turn to both sides to develop rotation in both directions.

- **Backward quick steps into strides:** Facing the back wall, do six to eight short strides backward and then longer strides backward to the front wall.

- **Sidestep into backpedal:** Face the side wall, step sideways four times, then turn 90 degrees toward the back wall and backpedal at medium speed. Repeat to the other side wall so you are working movement to both sides, not just one side.

Change of Direction Speed

Side to side

- **Lateral shuffle linear:** Face the front wall and shuffle side to side, touching the side walls when you get there.
- **Cone drill wide shuttle forward and backward:** Set up two cones or cans of balls about shoulder-width apart. Start with one leg by one cone or can and then wide shuffle with the other leg to the cone or can; the landing should be solid and balanced. Go back and forth. As you get stronger, widen the cones or cans.
- **Ladder forward zigzag:** Using an agility ladder, alternate jumping from one side of the ladder to the next using both feet.

Forward and backward

- **Three-step drop linear:** Put a line using painter's tape near the back wall to the short line in the middle of the court. Start at the back wall, and take three steps forward and then three steps backward along the line. Keep repeating based on level of play and fitness level. Start at 3 sets at 15 seconds progress to 3 sets at 25 seconds.
- **Cone drill three-step drop:** Put five cones starting near the back wall and space them approximately 3 feet apart up to the short line. Face the side wall, and starting at the cone near the back wall, run three steps forward toward the side wall and then three steps backward toward the second cone. Continue facing the side wall, and run three steps forward toward the side wall, then three steps backward toward the third cone. Keep repeating until you do all five cones. The number of sets and how fast you go is based on level of play and fitness level.
- **Ladder eight-step drill sideways:** Line up alongside the ladder and begin with the lead leg. The steps progress as follows: 2 steps in, 2 steps over the ladder, 2 steps back in, 2 steps back to starting position.

Hip turn

- **Linear running hip turn:** Face the front wall, then cross over to the right side and run to the right wall. Repeat, but cross over to the left side and run and touch the left wall.
- **Cone drill hip turn:** Be in the ready position with a cone to the left of you. Lift your right leg over the cone, rotating your hip over the cone toward the left side wall (figure 10.1). Do the same to the right side.

Figure 10.1 Cone drill hip turn.

- **Ladder jumping crossover with three on each side:** Starting on one side of the ladder, hop over the ladder with your outside leg, landing on that same foot on the opposite side of the ladder. Then three quick steps are taken and you cross the outside leg over the ladder again (figure 10.2). Repeat down the length of the ladder.

Figure 10.2 Ladder jumping crossover with three on each side.

Up and down

- **Cone jumps:** Put a cone down in front of you, and jump left to right over the cone (figure 10.3). You can do these with lines or an aerobic step and build up to cones and then boxes. Remember to land softly with bent knees to protect your joints.
- **Ladder hopscotch:** Jump forward using one-legged hops through an agility ladder, as though playing a game of hopscotch.

Figure 10.3 Cone jumps.

Speed Drills

The quicker you can get from point A to point B, the quicker your first step will be—a must in racquetball. The following drills are geared toward improving speed.

Line Drill

Use the four different lines.

Start at the back wall in a down and ready position.

Use a stopwatch and see how long it takes you to run and touch the dotted line and return to the back wall, run to the short line and return to the back wall, run to the service line and return to the back wall, and finally run to the front wall and return to the back wall. This is one set.

Do the appropriate number of sets for your level of play. Time all of them.

Sidewall Drill to Shadow Hit

Shuffle side to side with a racquet in your hand.

Start at the dotted line in the middle.

Shuffle to the right side wall, then turn, set up, and shadow hit.

Immediately shuffle to the left side wall, then turn, set up, and shadow hit.

Go back and forth between the side walls, five times to each wall or more if you can. This is one set.

Do the appropriate number of sets for your level of play. Time all of them.

Agility

Agility for a racquetball athlete can be most clearly defined as the ability to maneuver your way around the court as you are getting into position to hit the ball as it comes off the wall at different angles, heights, and speeds, all while having a sense of where your opponent is on the court. We can also call this being light on your feet or being on the balls of your feet—in other words, being able to make adjustments on a dime.

If you think of agility in terms of football, it would best be described as a running back approaching the line knowing there are guys ready to hit him from all directions. He recognizes an opening and accelerates toward it, but he finds a bigger athlete running toward him. In an instant, the running back is able to maneuver his body and feet to make the quick adjustment to avoid the collision. When you watch Jason during a rally in racquetball, his mind is intent on getting to every ball, no matter who is in his way. If a ball is in front court and his opponent is between him and the ball, Jason has the ability to make the same quick footwork and body adjustments to get around the opponent to get to the ball.

Concentrating your efforts on maneuvering your body around the court and around your opponent will not only enable you to get to more shots but also enhance your ability to perform the techniques and shots you've learned once you get there because you will have more time.

Your shot selection will also be enhanced because you will have more time to think. (*Where am I? Where's the ball? What's the best shot to hit?*)

There are specific exercises that develop your agility and help you be lighter on your feet on the court so that when the ball is moving in excess of 100 mph (161 km/h), you can react to the ball in a split second. The foundation of all movement skills begins with the specific ability of being light on your feet or on the balls of your feet. Your conditioning program will begin with exercises that enhance this skill.

Agility Drills

- Do one or two sets at first, 5 repetitions in each set, based on your fitness level.
- Time each set and write it down in your fitness log.
- Work your way up to three or four sets, 5 to 7 repetitions in each set, for intermediate players and five or six sets, 8 to 10 repetitions in each set, for advanced players. Try to shave off seconds from your time in each set.

Agility Exercises

Ankle Flips

This is a skipping motion done with knees locked so that the only moving parts are the ankles. Skip forward, curling the toes upward, then accelerate the ball of the foot down onto the court (figure 10.4). Do this exercise down the length of the racquetball court 3 times.

Figure 10.4 Ankle flips.

Cone Drill: Forward Zigzag

Place cones or cans of balls 2 feet (.6 m) apart lengthwise on the court. Run in and out in a forward zigzag from back wall to front wall. This is a quick shuffle through the cones, traveling up and down the court 3 times with balance.

Cone Drill: Backward Zigzag

This time run in and out in a backward zigzag from front wall to back wall. This is a balanced backward shuffle, traveling up and down the court 3 times. Be careful moving backward.

Cone Drill: Sideways Zigzag

This time run sideways, both forward and backward. Done with great posture, this should be done 3 times up and down the court facing the same wall the entire time. This ensures that you are traveling right and left in equal measure.

Large Star

Use painter's tape to put six Xs on the floor in the court, one in each corner (front left corner, front right corner, back left corner, back right corner), one on the dotted line on the left side wall, and one on the dotted line on the right side wall (figure 10.5).

Start at the dotted line in the middle, down and ready with your racquet in your hand.

Use a stopwatch and see how long it takes you to go to each X individually. Each time you get to an X, swing a forehand if you are on the forehand side or a backhand if you are on the backhand side, always going back to the middle before going to the next X. This is one set.

Do the appropriate number of sets for your level of play. Time all of them.

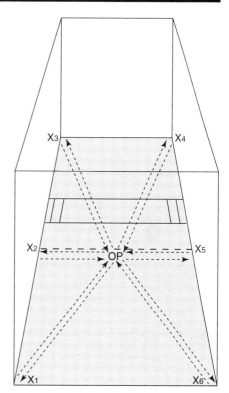

Figure 10.5   Large star drill.

Small Star

Use the four corners of the 6- by 6-feet (1.8 by 1.8 m) center-court box instead of the full court (figure 10.6).

Start in the middle of center court, down and ready with your racquet in your hand.

Use a stopwatch and see how long it takes you to go to each corner individually. Each time you get to a corner, swing a forehand if you are on the forehand side or a backhand if you are on the backhand side, always going back to the middle before going to the next corner. This is one set.

Do the appropriate number of sets for your level of play. Time all of them.

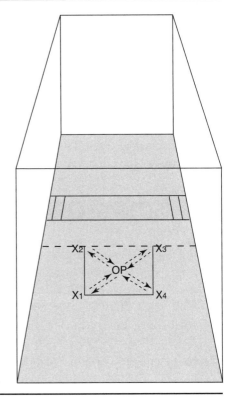

Figure 10.6   Small star drill.

Power and Strength

Power is speed multiplied by force. In other words, how quickly and with what force can you move? In sports we think of *explosive* when we think of power. How quickly can you act, react, or move with definite force? An example is a drive serve, which involves speed with force, equaling power.

Strength is determined by the number of muscle fibers that are engaged in a certain movement. The denser fibers are called on to create movements that represent strength. A strong forehand shot engages more muscle fibers than a weak forehand. In developing strength, it is important to understand that strength training entails breaking down already existing muscle fibers by the overload principle, and then that muscle heals and regenerates thicker, denser, and stronger muscle fibers. You have to break down a muscle to build it up.

Core strength is the popular term for abdominal and back strength. Each abdominal muscle has an attachment to the spine, so as you break down and train your different abdominal muscles, you are creating thicker, denser, and stronger spinal attachment muscles as well. Your core consists of upper, lower, center, and oblique muscles, so your core workouts have to incorporate all of these muscle groups. Your upper body and lower body are held together by your abdominal muscles. When you pivot, turn, sprint, and hit the ball, you are using your core strength. Everything revolves around an athlete's core strength—quickness, agility, timing, and power.

When thinking of power and strength in sports, an image that often comes to mind is a lineman in football who has to start from a stationary position and in an instant must move forward and encounter another 375-pound (170 kg) athlete trying to run him over. He's recruiting power from his legs, his core (abdomen and lower back), and his upper body.

During many extended rallies in racquetball, you can watch a player such as Jason recruiting the same power and strength from his body. If Jason sees the ball pass him, in an instant he rotates his hips backward and explodes into the back court with a sprint followed by an explosive dive. After hitting his shot he pops back up to his feet to get back into position. This is a combination of power and strength.

Having strength and power in any sport is an added benefit. By adding the following strength and power exercises to your weekly conditioning program, you will see a significant jump in your overall game. You will have more power not only on your forehand and backhand but also on your drive serves, which will give your opponent less time to react, forcing more weak returns and giving you an opportunity to score easier points on your serve. With your explosive movements, you will get to more shots that are a little out of your reach, and you will be able to pop the ball up to the ceiling to buy yourself time so you can recover and push back quickly into good center-court position. This will have you controlling center court, which will improve your winning percentage in rallies as well.

- Do one or two sets at first, 5 repetitions in each set, based on your fitness level.
- Time each set and write it down in your fitness log.
- Work your way up to three or four sets, 5 to 7 repetitions in each set, for intermediate players and five or six sets, 8 to 10 repetitions in each set, for advanced players. Try to shave off seconds from your time in each set.

Power and Strength Exercises

Leg Power and Strength

- **Forward lunges with weights:** Do this exercise only after you have done it with no weights and worked your way up based on your level of play and conditioning (figure 10.7).

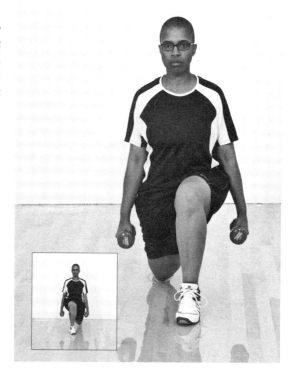

Figure 10.7 Forward lunges with weights.

- **Crossover lunges with weights:** Do this exercise only after you have done it with no weights and worked your way up based on your level of play and conditioning.
- **Descending squats to aerobic step, then low aerobic step, then floor, no bending over:** Legs should be slightly wider than shoulder-width apart. Squat with weight back as if you are going to sit on the aerobic step (figure 10.8).

Figure 10.8 Descending squats.

- **Box jumps with weights:** With both feet together, start by just jumping over a line, then jumping onto an aerobic step, then onto a small box a foot (.3 m) high, then increase to a higher box as you get more explosive and can jump higher. Once you are doing this well with no weights, start with very light weights (figure 10.9). Make sure you jump and land softly with knees bent, not with your knees straight and locked.

Figure 10.9 Box jumps with weights.

Core Power and Strength

Most conditioning coaches use medicine ball drills to increase core strength and power. Here are a couple that are effective:

Medicine ball toss sideways

Medicine ball toss downward

Upper-Body Power and Strength

Most conditioning coaches use medicine ball drills to increase upper-body strength and power. Some that we like are listed here.

Medicine ball forward push

Medicine ball shoulder toss: Point your shoulder towards the wall and hold the ball with both hands at the height of the right shoulder. Now turn while throwing the ball to a target at head height on the wall and then let it bounce once. After the bounce, pick up the ball and then turn and throw from the left shoulder, keeping in mind that the throw includes a rotation of the body followed by the throw.

Medicine ball underhand throw: With good posture, squat down. Swing ball between the legs and throw to a target at chest height on the wall.

Power Drills

A powerful first step will get you to center court more efficiently and ready to defend.

Step-Up

Find a flat bench or aerobic steps about 6 to 12 inches (15 to 30 cm) high and stand in front of it; lower height based on your fitness level.

Using one leg at a time, step up on the bench with full range of motion and then down. Five times on each leg is one set (figure 10.10).

Do the appropriate number of sets for your level of play. Time all of them.

Figure 10.10   Step-up drill.

Lunge

You can do this drill on the racquetball court, in the aerobics room, or on a basketball court.

Get into a down and ready position.

Lunge forward as if you are taking a shot, then push back to get into the down and ready position (figure 10.11). Five times on each leg is one set.

Cross over to the left or right as if you are taking a shot, then push back to get into the down and ready position. Five times on each leg is one set.

Do the appropriate number of sets for your level of play. Time all of them.

Figure 10.11   Lunge drill.

Balance

Balance means an athlete has control of all body parts at the same time regardless of what is actually going on. A balanced athlete knows how to lower his center of gravity so he has the fastest hand–eye and foot–eye coordination possible. A balanced athlete can move quickly in all directions, knowing where his upper body and lower body are at all times. Balance is trainable, and all elite athletes spend a considerable amount of time on this area of fitness. A balanced athlete can recover from almost anything, and an imbalanced athlete crashes and burns.

When you think of a figure skater gliding around the ice performing jumps, turns, and spins while in total control, this is the epitome of a balanced athlete. When Sudsy Monchik stepped into the court and hit his serve with blinding speed or backpedaled into the back court and hit the most powerful backhand ever, it was his ability to keep his head stable and maintain perfect body control on every shot that made him one of the most balanced racquetball players ever.

In racquetball, balance is the ability to maintain bodily equilibrium, which comes from strengthening the core body parts. Balance is one of the ingredients of conditioning that many racquetball players overlook, but it is a key factor that allows you to perform the mechanics involved on the forehand and backhand side with total confidence. With this level of confidence your shots, serves, and return of serves become more consistent, accurate, and powerful, which puts total pressure on your opponent.

Balance Exercises and Drills

Adding balance exercises to your weekly conditioning program will lead to a tremendous amount of improvement in your overall game. In addition to the two drills presented here, you can also add ladder drills that focus on balance.

- Do one or two sets at first, 5 repetitions in each set, based on your fitness level.
- Time each set and write it down in your fitness log.
- Work your way up to three or four sets, 5 to 7 repetitions in each set, for intermediate players and five or six sets, 8 to 10 repetitions in each set, for advanced players. Try to shave off seconds from your time in each set.

Line Drill on Court

Balance on one leg next to a line, then jump over the line with the same leg, and land your jump with control (figure 10.12). Then jump back over the line and stick your landing. Going back and forth is one set. Do the appropriate number of sets for your level of play. Time all of them.

Figure 10.12   Line drill on court.

Dotted Line Drill

Facing the opposite side wall, balance on one leg on the dotted line, then jump with the same leg onto each dash line, not the space in between, and land your jump with control (figure 10.13). Go from one side of the court to the other, then change legs, turn around, and go back using the opposite leg in the same way. Going back and forth is one set. Do the appropriate number of sets for your level of play. Time all of them.

Figure 10.13 Dotted line drill.

Flexibility

Flexibility is the ability to elongate the tissues and fibers in your muscles. It can be increased by proper stretching routines done on a consistent basis to get a fuller range of motion. Your ability to reach, act, and react depends on your level of flexibility. Flexibility is something we all need to work on all the time.

Stretching involves positioning your muscles in a way that encourages them to recruit more fibers by warming the muscle. Properly warmed muscles, therefore, have an enhanced range of motion. A stretching workout enhances circulation, blood flow, and oxygen to certain areas of your body and therefore increases your metabolism in that body part. In sports, your body works on the amount of oxygen, water, and blood flow to each muscle group. Stretching workouts also raise your body's core temperature and warm up your muscles, tendons, and ligaments. Post exercise stretching cleans out the lactic acid from these areas for faster recovery time. There is a lot of controversy around stretching workouts, so we suggest that you read this section carefully to understand how you can stretch properly.

During all of Jason's matches, there comes a point where he needs to put his body into extreme positions just to get to the ball. He sometimes has to lunge into a full extension to retrieve the ball, and in the same rally he has to extend into a full dive in the prone position. Jason is the greatest diver of all time, so this occurs numerous times in every match. His dedication to flexibility not only allows him to stay in the rallies but also keeps him injury free.

As a racquetball player, it is critical to be flexible and to have a full range of motion because you are often put into positions where you are stretching or reaching for the ball, and flexibility helps prevent muscle strains.

Your workout should include three styles of stretching, all of which are beneficial when used at the correct time in a workout session.

1. Dynamic stretching, which is stretching while you are moving.
2. Ballistic stretching, which is stretching while you are skipping.
3. Static stretching, which is stretching while standing still, sitting, or lying on the ground.

It has been proven through many studies on many types of athletes that it is best to begin every workout session or racquetball match with dynamic stretching. You will warm the muscles with many different exercises while stretching at the same time. Ballistic stretching will also be added to your warm-up, but it is more intense and should be done when your muscles are warm. You also have the option of static stretching, but this type of stretching should be done when you are completely warm and you believe there are body parts that need specific stretches to get you ready to compete at your highest level.

Be aware that static stretching first, when your body is not warmed up, is very dangerous because it can lead to muscle strains. Think of a brittle rubber band; if you pull it apart, it will break. The same is true for your muscles; if you start stretching before you are sufficiently warmed up, you can strain a muscle. This can lead to more injuries and lower levels of performance on the court.

Stretching Exercises

- Do 1 or 2 sets at first, 5 repetitions in each set, based on your fitness level.
- Work your way up to three or four sets, 5 to 7 repetitions in each set, for intermediate players and five or six sets, 8 to 10 repetitions in each set, for advanced players.

Dynamic Stretches

Most all conditioning coaches use these stretches to increase flexibility. Dynamic stretches involve movement that causes the muscle to extend, but not beyond its normal range of motion. Here are some of our favorites:

- **Walking lunges with a twist:** Do a lunge, and when you are in the lunge position, twist with control to one side and then the other.
- **Walking Frankenstein:** With your arms stretched out straight in front of you as you are walking, lift your legs straight up so your toes touch your hands (figure 10.14).
- **Knees to chest walking:** Your knees come up in front of you one at a time (figure 10.15a).
- **Quad stretch walking:** Your knees come up and your heels go behind you; try to touch your heels to your butt (figure 10.15b).

Figure 10.14 Walking Frankenstein.

Figure 10.15 *(a)* Knee to chest walking. *(b)* Quad stretch walking.

Ballistic Stretches

Most conditioning coaches use ballistic stretching to increase flexibility. Ballistic stretches differ from dynamic stretches because, while they involve stretching while moving, they cause the muscle to move beyond its typical range of motion. This type of stretch usually involves a bouncing motion. Some of our favorites include:

- **Wide skips forward:** Skip with a wider step, trying to get your knees up into your armpit area.

- **Wide rotation skips backward:** Do wide skips while moving backward, and when your knees are up high in front of your body, add leg circles to the left or right wall, opening up the hips and groin.

- **Skipping knees to chest:** Skip with high knees up in front of your body.

- **Skipping Frankenstein:** With your arms stretched out straight in front of you as you are skipping, lift your legs straight up so your toes touch your hands (figure 10.16).

Figure 10.16 Skipping Frankenstein.

List of Key Words

• Aerobic conditioning is when you are doing a cardio respiratory workout (e.g., running, biking, stair stepper, elliptical trainer) for longer than 3 minutes in duration. Usually a good aerobic workout lasts 20 to 35 minutes, and your body is burning fatty acids as fuel. This workout prevents fatigue on the court and improves accuracy and recovery time.

• Strength training is when you are breaking down and building up your muscle tissue for more power and speed. The lighter weights and lots of repetition cleanse and prepare your muscles for a heavier power workout. Lean muscle tissue is your fastest neuroelectrical conductor and the most efficient tissue that absorbs shock when you are on the court.

• Flexibility of your tendons and ligaments helps prevent injury and will add to your quickness and recovery. Racquetball is a game that involves a lot of stretching, reaching, and sometimes lunging, so stretching before and after each workout is key.

• Speed play is a combination of anaerobic quickness, agility, balance, and speed. This type of training should be fun. It balances your right and left brain hemispheres so that you can see, do, and make more moves on the court. You have to be able to hit the ball from anywhere. Speed play improves timing, balance, and recovery skills, all of which are necessary in order to win.

Static Stretches

Many conditioning coaches use static stretching to increase flexibility. This type of stretching is done when at rest, with the goal of increasing a muscle's length so that you have more flexibility during play.

Hamstring standing	Hamstring sitting
Quad standing	Calf standing
Quad sitting	Groin sitting

Stretching Programs

What follows is a sample conditioning and stretching program that includes all the sections: speed, agility, power and strength, balance, and stretching. We recommend that you use this sample program two times each week, allowing a two-day rest between workouts. On subsequent weeks as you start to master these exercises, you can choose two or three different exercises from each of the categories and work to master them. The idea is to keep yourself from getting bored so that you will continue to work out; you can change your conditioning program as you see fit, as long as you use the exercise sequence of two flexibility, one agility, two flexibility, two agility, two balance, three speed, two power and strength, and four flexibility. Always work flexibility first to get your body warmed up, and progress to the areas of focus for that week. Remember that quality is more important than quantity when performing the movements. You want to master the movements much the same as your racquetball technique.

Sample Program

Walking lunges with a twist (flexibility)

Walking Frankenstein (flexibility)

Ankle flips (agility)

Wide skips forward (flexibility)

Wide rotation skips backward (flexibility)

Cone drill: forward zigzag (agility)

Cone drill: backward zigzag (agility)

Ladder drill (balance)

Ladder drill (balance)

Backward swivel turn and run (backpedal speed)

Three-step drop linear (change of direction speed)

Lateral shuffle linear (change of direction speed)

Medicine ball toss sideways (core strength and power)

Ladder swivel (core strength and power)

Quad sitting (flexibility)

Hamstring sitting (flexibility)

Calf standing (flexibility)

Groin sitting (flexibility)

Make sure you consult your medical doctor concerning your physical ability to perform these exercises and take part in these conditioning programs.

Do not start any of these exercises or programs without a proper warm-up. Ideally, you should warm up for 10 to 12 minutes at a low intensity level. This raises your core body temperature and brings more blood, oxygen, and water to the muscles, supplying them with more energy and fuel so they can act and react faster. If you do not warm up properly, your body will be cold; your muscles will act and react slower, and you will have a tendency to strain tendons and sprain ligaments because there is not enough blood flow. You can jog or get on an exercise bike, a stair stepper, or an elliptical trainer to create the rhythmical circular motion needed to warm up the large muscle groups. This will not only improve performance but also help prevent injury.

At the introductory level of conditioning training, your workload, your intensity level, and your knowledge of the exercises will be limited.

As you advance to an intermediate level of training, you will start to see improvement in your movement technique, your range of motion, your conditioning level, and most likely your racquetball game. Now is the time to increase your workload and the level of intensity (speed) of each movement or exercise.

When you think you have mastered most of the drills and can move through the program with efficiency, move to a more advanced level of training by adding a few more exercises, increasing your speed through the movement drills, and diminishing the rest time between exercises and sets.

Basic Guidelines for Safe Exercise Progression

Levels are based on number of repetitions, number of sets, weight, speed of exercise, and intensity level.

Let's pick 1 to 10, with 1 being the easiest and 10 being the hardest.

Unconditioned or untrained person (level 1 to 3): Do 10 to 30 percent of maximum.

Beginner (level 4 to 6): Do 40 to 60 percent of maximum.

Intermediate (level 6 to 8): Do 60 to 80 percent of maximum.

Advanced (level 8 to 10): Do 80 to 90 percent of maximum.

Training for Peak Play

Training is an athlete's approach to optimizing his playing potential. In this section, we will teach you the latest concepts for reaching peak play.

One of these concepts is periodization, which is cutting-edge research for elite athletic training to reach peak play. Periodization involves looking at the whole year and breaking down your calendar into preseason, in-season, and postseason. The racquetball season is usually as follows:

- Preseason starts in July and usually lasts for six to eight weeks, or until the end of August. You want to focus on getting back into a routine, with aerobic conditioning being the most important. These workouts are long in duration and low in intensity and are great for fat burning and cleansing.

- In-season usually lasts from September through May, which is a nine-month stretch and extremely long. To keep from overtraining or burning out, you have to understand the cycles of training. You can only play at your best for an average of six to eight weeks at a time because of fatigue, both physical and mental, and the possibility of sustaining injuries. Playing a lot of tournaments over a long period of time exhausts you, so you have to match your tournaments to your peak play cycles. You can basically prepare and peak four times a season for major tournaments. After every six to eight weeks, you need to take a recovery cycle in which you rest and stretch and heal. Take a week off on low maintenance and repair.

- Postseason begins right after your playing season ends in June, and you should take three weeks off for a full mind and body recovery. Rest, relax, and enjoy your time off, and then gradually start back with aerobic exercise, ideally for fun outside such as running, hiking, and biking.

Recovery Cycles

Your body thrives on stress with recovery cycles. Work hard and then eat a healthy, balanced diet; always hydrate with lots of water; and add a sports drink if you need extra electrolytes to prevent muscle cramping.

There are many different types of recovery.

- **Recovery from your match and tournament.** Physically your muscles have been broken down, and you are filled with the waste product lactic acid. Therefore you need to take a few days off and stretch, hydrate, eat well, and put your legs up to drain all the waste toxins through your kidneys. Get a massage, and focus on other parts of your life.

- **Recovery from injuries.** This takes anywhere from six to eight weeks if it is serious to just a few days if it is minor. Rest, ice (no longer than 20 minutes), and elevate twice a day for one week. Monitor your healing; if it persists, seek a medical opinion and then start physical therapy, if necessary. Diet, water, rest, and recovery are what you need. During this recovery, you want to continue visualizing perfect play to keep your mind in the game.

- **Postseason recovery.** Take three weeks off, and then start back up with your aerobic conditioning and overall fitness. Slowly add strength training (weights) and cross-training (other sports such as yoga, hiking, and biking). Never go longer than three weeks without exercise or you will lose all to most of your muscle tone and aerobic fitness.

Training Schedule

Your schedule is determined by what goals you set for yourself. The loftier your goals, the more extensive your schedule should be. A training schedule is as important as a work schedule or a school schedule and cannot be compromised.

In the charts appearing on the next page, you will see how to set up a preseason, in-season, and postseason training program using the components of flexibility, speed play, aerobic conditioning, and strength training. Give yourself adequate time to prepare. Follow the three seasons of training and you will reach peak play more often.

Step 1: Six to eight weeks out

Start with an aerobic conditioning program of running, biking, stair stepping, and so on for 25 to 35 minutes, and build up to 35 to 45 minutes, three or four times per week.

- Begin strength training with light weights for endurance and cleansing, two or three times per week.
- Begin practicing and drilling on the court by yourself (no playing yet), three to five times per week.

Step 2: Four to six weeks out

Continue the aerobic conditioning program three times per week, and add speed play for 15 minutes once a week.

- Continue strength training, and increase to heavier weights two or three times per week for power and speed.
- Continue practicing and drilling by yourself, but add some movement and service drills, plus play with someone once per week (choose a partner one level below you so you can work on your game and not feel pressured).

Step 3: Two to four weeks out

Continue aerobic conditioning two times per week for up to 35 minutes and speed play one or two times per week for 15 minutes.

- Continue strength training two or three times per week with lighter weights and more repetitions to begin your maintenance program.
- Continue practicing by yourself one or two times per week, and play two times per week with someone a level below you as well as someone a level equal to you so you can put your skills to the test.

Step 4: Zero to two weeks out

Continue the aerobic conditioning one or two times per week for 20 minutes and speed play two times per week for 15 minutes.

- Continue strength one or two times per week, tapering to lighter weights and fewer repetitions to enter your peak play mode.
- Continue practicing by yourself once per week, and play three times per week with someone one level below you, one level equal to you, and one level above you to push you a little bit to get you ready for peak play and the season.

Specific Training Schedules

PRESEASON

Monday	Tuesday	Wednesday	Thursday	Friday	Saturday	Sunday
DR_1	DR_1	DR_1	Off	DR_1	DR_1	Off
DR_2	DR_3	DR_2	FLEX	DR_2	DR_3	FLEX
DR_4	DR_5	DR_4	MENT	DR_4	DR_6	MENT
ST	AC	ST		ST	SP	
AC	FLEX	AC		AC	FLEX	
FLEX	SP	FLEX		FLEX		
	MENT					

IN-SEASON

Monday	Tuesday	Wednesday	Thursday	Friday	Saturday	Sunday
$DR_{1,2,3}$	SP	Off	$DR_{1,3,5}$	$DR_{1,2,4}$	$DR_{1,3,5}$	Off
ST	AC	FLEX	ST	AC	AC	FLEX
PLAY	MENT	MENT	FLEX	MENT	SP	MENT
FLEX	FLEX		Play	Play	FLEX	
				FLEX		

What drills you do is personal based on what you need to work on.

Remember that since the racquetball season is so long, you need to rest before each tournament, physically, mentally, and emotionally. Start to visualize and rehearse perfect technique and on-court strategies. After each tournament, rest, hydrate, stretch, and relax for a few days until your body feels energized and ready to go to the club again. This is called stress with recovery cycles, giving you the best possible chance of playing all season without serious fatigue or injuries.

POSTSEASON

Monday	Tuesday	Wednesday	Thursday	Friday	Saturday	Sunday
ST	AC	ST	Off	ST	End	Off
AC	FLEX	AC	FLEX	SP	FLEX	FLEX
FLEX	MENT	FLEX	MENT	FLEX	MENT	MENT
	SP					

Remember, try not to go longer than 3 weeks without exercise or you will lose muscle tone and aerobic fitness.

TOURNAMENT WEEK

Monday	Tuesday	Wednesday	Thursday	Friday	Saturday	Sunday
AC	SP	AC	Off	TOURN	TOURN	TOURN
PLAY	$DR_{1,3,5,etc}$	$DR_{6,7,8}$	MENT	FLEX	FLEX	FLEX
MENT	MENT	MENT	FLEX		MENT	
FLEX	FLEX	FLEX			FLEX	

How many days you take off before a tournament is personal preference, so you need to figure out what works for your individual needs.

Key

DR = drill

DR_1 = drop and hit forehand

DR_2 = set up and hit forehand

DR_3 = drive serves from all 3 positions

DR_4 = return of serve footwork to both the forehand and backhand sides

DR_5 = relocation out of the box after a drive serve

$DR_{6, 7, 8, 9, 10, 11, 12, etc.}$ Above are 5 drills named as examples. Now assess your weaknesses, pick a drill that will attack that weakness and name it (backhand ceiling balls=DR_6, forehand wide angle pass=DR_7, high lob nick serves to the backhand side=DR_8, etc.), and start practicing so it will become a strength.

ST = strength training (weight training builds power, explosion, and speed)

FLEX = flexibility (prematch and postmatch stretching)

SP = speed play (anaerobic quickness, agility, balance, and speed)

AC = aerobic conditioning (cardiorespiratory training for endurance)

MENT = mental toughness

TOURN = tournament

PLAY = play games/matches. Close to a tournament, play to win. Far from a tournament, play to improve.

Training Log

Keeping a log is the same thing as keeping a journal. You need to record not only your drilling sessions but also all aspects of your training and preparation. Total preparation requires the mind, body, and spirit, so think about proper diet, hydration, sleep, visualization, and practice. See appendix A on page 275 for a sample template that you can customize for your own training and drill sessions. Also see http://bit.ly/fbCfh0 for downloadable logs.

Training Log Questions

1. Were you 100 percent prepared for your training—mentally, physically, emotionally, and spiritually?
2. Did you eat a balanced diet, hydrate adequately, and get enough sleep?
3. What did you drill?
4. What were your percentages when drilling?
5. Did your serve improve?
6. How much cardio did you do today versus footwork and drills?
7. How was your backhand ceiling ball?
8. Did you stretch?

Tournament Log

Keeping track of your strengths and weaknesses and your opponent's strengths and weaknesses will allow you to create great practice sessions so you can fix those weaknesses as well as develop a game plan to exploit your opponent's weaknesses. Jason is a genius in his prematch preparation and journals; he records everything from who he is going to play to how he can make his opponent the most uncomfortable. See appendix B on page 277 for a sample template that you can customize for your own tournament log. Also see http://bit.ly/fbCfh0 for downloadable logs.

Tournament Log Questions

1. How motivated, optimistic, and self-confident was I going into the match?
2. Did I visualize the night before and create positive affirmations as I watched myself play?
3. Did I hydrate well, eat correctly, and sleep well before the tournament?
4. Did I play well and win? Or did I play well and lose?
5. What went well for me today? Be specific (mentally, physically, emotionally, skills, etc.).
6. What did not go well? Be specific. Can you "see" the corrections you want to make in your head?
7. Were my shots consistent and accurate?
8. What were my opponent's strengths and weaknesses?
9. Did I have a variety of options and game plans that I could call on during the match?
10. What on-court recovery techniques did I use?
11. Did I erase the negative and plug in the positive?
12. How was my self-confidence, focus, and concentration?
13. Did I get into the zone (peak play)?
14. What do I need to work on?
15. Did I have fun out there today?

You need this information in order to evaluate your performances and see what is working and what is not working so you can make adjustments where necessary. By keeping a log, you take the guesswork out of everything and have the facts at your fingertips. Always keep a winning game, but change a losing game. Remember your successes, and learn from your mistakes. If you played well, keep doing what you are doing. If you got sick or injured, maybe you are overtraining, so back off. If you were tired during your matches, look at how much rest you got, what you ate, your stress level, your water level, and so on, and make the necessary changes so history doesn't repeat itself.

Summary

When you look at starting a conditioning and flexibility program, think of all the skills you need in order to compete at the next level. Racquetball is a game of speed, timing, balance, strength, and flexibility, and each of these aspects of your game is trainable and can improve with practice. Great athletes are made, not born. They are made by their own hard work. Think about it—if you had better footwork, better balance, more forward speed, better hip rotation and balance, more agility when you need to change direction on a ball, better posture when you hit your shots, more power on your serve, less soreness, and better endurance, what would happen to your game? Better yet, what would happen for you as an athlete? When you are in great physical condition, it affects your mind, self-confidence, and willingness to persevere through the good times and bad. Once you are in great physical condition and more flexible, you can start to train for peak play. At this point there are no limits on where your game can go, and better yet, there are no limits on your success.

Chapter 11

Playing Doubles

Doubles is primarily a game of strategy and court positioning when you get into the intermediate and advanced levels of play. You can no longer just bang the ball, stand anywhere, and have two players play singles out there on the court. One of the biggest myths of doubles is that if you are a good singles player you'll be a good doubles player, but that couldn't be further from the truth. No matter how talented you are individually, doubles involves two people joining their skills and unifying into a singular working unit. In doubles you must move and work independently and together all at the same time. How often do you read in the newspaper or hear a commentator say that the recently obtained superstar of a particular team is a great player in his own right but does not know how to gel with the team? Instead of helping the team, the player can actually hurt the team. Teamwork is the key to success. Doubles is truly an art; it is like playing the game of chess at 100-plus mph (161 km/h). Figuring out all the elements is critical:

- Where do both players stand and position themselves for the best court coverage?
- What shots do both players want to hit during a rally to put their opponents on the defense?
- What serves do both players want to use in any given situation in developing a good service strategy?
- How do both players want to return serve based on their opponents' positioning when creating a smart return of serve strategy?
- How do both players move as one on the court like good dance partners?
- How do both players come together and create a team?

It is like any other team sport: basketball, baseball, football, soccer. Having the right players working together is the key to achieving success. Remember what *team* stands for: together everyone achieves more.

In this chapter, we cover all the elements that can make or break a doubles team: the seven secret components, court positioning, service strategy, return of serve strategy, and drills for doubles only.

Seven Secret Components

These are the critical components that make up a great doubles team, and we recommend you address all seven when you are picking a partner if you want to be a successful team that stays together, grows together, and wins championships together. This is a sign of a great relationship, which is what doubles is all about. The last thing you want to do is keep changing partners. As you spend more time with your partner, you will learn what shot your partner will take in given situations and where your partner will move after a shot. The longer you stay together and get to know each other's strengths and weakness and idiosyncrasies, the more you gel as a team, and the end result will take care of itself.

1. Chemistry

Natural chemistry plays a big part when playing doubles. Chemistry is defined as a mutual attraction or rapport. You want to ask yourself these questions when picking a partner.

- How well do you gel together as one unit on the court? Do you move together and cover for each other instinctively?
- How well do you work together as a team and cooperate with one another on all facets of the game such as game plans, court positioning, and strategy?
- How do you feel about your partner? Do you respect, like, have fun with, believe in, and trust this person?
- Are you in sync both physically and mentally?

Basically, players should be able to get along. The better the friendship, the better the partnership. Doubles is a game of saves and covering one another. Chemistry plays a big role in each player's accountability and willingness to take responsibility for the area of the court that becomes unattended. Chemistry makes it easier to say, "My mistake," rather than, "Where were you on that shot?"

2. Communication

Communication is the key in any relationship, and doubles is just another relationship. You must be able to talk to each other and share your thoughts and know what the other thinks out there before, during, and after the match. You should discuss your overall game plan with each other and know what serves you will be hitting, what's the best return of serve, what court coverage you will be using, what shots work against this particular team, how to use your time-outs, and so on. There needs to be a leader on the court calling the plays, serves, return of serves, and so on and also calling the shots if they are questionable, such as "Mine," "Yours," or "Switch" (switch sides if necessary to cover a shot that is irretrievable by your partner). The last thing you want is for both players to go for the same shot. This can result in one of three things:

1. It puts you and your partner in the same area of the court, leaving the rest of the court open and uncovered for your opponents to now have an easy shot to hit, with an added scoring opportunity.

2. You lose the point because you hit each other's racquet instead of the ball and dump it into the ground for a skip.

3. You leave the ball up for a setup when one of you could have put the ball away and ended the rally.

Usually the stronger and more experienced player is the leader, making adjustments when things are not going your way.

3. Contrasting Game Style

When you are playing doubles, the best teams generally have partners with contrasting game styles; the differences tend to complement one another and balance things out. Let's take a look at two different game styles.

Power Versus Control   Power is when one partner hits harder than the other. Control is when the other partner complements the power with higher-percentage shots.

Cliff Swain and Jason Mannino are a great example of power versus control. They never lost a doubles match in their careers. Why? Cliff was a dominant power player with a huge serve. Jason was more of a methodical high-percentage player with the best lob serve and the greatest high-percentage shots, with exceptional getting ability. This balanced their team out because they were able to throw everything at their opponents and totally keep them off balance and guessing.

Shooter Versus Retriever   Shooter is when one partner is more aggressive but in a high-percentage way because she relies on the speed of her partner, the retriever. Retriever gets to everything, putting tremendous amount of pressure on the other team.

4. Contrasting Personality Types

Often players do not take their mental states into account. If two players have the same personality traits, one cannot complement the other, and they cannot feed off each other in a troubled situation. When you are playing doubles, the best teams generally have partners with contrasting personality types; the differences tend to complement one another and balance things out. Let's take a look at two different personality types.

Emotional Versus Levelheaded   Emotional players can be subdued by levelheaded players in a crisis. If there were two emotional players on the same team, they would have a tendency to rush their shots and not think clearly in a tough situation because their balance would be off. This is why Sudsy Monchik and Jason Mannino were a good team; if Jason spun out of control, Sudsy would be able to reel him back in. On the contrary, if you had two levelheaded players on the court, they would probably not be aggressive enough and therefore would not be able to create many scoring opportunities.

Calm Versus Psyched Up   A calm player typically has trouble getting psyched up and using emotions to raise his level of play to the intensity of the moment. A psyched-up player can be responsible for pumping up his emotionless partner so the team can take advantage of prime opportunities to score points at crucial times in the match.

5. Specialty Positions

When you take a look at any other sport, there are specialty positions. In football there is a running back, wide receiver, punter, defensive lineman, quarterback; in baseball there is a shortstop, catcher, pitcher, center fielder; in basketball there is a forward, guard, center. Athletes playing in these positions are skilled in their specialty, and they know what to do no matter what. In racquetball, it is no different. Knowing how to play a particular position takes a special skill and will usually enhance the team's performance.

Lefty/Righty Team   This is one of the most advantageous combinations for a doubles team because both forehands are on the wall, covering down-the-line and crosscourt shots. The stronger of the two players should cover the middle as well.

Right Side/Left Side Team   In this combination, both players are right-handed or both are left-handed. This is the most widely used combination in doubles teams because of the number of righties and lefties playing. Usually the stronger and more dominant player plays the left side, or backhand side, if the partners are two righties (reversed for lefties), and is classified as the shooter, whereas the weaker and less experienced player plays the right side and is usually classified as the retriever. In these specialty positions, the left-side player covers two-thirds of the court, which includes the middle, because as a general rule a player's forehand is stronger than his backhand. Also if the right-side player moved over to take the ball in the middle with his forehand, that would pull him completely out of position.

Front/Back Team   This is the least used combination for a doubles team at the higher level of play and should not be a deliberate position. Usually the stronger and more dominant player plays the back court (dotted line and back) and is the shooter, while the front-court player (dotted line and up) is the weaker and less experienced player and is the retriever. The top player floats into the front position every now and then but immediately goes back into her original position because the front/back formation is very vulnerable to down-the-line passes, pinches, and splats. Ideally, you would use this combination only when you as a team are being overpowered or your opponents are able to kill and splat on you continually.

All great teams use this combination, at times, and then will switch as needed back and forth between combinations. Playing doubles is like dancing: you want both partners to move as one. You need to adjust and adapt to the situation that is presented to you.

6. Control

The elements in a match such as attitude, tempo and rhythm, positioning, service strategy, game strategy, and shot selection must be controlled in order to create the best unity between doubles partners.

Attitude   Attitude is everything. Having a positive attitude toward yourself as well as your partner will go a long way in the success of your team. Putting yourself or your partner down will not work. Don't roll your eyes, throw your hands up, or even say something negative or criticize your partner because this can and will be destructive in the long run. Instead of saying, "How could you skip that ball?" it would be better to say, "Great shot, but swing level next time."

By having the utmost mutual respect for one another and complimenting one another, you will be creating a safe, comfortable, and confident environment for both of you to play in. This is a winning formula.

Tempo and Rhythm   You and your partner want to find the right tempo and rhythm, which in essence is the timing and pace of the game that works best for you. The last thing you want to do is play your opponents' game and not your own. If you like to play a slow and methodical game, then slow the game down by utilizing the 10-second rule and lob serves. If you like a faster-paced game, then speed it up and use lower and harder serves. In chapter 7 we discuss this at length, and it is the same for doubles as it is for singles; the only difference is you have a partner to consider and two opponents to contend with instead of one.

Court Positioning   The key is to be constantly moving into position, creating both offensive and defensive opportunities and at the same time trying not to leave any part of the court uncovered, which is fatal in doubles. With proper positioning on the court, you can often take advantage of the situation and use your partner to legally block out a shot you or your opponent hits, very similar to a pick in basketball.

Service Game Strategy   The doubles game is so fast that it's difficult to move into proper center-court position quickly enough when serving to establish control of center court, so choosing the right serves (discussed later in this chapter) is critical. Since getting back quickly is an issue, as a general rule you do not want to serve to your partner's side of the court, except if you hit a wraparound or jam serve, because she will not be able get out of the doubles box and back into good court position without getting in the way of the back-court defensive player. This can result in a hinder or penalty hinder.

Game Strategy   The name of the game in doubles is to play to the weaker player on the team, and this holds true at all levels of play, creating lots of offensive opportunities for your team. Although you are focusing on the weaker player, you also want to keep the ball away from the stronger and more experienced player, who is playing aggressively and trying to dominate the court by shooting the ball. By assessing your opponents' strengths and weaknesses and playing into the weaknesses of the opposing team's court position, shot selection, serves, and return of serves, you force lots of mistakes that you can convert into scoring opportunities.

Shot Selection   There are two variables in doubles that you do not have in singles:

1. You are playing against two opponents, unlike singles where you have only one opponent.
2. You have a partner on the court with you, unlike singles where you are playing alone.

Awareness of this will help you choose better shots, which will help you control the match better. Later in this chapter, we discuss in detail the specifics of shot selection strategy for doubles.

7. Shots for Doubles Plays

All the shots we discuss in chapter 4 should be used in both singles and doubles, but some shots are more effective in doubles play because the number of players on the court and the teams' court positions create a smaller margin of error.

Pass Shot   The pass shot is critical in doubles because it moves your opponents out of the middle and into the back court. This gives you and your partner a chance to get into better court position and forces your opponents to shoot around both of you. The down-the-line pass is great when playing a front/back team because down the line is the farthest shot for them to have to reach. You also want to use it against two righties or two lefties because one player must cover the backhand side, which is usually weaker. The wide-angle pass is also a good shot when playing against two righties or two lefties because the backhand player doesn't have the correct angle to hit the ball effectively or hit it at all.

The jam pass is a variation of a wide-angle pass, but instead of hitting the side wall between the short line and the dotted line, you hit the side wall on a fly, closer to the front wall so the ball goes into the middle of the court. This is one of the best shots against a lefty/righty team because it goes to both players' backhands. The pass down the middle is a variation of the pass down the line and does exactly what the name depicts, goes down the middle; this shot is used against a lefty/righty team because it goes to both players' backhands and handcuffs them.

Reverse Pinch   The reverse pinch is sometimes useful in the front court when your opponent is behind you because you can block him out with your body, both visually and physically. A right-handed player will hit the ball from the right side of the court and hit the reverse pinch into the left corner. A left-handed player will hit the ball from the left side of the court and hit the reverse pinch into the right corner. That is a tough shot for your opponent to see and move up to get.

Z Shot The Z shot is a great defensive shot because it pulls your opponents into the back court. Because the ball hits three walls consecutively and comes off the second side wall with natural spin and speed, it is more difficult to return than just a ceiling ball. And the fact that there are two more players on the court in doubles than in singles makes it a frustrating shot for your opponents to return.

Court Positioning

Court positioning is just as important for your doubles game as it is for your singles game. With four players on the court, putting yourself and your partner in the right position to get to a majority of the balls can win or lose a match. Regardless of what court positioning you choose to use (the different court coverage formations are discussed in detail later), you must be aware of everyone's position at all times. Depending on where your opponents and partner are on the court, you will need to move with necessary ebb and flow. You must move quickly to establish your proper court position independently, but that will be determined by the shot that is hit as well as the position your opponents and partner establish.

The downfall of most doubles teams is that the partners act as if they are playing singles and are very haphazard about where to go after the serve, after the return of serve, and during the rally. When you play doubles, you want to be like a piece on a chess board, knowing how to position yourself on the board and that every move can cost you.

No matter what court position you choose to play, make sure you and your partner are never within 5 feet (1.5 m) of the side wall; that is a cardinal sin in doubles. You want to leave those 5-foot lanes open for crosscourt, down-the-line, and wide-angle passes.

Core Court Positions

There are two core court positions you need to know when playing doubles: side by side and front/back. All variations stem from these two positions.

Side by Side

In the side-by-side formation, the court is divided in half vertically, and one person plays the right side and the other person plays the left side, with both partners hovering around the dotted line and back, staying even with one another (figure 11.1). Both players are roughly equal in ability level. With two righties, the stronger player plays the left side and the other player plays the right side. With two lefties, the stronger player plays the right side and the other player plays the left side. With one lefty and one righty, the left-handed player plays the left side and the right-handed player plays the right side.

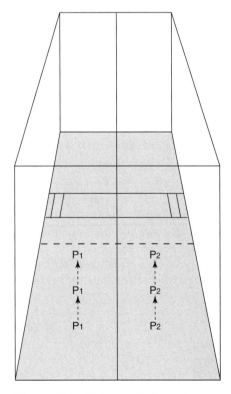

Figure 11.1 Side-by-side formation.

This type of positioning is vulnerable to crosscourt and wide-angle passes when both players are on or in front of the dotted line and is vulnerable to kills, pinches, and splats when both players are sagging back in deeper court. If both players move up to cover an up-front shot, that would leave the whole back court open for your opponents to hit to; if both players move back to cover a shot hit to the back court, that would leave the whole front court open for your opponents to hit to. Also if both players go for a shot hit down the middle, it could be a little confusing as to who takes it. This uncertainty could lead to mistakes.

Front/Back

In the front/back formation, the court is divided in half horizontally; one person plays the front court from the dotted line and up, and the other person plays the back court from the dotted line and back (figure 11.2). Generally the front-court player positions herself somewhere between the dotted line and the short line in the middle, and the back-court player positions herself somewhere between the dotted line and the back wall in the middle. These positions fluctuate based on what shots their opponents are hitting. If their opponents are hitting a lot of kills, pinches, and splats, the front-court player will be farther up. If their opponents are hitting a lot of passes and ceilings, the back-court player will be farther back. The front-court player is fast, is a great retriever, and rekills shots that are left up. The back-court player is a bit slower but is a great shooter who runs down pass shots and well-hit ceiling balls and creates offense from deeper in the court. This type of court coverage is used with a stronger and weaker player on the court so that the weaker player is not overpowered. The stronger player plays in the back court.

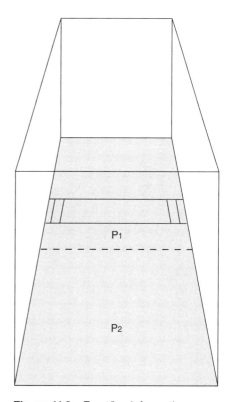

Figure 11.2   Front/back formation.

This type of positioning is vulnerable to down-the-line and crosscourt passes. When going down the line, it's harder to get to the ball because it covers a shorter distance, which cuts down your reaction time. The crosscourt pass is an excellent choice because the front-court player is in good position to sit on the kills, pinches, and left-up side wall shots. The biggest disadvantage of this court position is that the opponents can isolate one player over the other and exploit that one player, leaving the other player completely out of the play. This type of strategy can disrupt the other player's timing because he may not be hitting many balls. Use this to your advantage: If you hit kills and pinches, the front-court player is in the play and the back-court player is left out; if you hit passes and ceiling balls to the back court, the front-court player is left out.

Intermediate and Advanced Court Positions

Once you learn side-by-side and front/back court positioning, you are ready to move up to the intermediate and advanced positions, which are combinations or variations of the two core formations. As you improve as a doubles player, you will learn that you do not play just one type of court position; rather, you are always mixing and matching, moving and dancing, ready to cover anything your partner cannot get to.

Two-Thirds Side by Side

This is the same as side by side, but instead of dividing the court in half, you divide the court two-thirds to one-third. For two right-handed players, the stronger player takes the backhand (left) side and will cover two-thirds of the court, which includes the middle (figure 11.3). This makes the team stronger because the left-side player will be using the forehand in the middle (rather than the right-side player using the backhand). For two left-handed players, the player with the stronger backhand plays two-thirds of the court and takes the middle using the forehand.

This type of positioning is vulnerable to shots that are hit to the middle when the player assigned to those middle shots is out of position. His partner must pay close attention and cover for him, taking that middle shot when needed. Also, the one-third-court player may have a tendency to stick her racquet into the middle, using her backhand to play the shot, and that is not good. It takes discipline to let the ball go to a partner's forehand. Just as in the front/back positioning, the two-thirds-court player can be doing most of the work and can get tired, and her partner can lose her timing because she is not hitting as many balls. Lastly, this formation opens up opportunities for opponents to exploit because the two-thirds-court player can be pulled out of position.

L Formation

The court is divided into an L, and the stronger player covers the L on the court (figure 11.4). This is designed for a strong and weak player that want to play one level up, but the weaker player is not proficient at shooting balls off the back wall or hitting good ceiling balls.

This type of positioning is very vulnerable because the stronger player is pulled out of position a lot while covering most of the court, which leaves lots of openings for opponents to capitalize on.

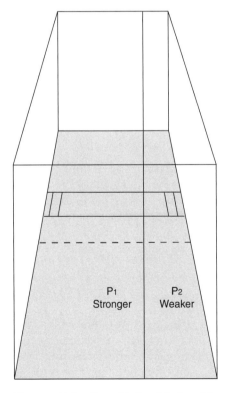

Figure 11.3 Two-thirds side-by-side formation.

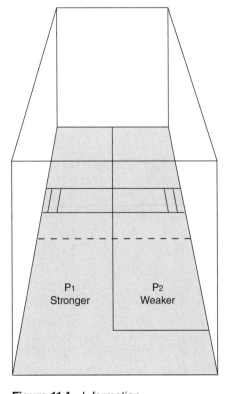

Figure 11.4 L formation.

Modified Side-by-Side, or S Formation

This is the court position most widely used by the pros and top amateur players. It is a true combination of the side-by-side and front/back positions, allowing players to maneuver around the court and make adjustments when necessary based on where the shooter is and what her tendencies are. If your opponent is shooting from the right side of the court and is deep, then the right-side player should be behind the dotted line, slightly to the right of center court, defending the down-the-line, the crosscourt, and wide-angle pass; the left-side player should cover the crosscourt kill, splat, and pinch from between the dotted line and the short line, slightly to the left of center court (figure 11.5a). If your opponent is shooting from the left side of the court and is deep, then the left-side player should be behind the dotted line, slightly to the left of center court, defending the down-the-line, the crosscourt, and the wide-angle pass; the right-side player should cover the crosscourt kill, splat, and pinch from between the dotted line and the short line, slightly to the right of center court (figure 11.5b).

Your position as the front-court player will change based on the shot. If your opponent has a tendency to pinch and splat a lot, you should be closer to the short line; conversely, if your opponent is passing a lot, you should be closer to the dotted line. Your position as the back-court player will also change. If your opponent is hitting more wide-angle passes and ceiling balls, you should be farther from the dotted line and deeper in the court.

The best way to describe this positioning is like a zone defense in basketball, in which you hang in your zone and cover the player who winds up on your side or in your zone. You are forever moving and floating around the court, never standing still or flat-footed, so you can anticipate defensive coverage and offensive opportunities.

This type of positioning is the hardest to exploit because it puts a tremendous amount of pressure on your opponents to hit perfect kill shots up front and passes or ceilings deep. The front-court player is in great position to move forward and dig out the balls that are left up, and the back-court player is deep enough to track left-up pass shots and long ceiling balls. All in all, almost everything is covered—except the perfect straight-in kill shot—so your opponent believes perfection is the only way to win. And when players try to hit perfect shots all the time from all over the court, mistakes are inevitable.

When you and your partner are facing this formation, there are certain shots you can hit to combat your

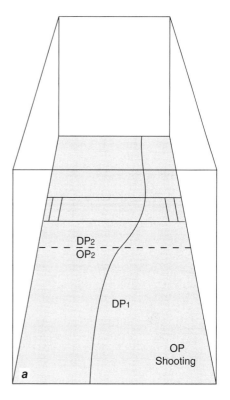

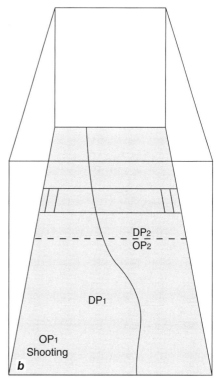

Figure 11.5a-b Modified side-by-side, or S formation.

opponents' great positioning. Try the Z shot, lower and harder wide-angle passes, and ceiling balls from right to left, pulling your front-court player back then up, back then up, and back then up.

Shot Selection Strategy for Doubles

Shot selection is no different for doubles than for singles; you use the formula A + B + C + D = E (see chapter 6 for details). Just remember there are two extra people on the court. Therefore your choice of shots needs to be smarter and more precise because you have to get the ball past two players instead of one, and you do not want to hit your partner. This makes doubles less forgiving—you have less room for error compared to singles. Killing and pinching the ball are not as common in doubles because these shots are more difficult to make with four people on the court. This is why the wide-angle pass is extremely important in doubles. The ball changes directions drastically with this shot while taking the floor out of play. The wide angle is the pass of choice because it is very difficult to get a down-the-line or crosscourt pass by two people, and the wide-angle pass brings both players into the shot, creating confusion because they will both be going for the ball at the same time. This is the epitome of high-percentage racquetball. However, you don't want to discount putting the ball away. You just want to do so when given the right opportunity—when your opponents are not in good position, the shot is open, you are in setup position with your feet stopped and set, and the ball is knee high and lower.

When you do not have an offensive shot and must go defensive, and the opportunity presents itself to hit a Z or a ceiling ball, the Z shot is more effective. Like the wide-angle pass, the Z creates confusion because the two players will be going after the ball at the same time since it goes through both sides of the court before landing. Choosing the right shot at the right time in doubles is twice as important.

Service Game Strategy

Before you decide on what serve to hit, you want to know your opponents' strengths and weaknesses, as well as your own, and take advantage of serving to your opponents' weaknesses. Pay close attention to what style players you are playing—a lefty/righty team or two righties or two lefties—because that will help determine what serves you will use. Keep in mind that certain serves work better against a particular player or team. Having a precise service game strategy is extremely important for doubles because the serve sets the tone of the match.

Once you know the following information, you and your partner can come up with a service game strategy:

1. Lefty/righty team: Serve to the middle, where both players are on their backhands. This is a weakness, and there might be a little confusion between the players. Try a half lob down the middle, half lob nick to the middle, drive wrap to the middle, or drive jam to the middle.

2. Two righties or two lefties: Use the Z serves because they are very effective. Start out with high-lob Z serves to see if they cut them off, then start bringing them down to three-quarters, then one-half, then a hard lob Z, concentrating on which you have the most success with. Try half lobs right along the wall, such as drive serves, drive wraps, and drive jams. The height, speed, and angle of the ball will play a huge role in your opponents' comfort level.

Return of Serve Strategy

Pass, pass, pass!

The best return of serve for doubles is a pass, if possible, trying to keep your opponents from getting back into good center-court position. If you cannot attack early, then go to the ceiling, which still gets the serving team into the back court, your number one goal. Once the serve is hit, if the non-serving partner is slow getting back out of the service zone, that is a great opportunity for you to step up and blast the ball back to that side with a hard passing shot.

Wide angles are Jason's favorite, and he is good at them. After a particular match, Kane Waselenchuk (the number one pro player in the world, 2008-2009) came up to him and said, "You hit six wide-angle passes in a row, starting with the return of serve. I don't think I've ever seen that before." Jason laughed and said, "That's what I do, bro." As you learned in chapter 5, it's more difficult to kill the ball from 39 feet (11.9 m) back because the odds are stacked against you, let alone having two people trying to retrieve the ball. What Jason likes to do and what we advocate is to wear your opponents down by hitting a ton of passes. Even if the retrieving team is up close in the front of the court, when you hit enough passes, you get them on their heels. Your pass-kill shots then become more effective, and you can even throw in a kill shot.

Remember, when you are developing a return of serve strategy for doubles, think *pass* first, second, and third, and then think *ceiling* when you can't pass. Both of these shots get the opposing team to the back court and allow you and your partner time to come in and reestablish yourselves in the front court.

Doubles Drills

Drilling is especially important in doubles because you will be hitting different shots and serves more frequently. In singles, you need only be concerned about the strengths and weaknesses of two players (you and your opponent), whereas in doubles, you must be concerned about four. In singles, you have to hit the ball around only one player, whereas in doubles, you must know where three other players are on the court besides yourself. Given these facts, you must hit many different shots and serves effectively to succeed. Proper drilling is a major factor of your success.

Chapter 8 covers all the details on drilling and shows you how to keep track of everything you do.

Partner Reaction

This is a timing drill that partners can do to sharpen their swords. Cliff (lefty) and Jason (righty) always did this before they played. They simply stayed at the dotted line, Cliff on the left and Jason on the right, and hammered the ball back and forth at each other in order to get used to the pace. This would make their hands, feet, and brains quicker at game time.

Z and Jam Serve Returns

In doubles you should expect to see a lot of Z serves and jam serves. During warm-up and when you drill with your doubles partner, you can hit 15 or 20 Z serves in a row and 15 or 20 jam serves in a row and have your partner return them, and then switch roles. This gets you both comfortable with what's likely to occur in the match and the serves you are most likely going to use.

Wide-Angle Pass With Partner

One of the most prevalent shots in the game of doubles is the wide-angle pass. You can position your partner in several different spots near the side wall and try to hit the ball around her, practicing from different spots on the court that you expect to be shooting from. This can help you visualize the shots as they will occur in the match.

Reverse Pinch

Quick-reverse pinches are used a lot at the higher levels. When an opponent misses a shot in the front of the court, the corner is likely open (except when the ball is coming off the back wall or when your opponents have time to get into position). You and your partner can drill by shooting left-up pinches and passes that kick off the side wall in the front of the court and shooting reverse pinches from these setups.

Overhead Passes

On the forehand side, try to shoot as many overhead passes as you can off of short ceiling balls or off of Z serves, creating more offense. Have your partner or you hit short ceiling balls or Z serves, and then hit an overhead crosscourt or overhead wide angle. This shot helps solicit weak returns because your opponent wants to shoot your return, which is extremely difficult and typically leaves some kind of offensive opportunity on the next shot.

Summary

Although doubles may seem complicated, it is actually a ton of fun. There are many things to consider about doubles, as we've discussed in this chapter, but in the end it all comes down to applying your team's strengths and weaknesses to your opponents' strengths and weaknesses, just like in singles. Remember that the key to doubles is to pick the right partner for you, not necessarily the best player you can find. Together everyone achieves more (TEAM) should be the mantra for your doubles strategy, and being able to work together on the court is of utmost importance. Drill for the high-percentage racquetball you should be playing, and try to wear down your opponents while earning the right to kill. Playing the percentages in doubles is arguably more important than doing so in singles. The team that applies the most pressure on their opponents usually wins.

Appendix A
Training Logs

Sample training log

Session	Date	Time	Trainer	Comments
1	___ / ___ / ___	___ : ___		
2	___ / ___ / ___	___ : ___		
3	___ / ___ / ___	___ : ___		
4	___ / ___ / ___	___ : ___		
5	___ / ___ / ___	___ : ___		
6	___ / ___ / ___	___ : ___		
7	___ / ___ / ___	___ : ___		
8	___ / ___ / ___	___ : ___		
9	___ / ___ / ___	___ : ___		
10	___ / ___ / ___	___ : ___		
11	___ / ___ / ___	___ : ___		
12	___ / ___ / ___	___ : ___		
13	___ / ___ / ___	___ : ___		
14	___ / ___ / ___	___ : ___		
15	___ / ___ / ___	___ : ___		

From F. Davis and J. Mannino, 2011, *Championship Racquetball* (Champaign, IL: Human Kinetics).
http://bit.ly/fbCfh0

Drill worksheet

Today's date: _____ / _____ / _____

Drill strokes practiced	Court position # hits # attempts	Court position # hits # attempts	Court position # hits # attempts	Court position # hits # attempts	Comments
FOREHAND					
Down the line					
Crosscourt					
Wide-angle pass					
Pinch					
Reverse pinch					
BACKHAND					
Down the line					
Crosscourt					
(YOUR OWN) DRILL					

Record the number of good hits you make in the first box. Record the number of attempts in the second box.

Use the blank section to record other drills that you chose based on what skill you want to develop.

From F. Davis and J. Mannino, 2011, *Championship Racquetball* (Champaign, IL: Human Kinetics).
http://bit.ly/fbCfh0

Appendix B
Tournament Logs

Tournament log

Event	Date	Division(s)	Results	Answers to tournament log questions
	____ / ____ / ____			
	____ / ____ / ____			
	____ / ____ / ____			
	____ / ____ / ____			
	____ / ____ / ____			
	____ / ____ / ____			
	____ / ____ / ____			
	____ / ____ / ____			
	____ / ____ / ____			
	____ / ____ / ____			
	____ / ____ / ____			
	____ / ____ / ____			
	____ / ____ / ____			
	____ / ____ / ____			

From F. Davis and J. Mannino, 2011, *Championship Racquetball* (Champaign, IL: Human Kinetics).
http://bit.ly/fbCfh0

Index

Note: Page references followed by an italicized f or t indicate information contained in figures and tables, respectively.

A

advanced ball toss
   drive serve 61, 61f, 66t
   lob serve 68, 68f
advanced contact point
   backhand 42, 42f, 55t
   forehand 14, 14f, 28t
   serving: drive serve 62, 62f, 66t
   serving: lob serve 69, 69f
advanced court position footwork 138-141, 139f, 140f, 156t-157t
advanced defensive shots
   drills 129-130
   technique 126-128, 127f, 128f, 132t
advanced doubles court positions 269-272, 270f, 271f
advanced drills 206
advanced follow-through
   backhand 45-46, 45f, 55t
   forehand 17, 17f, 28t
   serving: drive serve 65, 65f, 66t
   serving: lob serve 72, 72f
advanced footwork
   drive serve 60, 60f, 66t
   lob serve 67, 67f
advanced grips
   backhand 33-34, 33f, 54t
   forehand 5-6, 5f, 7, 27t
advanced-level challenges ix, viii
advanced offensive shots
   drills 116-118
   technique 109-111, 109f, 110f, 111f, 121t-122t
advanced relocation after serve 89-90, 89f, 90f
advanced shot selection 163t
advanced stance
   backhand 36, 36f, 54t
   forehand 7-8, 7f, 27t
advanced step and swing
   backhand 39, 39f, 54t
   forehand 10, 10f, 28t
advanced strategies 195-198, 201t
adversity, overcoming 228-232
aerobic conditioning 256, 258, 259. See also conditioning
affirmations
   creation and usage 227-228, 233
   peak performance preparation 217, 222, 225
aggressive shots. See defensive shots; offensive shots
agility 244, 245-247, 246f, 247f
alone drills. See solo drills
angle of the ball
   drills for reading 24-25, 51-52
   offensive shots, reading 149, 150
   serve 76, 81, 83, 85, 153
   shot selection relevance 161, 174
arm drive 238
attacking forehand. See forehand
attitude. See positive vs. negative attitudes

B

back foot, hitting off of 14, 44. See also contact point
backhand 31-32, 55-56
balance with forehand 31, 46
   ceiling shot 125-126, 125f, 126f, 132t
   checklists 54t-55t
   contact point 41-44, 42f, 55t
   drilling and practice 46-53, 48f, 49f, 50f, 51f, 53f, 213
   follow-through 44-46, 45f, 55t, 126f
   grips 32-34, 33f, 54t
   mistakes 34, 36-37, 40-41, 44
   return of serve 93, 151
   stances 35-37, 35f, 36f, 54t
   step and swing 37-41, 38f, 39f, 54t
backhand lob Z serves 70, 70f
backpedal speed 239, 241
back wall shot. See "off the back wall" shot
balance 251-252, 252-253, 252f, 253f
balance of shots
   forehand/backhand balance 31, 46, 55, 56
   offensive/defensive balance 128-129, 133
   offensive/defensive choices 164-165
ballistic stretching 254, 255, 255f
ball reads. See reading the ball
ball speed. See speed of ball travel
ball toss
   deception method 60, 68, 82
   drive serve 60-61, 61f, 66t
   lob serve 68, 68f, 73t
   mistakes 74-75
beginner skills. See also core skills
   drilling methods and tips 20-21, 48, 113
   literature vii
   shot development 101
Bleiler, Gretchen 228, 233
body language 223-224
body-mind connection 215, 216, 220, 225, 227
body positioning. See body language; follow-through; footwork; posture; stance; step and swing
bounce, in shots. See cutting the ball off; mid hop shot; "off the back wall" shot; short hop shot
breathing methods and exercises 217, 218, 227
broad focus 229
burnout 231

C

ceiling ball/shot. See also "go up to the ceiling" return
   backhand 125-126, 125f, 126f, 132t
   as defensive tool 107, 123, 129
   drills 129, 207, 210, 211, 212
   forehand 123-124, 123f, 124f, 132t
   higher-level 127, 127f, 132t
   mistakes 131

offensive shots following 108
on return of serve 92
center-court position 137, 138, 138f, 157. See also court position
   match strategy 194
   mistakes 138, 147
   positioning of opponent 92
   rally positions 142-146, 142f, 143f, 144f, 145f, 146f, 147
   rules of thumb 146
   self-positioning, defensive shots 126
   self-positioning, post-serve 87, 91, 100, 148, 154-155
   self-positioning, return-of-serve 92, 95, 96, 97
   what to look for 149-150
centering (emotional) 218, 219, 223
change of direction speed 239, 241-243, 242f, 243f
checklists, game plans and strategies
   core, intermediate, and advanced 201t
   game evaluation worksheet 191-192
checklists, skills 208
   backhand 54t-55t
   court position footwork 156t-157t
   defensive shots 132t
   drive serve 66t
   forehand 27t-28t, 208
   offensive shots 121t-122t
   return of serve 177t
   shot selection 163t, 177t
chemistry, doubles players 264
closed vs. open stance 140-141
combination drills
   partner drills 212-213
   progression 208-209
   solo drills 210-211
communication, doubles play 264-265
competition
   overview 203
   player assessment for game plans 184-190, 191-192
   playing the ball, not the opponent 197, 198
   return of serve consideration 173, 174
   shot selection consideration 161, 163t, 164-165, 185-186
   watching and reading individuals 150, 152-153, 173, 174
concentration. See focus and concentration
conditioning
   aerobic 256, 258, 259
   agility 244-247, 245f, 246f, 247f
   balance 251-253, 252f, 253f
   flexibility 253-256, 255f
   plans for athletes 237, 239, 256-257, 258, 259, 260t
   power and strength 247-251, 248f, 249f, 250f, 251f, 259
   speed 238-244, 242f, 243f
   training schedules 258, 259, 260t
   types/key words 256, 258

279

consistency
  backhand drills for 47-53
  forehand drills for 20-21, 22, 25
  importance 1, 31, 46, 55-56
  serve 85
contact point
  backhand 41, 55t
  backhand: ceiling shot 125-126, 125f
  backhand: intermediate and advanced
    42, 42f, 55t
  court position 157t
  defined 13, 41, 61
  forehand 13, 28t
  forehand: advanced 14, 14f, 28t
  forehand: ceiling shot 124, 124f
  forehand: intermediate 13, 13f, 28t
  four racquet contact points 13, 14, 15,
    15f, 42, 43, 43f, 68, 71
  high-level ceiling shot 127, 127f
  mistakes 14, 44, 75, 99
  offensive shots 105, 105f, 106, 107,
    108, 121t-122t
  return of serve 92, 94, 94f, 99
  serving: drive serve 61-62, 62f, 66t
  serving: lob serve 69, 69f, 73t
  splat shot 110
  watching and reading 150
  Z shot 128
control of gameplay/match
  doubles 266-267
  game tempo and rhythm 183, 184,
    187, 196-197, 198, 266
  mental toughness 215, 219, 232
core doubles court positions 268-269,
  268f, 269f
core drills 205-206
core fitness and strength
  benefits 219, 247
  exercises 221, 250
core skills
  backhand 54t-55t
  court position footwork 138-141, 139f,
    140f, 156t-157t
  defensive shots 123-126, 123f, 124f,
    125f, 126f, 132t
  drive serve 66t
  forehand 27t-28t
  lob serve 73t
  offensive shots 102-103, 102f, 103f,
    104t, 121t-122t
  return of serve drills 95, 96-97
  return of serve shot selection 177t
  shot selection 163t, 177t
core strategies 194-195, 201t
counterpunching style 189
court position 137, 157. See also center-
    court position
  after return of serve 92, 95, 149
  after serve 87, 91, 99, 100, 148-149
  checklists 156t-157t
  defensive shots and maneuvering 101,
    123, 126, 128
  doubles play 263, 267, 268-272, 268f,
    269f, 270f, 271f
  drilling and practice 154-155
  eight court positions 142-146, 142f,
    143f, 144f, 145f, 146f, 163t, 166-
    170, 166f, 167f, 168f, 169f, 170f
  match strategy 194
  mistakes 91, 138, 147, 152
  opponent assessment 185
  rallying 142-146, 142f, 143f, 144f,
    145f, 146f, 154, 166-170, 166f,
    167f, 168f, 169f, 170f
  return of serve 151-152, 151f, 172

rules of thumb 146
shot selection 166-170, 166f, 167f,
  168f, 169f, 170f, 170t
splat shot use 110
court size 137
crosscourt hits
  anticipating 150
  doubles vulnerability 269
  kill, pass-kill, and pass shots 103, 107,
    108, 168, 169, 170, 170t
  off lead foot 15, 15f, 43, 43f, 103
crossover and lunge step 140, 140f, 156t
crossover step
  mistakes 99, 141
  return of serve 92, 94, 94f, 98, 99
cue words 218, 226, 228
cutting the ball off. See also mid hop shot;
    short hop shot
  drills 116-117, 213
  mistakes 120
  technique 109, 109f, 121t

D
deception 58, 82
  footwork 67, 82
  hitting contact point 14, 41, 42, 55t
  serve ball toss/contact point 60, 62,
    68, 71, 82
  serve placement 82
  serve speed 67
defensive shots 101
  balance with offensive 128-129, 133,
    164-165
  checklists 132t
  core techniques and basic shots 123-
    126, 123f, 124f, 125f, 126f, 132t
  drilling and practice 128-130
  intermediate and advanced techniques
    126-128, 127f, 128f
  mistakes 131-132
  shot selection 161, 164-165, 164f
detective work 189-190. See also pattern
    reading
distractions 231-232
dominating serves and returns. See return
    of serve; serves and serving
doubles play
  components to success 264-268
  court positioning 263, 267, 268-272,
    268f, 269f, 270f, 271f
  drills 273-274
  overview 263-264, 274
  shot selection 267-268, 272-273
down the line hits
  doubles 267, 269
  drills 212-213
  kill, pass-kill, and pass shots 103, 107,
    108, 168, 169
  mistakes 119
  off lead foot 15, 15f, 43, 43f, 103
  from positions 1-7 166, 167, 168, 169
down and ready position
  backhand drills 49, 49f, 50, 50f
  court position/center court 138-141,
    139f, 149, 156t-157t, 157
  court position drills 154-155
  forehand drills 21, 21f, 22, 26
  mistakes 98, 141
  offensive shots 104-105, 104f
  relocation, post-serve 87, 148, 154-155
  return of serve 92, 93, 93f, 98, 151
  return of serve drills 95, 96, 97
drills. See also partner drills; solo drills
  backhand 46-53, 48f, 49f, 50f, 51f, 53f,
    213

conditioning: agility 245-247, 245f,
  246f, 247f
conditioning: balance 252-253, 252f,
  253f
conditioning: flexibility 254-256, 255f
conditioning: power and strength 248-
  251, 248f, 249f, 250f, 251f
conditioning: speed 239-244, 242f,
  243f
court position 154-155
defensive shots 128-130, 207, 210, 211,
  212
development and planning 207
doubles play 273-274
enjoyment 206-207, 256
forehand 18-27, 20f, 21f, 23f, 24f, 26f,
  29
game plan and match strategy 199-201
game scenarios 213-214
offensive shots 112-118, 210, 212
pregame warm-ups 223
progression 112-113, 205-206, 208-
  209, 214, 257
relocation, post-serve 91, 154-155, 210
return of serve 95-98
serve 85-86, 210
shot selection 179-181
in training regimen 259, 260t
drive serve 58, 66t
  ball toss 60-61, 61f, 66t
  contact point 61-62, 62f, 66t
  drilling and practice 85-86
  follow-through 65, 65f, 66t
  footwork 58-60, 59f, 60f, 66t
  hitting off lead foot 63-64, 63f, 64f
  mistakes 74-76, 81
  placement 76-78, 77f, 78f
  relocation, post-serve 87-89, 88f, 89f,
    148, 155
  return of serve drills 95-96
  return of serve policy 175, 177t, 179
  serving positions and options 83t
  wrap, jam, and nick serves 64, 64f, 76,
    77-78, 77f, 78f, 81, 175, 177t
  Z serve 63, 63f, 76, 77, 77f, 81, 175,
    177t
drop and hit drills
  backhand 47, 48, 48f
  forehand 18, 19, 20-21, 20f
  limitations 214
  offensive shots 112, 113, 114, 116,
    117-118
  pregame warm-ups 223
  progression 112
  serve 85
dynamic stretching 254, 255f

E
early racquet preparation (ERP)
  backhand: drills 48, 48f, 52
  backhand: stance 35, 36, 37, 54t
  forehand: drills 20, 20f, 24
  forehand: stance, step and swing 6, 7,
    8, 9
  offensive shots 105, 105f
  return of serve 151, 152
efficiency of movement 239
emotional state
  centering and focus 218, 219, 223
  control, mental toughness 215, 219,
    223
  opponent assessment 187
  opponent exploitation 193
  personality types (doubles) 265
  positive attitudes and 225-226

ERP. See early racquet preparation (ERP)
Evert, Chris 223-224, 231

F
Fast Fit Training System 237
fears of failure and success 229-230
fitness. See also agility; balance; conditioning; flexibility; power and strength; running speed
    abdominal muscles 219, 221, 247
    racquetball component 237, 239, 244, 253-254
five-step drilling approach 18-27, 47-53, 214
    drill progression 112
    practicing positions 18f, 19f
flexibility 253
    exercises and drills 254-256, 255f
    as racquetball component 237, 253-254, 256, 262
focus and concentration
    centering and visualization 218-219, 223, 229
    development 228-229
    different focus types 229
    match strategy 197, 199, 231
follow-through
    backhand 44, 55t
    backhand: ceiling shot 126, 126f
    backhand: intermediate and advanced 45-46, 45f, 55t
    contact point lead-in 13
    court position 157t
forehand 16, 28t
    forehand: ceiling shot 124, 124f
    forehand: intermediate and advanced 17, 17f, 28t
    high-level ceiling shot 127
    incomplete 16, 18, 44, 45, 46, 65, 72, 75, 99
    lob serve 73t
    mistakes 18, 44, 45, 46, 75-76
    offensive shots 105, 105f
    return of serve 92, 94, 94f
    serving: drive serve 65, 65f, 66t
    serving: lob serve 72, 72f
    step and swing lead-in 10
foot speed 238, 240, 244
footwork
    agility 244
    center court/return of serve 139-141, 139f, 140f, 155, 156t-157t
    deception method 67, 82
    drive serve 58-60, 59f, 60f, 66t
    lob serve 67, 67f, 73t
    mistakes 74, 98, 141
    offensive shots 104-105, 105f, 106, 121t
    opponent assessment 187, 193
    relocation, post-serve 87-90, 88f, 89f, 90f, 155
    return of serve drills 96, 97
forehand 3-4, 29
    balance with backhand 31, 46
    ceiling shot 123-124, 123f, 124f, 132t
    checklists 27t-28t, 208
    contact point 13-14, 15, 15f
    drilling and practice 18-27, 20f, 21f, 23f, 24f, 26f
    follow-through 16-18, 17f
    grips 4-6, 5f
    mistakes 14, 18
    power 11
    return of serve 93, 151
    stances 6-8, 7f
    step and swing 9-12, 10f

front/back split, doubles
    court position 269, 269f
    specialty teams 266
future, playing in 197, 198, 226, 227

G
game evaluation checklist 191-192
game plans 183, 199, 201t, 202. See also match strategy
    detective work 189-190
    development 184, 190, 193-194
    drilling and practice 199-201
    formula 189, 194
    match strategy vs. 183-184
    mistakes 194
    player assessment 184-189
    pregame plans 221-223, 235, 262
game situations 198-199, 200. See also score
game style, doubles play 265
goal setting 232-234
"go up to the ceiling" return
    drills 95, 96, 98, 213
    return selection/policy 175-176
grips
    backhand 32-33, 54t
    backhand: advanced 33-34, 33f, 54t
    backhand: intermediate 33, 33f, 54t
    forehand 4, 27t
    forehand: advanced 5-6, 5f, 7, 27t
    forehand: intermediate 4-5, 5f, 27t
    mistakes 6, 34
    guided imagery 220

H
half lob kick serve
    described 80, 80f, 82
    return of serve 97, 176, 177t
half lob nick serve
    described 79, 79f, 82
    return of serve 97, 176, 177t
hammer grip 4, 6, 32, 34
handedness
    doubles court positioning 268
    doubles specialty positions 266, 272
    opponents 188, 272
handshake grip 4, 32, 34
head placement 238
height of the ball.
    offensive shots, described 102-103, 104t
    offensive shots, reading 106, 149-150
    serve 82, 85
    shot selection relevance 161, 163t, 174
height of opponent 188
high lob nick serve
    described 79, 79f, 81
    return of serve 97, 176, 177t
high and lob serves. See high lob nick serve; lob serve
higher-level ceiling ball shot
    drills 129-130
    mistakes 131
    technique 127, 127f, 132t
hip drive and speed 238, 240
hitting zone 13, 14, 41. See also contact point
hydration
    pregame 222, 262
    recovery 258

I
incomplete follow-through 16, 18, 44, 45, 46, 65, 72, 75, 99
injuries 229
    fears 229-230

opponents 189
    recovery 258
    warm-up and stretching as preventive 195, 253-254
in-season conditioning 258, 260t
intermediate ball toss
    drive serve 61, 61f, 66t
    lob serve 68, 68f
intermediate contact point
    backhand 42, 42f, 55t
    forehand 13, 13f, 28t
    serving: drive serve 62, 62f, 66t
    serving: lob serve 69, 69f
intermediate court position footwork 138-141, 139f, 140f, 156t-157t
intermediate court positions 269-272, 270f, 271f
intermediate defensive shots
    drills 129-130
    technique 126-128, 127f, 128f, 132t
intermediate follow-through
    backhand 45, 45f, 55t
    forehand 17, 17f, 28t
    serving: drive serve 65, 65f, 66t
    serving: lob serve 72, 72f
intermediate footwork
    drive serve 59, 59f, 66t
    lob serve 67, 67f
intermediate grips
    backhand 33, 33f, 54t
    forehand 4-5, 5f, 27t
intermediate-level challenges ix, vii-viii
intermediate offensive shots
    drills 113-116
    technique 103-108, 104f, 105f, 106f, 107f, 108f, 109, 121t-122t
intermediate relocation after serve 88-89, 88f
intermediate shot selection 163t
intermediate stance
    backhand 35-36, 35f, 54t
    forehand 7, 7f, 27t
intermediate step and swing
    backhand 38-39, 38f, 54t
    forehand 10, 10f, 28t
intermediate strategies 195-198, 201t

J
jam serve
    as drive serve type 64, 64f, 76, 77, 77f, 81
    return of serve 96, 175, 177t, 273
journaling
    goal setting 234
    tournaments 262, 277
    training 261, 275-276
judgment, "off the back wall" shot 106, 121t
jump on the ball 149, 150, 152, 244
jumping exercises
    power and strength development 249, 249f
    speed development 240, 242-243, 242f, 243f
K
kick serve (lob)
    described 80, 80f, 82
    return of serve 97, 176, 177t
kill shot 142
    drills 113, 207
    mistakes 118-119, 160, 171, 172, 198
    shot selection/playing the percentages 159-160, 167, 168, 169, 170t, 171, 172, 178, 198
    technique 102, 102f, 104t, 121t
knee problems 186, 189

L

ladder drills
    balance development 252
    speed development 240, 241, 242, 242f, 243
lead foot, hitting off of. See also contact point
    backhand 41, 42, 43, 43f, 44
    forehand 13, 14, 15, 15f
    serving: drive serve 61, 62, 63-64, 63f, 64f, 75
    serving: lob serve 70-71, 70f, 71f, 75
learning brain 215
learning from problems/challenges 228, 231
left-handedness
    doubles teams 266, 272
    opponents 188, 272
L formation doubles court position 270, 270f
lob serve 66-67, 73t
    ball toss 68, 68f, 73t
    contact point 69, 69f, 73t
    drilling and practice 86, 207
    follow through 72, 72f, 73t
    footwork 67, 67f, 73t
    hitting off lead foot 70-71, 70f, 71f
    kick serve 80, 80f, 82
    mistakes 74-76, 81-82
    nick serves 79, 79f, 81-82
    placement 79-80, 79f, 80f
    power diffusion method 84
    relocation, post-serve 87, 90, 90f, 148, 155
    return of serve drills 96-97
    return of serve policy 175-176, 177t, 179
    serving positions and options 83t
    Z serves 70, 70f, 80, 80f, 81, 176, 177t
Loehr, James 216, 225
logs. See journaling
long-range and long-term goals 234
losing 231
low and hard drive serve. See drive serve
lower-body power generation 84, 247, 248
    backhand 36, 37, 39, 40
    exercises 248-251, 248f, 249f, 250f, 251f
    forehand 7-8, 10, 11

M

massage 218, 232
match strategy 183, 201t, 202. See also game plans
    core strategies 194-195, 201t
    doubles play 267
    drilling and practice 201
    game plans vs. 183-184
    game situations and 199, 200, 201
    mistakes 195
    rules of thumb 199
mental game. See also mental toughness
    backhand's role 31-32
    court position 157
    deception in hitting contact point 14, 41, 42
    deception in serving contact point 58, 62, 71
    deception in serving placement 82
    deception in serving speed 67
    forehand's role 3
    importance and power 1, 203, 215-216, 235
    offensive shots 108, 109
    return of serve 95, 100, 171
    serve 82, 100

    shot selection 159
    tactics 135
mental toughness 203, 215-216, 235. See also emotional state; mental game; peak play; routines and rituals; visualization
    fears 229-230
    overcoming adversity 228-232
    positive vs. negative attitudes 195, 196, 199, 223-226, 230, 232
    in training regimen 260t
"mid-hop or short-hop the ball" return of serve drills 97
mid hop shot
    drills 117-118
    mistakes 121
    technique 111, 111f, 122t
mind-body connection 215, 216, 220, 225, 227
mistakes
    backhand contact point 44
    backhand grip 34
    backhand stance 36-37
    backhand step and swing 40-41
    court position 91, 138, 147, 152
    defensive shots 131-132
    follow-through (incomplete) 16, 18, 44, 45, 46, 65, 72, 75, 99
    forehand contact point 14
    forehand follow-through 18
    forehand grip 6
    forehand stance 8
    forehand step and swing 11-12
    game plans, strategies, and situations 194, 195, 198-199
    offensive shots 118-121
    playing the percentages 160
    rallying 147, 171
    relocation, post-serve 91
    return of serve 98-99, 152, 172, 174, 176, 179
    serving and serves 74-76, 81-82
    shot selection 162, 165
    watching the server 153
modified side-by-side doubles court position 271-272, 271f
Monchik, Sudsy 46, 84, 223, 251, 265
monkey slump 227
movement drills. See combination drills
movement fundamentals 237-238
    agility 244
    balance 251-252
    flexibility 253-254
    power and strength 247-248
    speed 238-239
muscle memory 205, 206, 216, 220, 227
muscle relaxation 218, 227, 232

N

negative attitudes. See positive vs. negative attitudes
nick serve
    drive 64, 64f, 78, 78f, 175, 177t
    half lob 79, 79f, 82, 176, 177t
    high lob 79, 79f, 81, 176, 177t
nine practice positions. See practicing positions
nostril breathing 217, 218
nutrition
    pregame 222, 262
    recovery 258

O

Obremski, Dan 237, 239
"off the back wall" shot
    drills 113-114, 211, 213

    mistakes 119
    technique 104-106, 104f, 105f, 121t
off-balance correction shots 164, 211
offensive shots 101
    advanced techniques 109-111, 109f, 110f, 111f
    balance with defensive 128-129, 133, 164-165
    basic shots 104t
    checklists 121t-122t
    core techniques 102-103, 102f, 103f
    drilling and practice 112-118, 210, 212
    intermediate techniques 103-108, 104f, 105f, 106f, 107f, 108f, 109
    mistakes 118-121
    shot selection 161, 164-165, 164f
on-court distractions 231-232
on-court rituals 227, 229
one-step footwork 82
    drive serve 66t
    lob serve 67, 73t, 82
open vs. closed stance 140-141
opponents. See competition
orthodox vs. unorthodox players 189
overcoming adversity 228-232
overhead pass shot
    drills 115-116, 210, 274
    mistakes 120
    technique 107-108, 107f, 122t

P

pace of game. See tempo and rhythm of game
partner drills
    backhand 49, 51, 52, 53
    combinations 208, 212-213
    doubles play 273-274
    forehand 22, 24, 25, 26
    game scenarios 213-214
    return of serve 96, 97, 98
    serve 86
    shot selection 180
partner play. See doubles play
pass-kill shots
    drills 113
    technique 102, 102f, 104t, 121t
pass shots
    doubles 267, 273, 274
    drills 113, 114-116, 207, 274
    mistakes 119-120, 171
    popularity 103, 106
    on return of serve 92, 172
    shot selection/playing the percentages 159-160, 163t, 166, 167, 168, 169, 170, 170t, 171, 178, 198
    technique: core 102-103, 102f, 104t, 122t
    technique: overhead 107-108, 107f, 122t
    technique: sidearm 108, 108f, 122t
    technique: wide-angle 106-107, 106f, 121t
past, playing in 197, 198, 226, 227
pattern reading
    of opponent: game plan formation 184-190
    of opponent: serve and post-serve 152-153, 173, 174
    of opponent: skill and habits 150
peak play
    attitudes 223-225, 227-228
    defined 216
    fitness training 237, 258-261
    preparation 217-220, 221-223, 225-226, 262
pendulum swing 8, 12

penetrating backhand. See backhand
"perfect practice" concept 205, 206
periodization (training) 258
personality type, in doubles 265
pinch shot. See also splat shot
    anticipating 150
    drills 113, 212-213
    mistakes 119
    off lead foot 15, 15f, 43, 43f
    shot selection 166, 167, 168, 169, 170,
        170t, 171, 178
    technique 103, 103f, 104t, 110, 122t
pinpoint focus 229
pivot
    court positioning 140, 140f, 156t
    mistakes 98, 141
    return of serve 92, 93, 93f, 98
placement of serve 76
    drive serves 76-78, 77f, 78f
    lob serves 79-80, 79f, 80f
playing against the ball 197, 198
playing in the now 197, 198, 226-227,
        231. See also affirmations; muscle
        memory
playing the percentages 139, 142, 143,
        159-160, 198
positions. See center-court position; court
        position; practicing positions; serv-
        ing positions
positive vs. negative attitudes
    doubles play 266
    match strategy 195, 196, 199
    mental toughness 223-226, 230,
        232
postseason conditioning 258, 260t
posture 238. See also stance
power, physics of 11, 39, 84, 247
power base. See stance
power generation
    backhand grips 33, 34
    backhand stances, step and swing 36,
        39, 40
    backhand wrist action 33, 34, 39, 40
    drive serve 59, 60, 61, 62
    follow-through techniques and 16, 18,
        44, 45, 65
    forehand, and benefits 3, 11
    forehand grips 4, 5, 6
    forehand stances, step and swing 6, 7,
        8, 9, 10
    forehand wrist action 5, 9, 10, 12
    hitting zone/contact point 13, 14, 41,
        44
    lob serve differences 72
    serving 84
power and strength
    exercises and drills 248-251, 248f,
        249f, 250f, 251f
    as racquetball component 247-248
practice 214. See also drills; practicing
        positions
    game scenarios 213-214
    guidelines 205-206
    "perfect practice" 205, 206
practicing positions 18-20, 18f, 19f, 47
predictability. See deception; variety
pregame plans 221-223, 235, 262
preseason conditioning 258, 259, 260t
present. See playing in the now

R
"racquetball sports triangle" 1, 203
racquet choice 84
racquet preparation. See early racquet
        preparation (ERP)
racquet technology vii

rallies
    court position drills 154
    court positions 142-146, 142f, 143f,
        144f, 145f, 146f, 166-170, 166f,
        167f, 168f, 169f, 170f
    mistakes 147, 171
    pass shots 103
    return of serve role 92, 95
    shot selection 166-171
reaction time
    jump on the ball 149, 150, 152, 244
    opponents', post-offensive shots 109,
        111, 150
    opponents', post-power shots 3, 11
    opponents' return of serve 58
    return of serve 148, 151, 173
reading the ball
    drills for 24-26, 51-53
    off the back wall shot judgment 106
    return of serve 92, 99, 152-153
    shot selection 161
    watching for 76, 149-150, 153, 194,
        198, 199
    wide-angle pass shots 107
ready position. See down and ready
        position
recovery cycles 258, 260
referees
    bad calls 197, 198, 232
    questioning 187, 196
relaxation methods and exercises 218,
        227, 232
relocation, post-serve 87-90, 88f, 89f, 90f,
        148, 148f
    drilling and practice 91, 154-155, 210
    mistakes 91, 148-149
    of opponent 173
repetition and muscle memory 205,
        206, 216
return of serve 92, 139
    court position 151-152, 151f, 172
    doubles play 273
    drilling and practice 95-98
    footwork 139-141, 140f
    game plan development 186-187, 193
    manipulation of opponent 58, 78, 82,
        83, 92, 95, 99, 172
    mechanics 92-94, 93f, 94f
    mistakes 98-99, 152, 172, 174, 176,
        179
    relocation 87-90, 149, 155
return policy 174-176, 177t
    rituals 224-225
    shot selection 166, 171-176, 177t
    what to look for 152-153
reverse pinch shot
    doubles 267-268, 274
    drills 113, 274
    off lead foot 15, 15f, 43, 43f
    technique 103, 103f, 104t, 122t
rhythm of game. See tempo and rhythm
        of game
right-handedness
    doubles teams 266, 272
    opponents 188, 272
routines and rituals 221-223, 224-225,
        227, 229, 231
rules of the game. See also referees
    match control method 187, 196, 197
    running drills. See set up, run, and hit
        drill; toss, turn, shuffle, and hit drill
running speed
    drills 243-244
    exercises 239-243, 242f, 243f
    of opponent 188, 193
    racquetball components 238-239

S
score. See also game situations
    serve rules 57, 85, 101
    shot selection relevance 160, 161, 163t
    scout analysis 190
self-assessment
    in return of serve 173
    in shot selection 161, 163t
    in training 29, 53, 208, 261
    whole game 191-192
self-talk
    peak performance preparation 217-
        218, 222, 225, 227-228, 233
    positive and negative messages 224,
        225, 230
serves and serving 57-58, 70f, 85, 99-100.
        See also relocation, post-serve;
        return of serve
    consistency 85
    deception 58, 82
    doubles play 267, 272
    drilling and practice 85-86, 207, 210
    drive serve techniques and mechanics
        58-65, 59f, 60f, 61f, 62f, 63f, 64f,
        65f, 66t
    game plan development 186, 193
    lob serve techniques and mechanics
        66-72, 67f, 68f, 69f, 70f, 71f, 72f,
        73t
    mistakes 74-76, 81-82
    placement 76-82, 77f, 78f, 79f, 80f
    positions 63f, 70, 71, 81, 83t, 148f,
        152-153
    power 84
    reading the opponent 152-153, 173, 174
    rituals 224
    variety 82-83
serving positions 63f, 70, 71, 81, 83t, 148f,
        152-153
set up and hit drill
    backhand 47, 51-52, 51f
    defensive shots 130
    forehand 18, 19, 24-25, 24f
    offensive shots 112, 114, 115, 116-117,
        118
    progression 112
set up, run, and hit drill
    backhand 47, 52-53, 53f
    forehand 18, 19, 25-26, 26f
    progression 112
"seven secret components," doubles play
        264-268
"shoot the pass" return of serve drills 95,
        96, 97, 98
"short-hop or mid-hop the ball" return of
        serve drills 97
short hop shot
    drills 117-118
    mistakes 121
    technique 111, 111f, 122t
short players 188
short-range and short-term goals 233, 234
shotmaking. See defensive shots; offensive
        shots; shot selection
shot selection 159, 163t, 170t, 181
    doubles play 267-268, 272-273
    drilling and practice 179-181
    formula 160-162, 272
    mistakes 162, 165, 171, 172
    offensive/defensive choices 161, 164-
        165, 164f
    opponent assessment and game plan
        development 185-186, 193
    playing the percentages 159-160, 178
    rallies and rally positions 166-171,
        166f, 167f, 168f, 169f, 170f

shot selection *(continued)*
  return of serve 171-174
  rules of thumb 178
shuffling. See footwork; set up, run, and hit drill; toss, turn, shuffle, and hit drill
sidearm pass shot
  drills 115-116, 210
  mistakes 120
  technique 108, 108f, 122t
side-by-side doubles court position
  fifty-fifty split 268-269, 268f
  modified/S formation 271-272, 271f
  two-thirds split 270, 270f
skills. See also backhand; checklists, skills; defensive shots; forehand; offensive shots; return of serve; serves and serving
  lopsided/unbalanced 31, 46, 55, 56
  racquetball literature vii-ix
  self-assessment, whole-game 191-192
  self-assessment and training 29, 53, 208, 261
  self-assessment in return of serve 173
  self-assessment in shot selection 161, 163t
sleep habits 221, 222
slumps 230
solo drills
  backhand 48, 49, 51, 53
  combinations 208, 210-211
  forehand 21, 22, 25, 26
  return of serve 95-97
  serve 85-86
  shot selection 179
specialty positions, doubles 265-266
speed, running. See backpedal speed; change of direction speed; foot speed; running speed; starting speed
speed of ball travel
  maximums 3, 58, 92, 140
  serve options 58, 83
  shot selection relevance 161, 174
  watching and reading 149-150
speed play 256
spirit in sports 218, 226
splat shot
  anticipating 150
  drills 117
  mistakes 120
  shot selection 170t, 186
  technique 110, 110f, 121t
sports brain 216, 218, 219, 220, 228. See also muscle memory
squash grips 6
stance
  backhand 35, 54t
  backhand: advanced 36, 36f, 54t
  backhand: ceiling shot 125, 125f
  backhand: intermediate 35-36, 35f, 54t
  forehand 6, 27t
  forehand: advanced 7-8, 7f, 27t
  forehand: ceiling shot 123, 123f
  forehand: intermediate 7, 7f, 27t
  high-level ceiling shot 127, 127f
  mistakes 8, 36-37
  open vs. closed 140-141
  watching and reading opponents 150
starting speed 238, 239, 240
static stretching 254, 256
step length
  backhand step and swing 38, 39, 54t

drive serve footwork 59, 60
  forehand step and swing 9, 10, 11, 28t
step and swing. See also five-step drilling approach; step length
  backhand 37-38, 54t
  backhand: advanced 39, 39f, 54t
  backhand: ceiling shot 125, 125f
  backhand: intermediate 38-39, 38f, 54t
  forehand 9-10, 28t
  forehand: advanced 10, 10f, 28t
  forehand: ceiling shot 123, 123f
  forehand: intermediate 10, 10f, 28t
  high-level ceiling shot 127, 127f
  mistakes 11-12, 40-41
strategy 135. See also court position; game plans; match strategy; shot selection
strength training 256. See also conditioning; power and strength
stretching 253-256
success, fear of 230
Swain, Cliff 265
swing. See step and swing

T
tactics 135. See also court position; game plans; match strategy; shot selection
tall players 188
target hitting drills 114-115, 207
target serve drills 86, 207
teamwork, doubles play 263, 274
temperature, body 221, 232, 253, 254, 257
tempo and rhythm of game
  control, match strategy 196-197, 198
  doubles 266
  game plan development 184, 187, 193
  mistakes 198
tennis grips and swings 6, 12, 40
  10 second rule, strategy 184, 196, 197
  30/40/30 principle 139
  30 percent principle 142, 143, 160, 165, 166, 172, 175
  30-second reaction drills 211, 213
three-quarter lob Z serve 80, 80f
  relocation, post-serve 90, 90f
  return of serve 97, 176, 177t
time-outs 196, 197, 229, 232
toss, turn, and hit drill
  backhand 47, 49, 49f
  forehand 18, 19, 21-22, 21f
  offensive shots 112, 114-115, 116, 117, 118
  progression 112
toss, turn, shuffle, and hit drill
  backhand 47, 50-51, 50f
  defensive shots 129, 130
  forehand 18, 19, 22-23, 23f
  offensive shots 112, 114-115, 116, 117, 118
  progression 112
tournament logs 262, 277
training. See conditioning; drills; practice; training logs; training schedules
training logs 261, 275-276
training schedules 258, 259, 260t
two-step footwork 59, 66t, 82
two-thirds side by side doubles court position 270, 270f

U
unorthodox players 189
upper-body strength and power 250

V
variety. See also deception
  offensive shots 103, 106, 109
  of serve 76-80, 82-83, 83t
video analysis 190
visualization 218
  in court position drills 155
  in goal setting 233
  peak performance preparation 217, 221, 228
  steps 218-219, 220
  types 219-220

W
warm-up 257
  first game as 184, 195
  peak play preparation 217, 221, 222-223, 225
  stretching 253, 254
Waselenchuk, Kane 273
watching the ball. See reading the ball
weight distribution and transfer
  backhand contact point 41, 42, 55t
  backhand follow-through 44, 45-46, 55t
  backhand stance 35, 36, 54t
  backhand step and swing 37, 38, 39, 41, 54t
  drive serve 65, 66t
  forehand contact point 13, 14, 28t
  forehand follow-through 17, 28t
  forehand stance 6
  forehand step and swing 10, 11, 12
  lob serve 72, 73t
  mistakes 14, 41
  role in power generation 9, 10, 11, 12
wide-angle pass shot
  doubles 267, 272, 273, 274
  drills 114-115, 207, 274
  mistakes 119
  technique 106-107, 106f, 121t
winning shots. See defensive shots; offensive shots
wrap serve
  as drive serve type 64, 64f, 78, 78f, 81
  relocation, post-serve 89, 89f
  return of serve 96, 175, 177t
wrist action
  backhand 33, 34, 38, 39, 40, 41
  forehand 5, 9, 10, 12

Z
"the zone" 216-219, 220, 222, 226. See also peak play
zones, court
  offensive/defensive shot choices 164-165, 164f
  offensive shot options 170t, 181f
zones, practicing. See practicing positions
Z serves
  drive 63, 63f, 76, 77, 77f, 81, 175, 177t
  lob 70, 70f, 80, 80f, 81, 176
  mistakes 81
  relocation, post-serve 88-89, 88f, 89f, 90, 90f
  return drills 273
Z shot
  doubles 268, 272
  drills 130, 211, 213
  mistakes 131-132
  shot selection 170t
  technique 128, 128f, 132t

About the Authors

Fran Davis' career has spanned 30 years as a competitor and coach. She instructed top professional and world champion junior players, including Paola Longoria, Rocky Carson, Taylor Knoth, and Jason Mannino. She served as the U.S. national team coach for eight years; during her time as a player, she won four national championships.

Davis was selected by USA Racquetball as the Woman of the Year in 2009. In 2004, she was inducted into the Racquetball Hall of Fame for her excellence and dedication to the sport.

Davis is a staff writer for *Racquetball Magazine* and serves as a commentator for IRT Network (www.IRTNetwork.com). She lives in Seattle, Washington, where she enjoys biking, hiking, and spending time with her family.

Jason Mannino has been playing professionally and coaching for over 15 years. He has been ranked as the No. 1 player in the world during three different seasons and ended 2003 as the International Racquetball Tour (IRT) Player of the Year. In 1998, he received the IRT Most Improved Player Award; in 1996, he was named IRT Rookie of the Year.

Mannino served on the International Racquetball Board for over five years and was instrumental in developing the governance for the International Racquetball Tour. He now serves as president of the IRT.

Mannino has contributed to numerous articles for *Racquetball Magazine* and on the Men's Professional Racquetball Forum. He resides in California with his wife, Christina, and children Jason and Jared. In his spare time, he enjoys golf, racquetball, tennis, biking, and coaching the kids in sports.

To contact the authors, visit www.FranDavisRacquetball.com or send an e-mail to Fran@FranDavisRacquetball.com.

The Best Play Penn!
Shouldn't You?

OFFICIAL BALL

International
Racquetball
Federation

WORLD'S #1
SELLING BRAND.

pennracquet.com